"Until recently, there have been two groups of people: those who argue sex differences are innate and should be embraced and those who insist that they are learned and should be eliminated by changing the environment. Sax is one of the few in the middle—convinced that boys and girls are innately different and that we must change the environment so differences don't become limitations."   —*Time*

"Convincing . . . Psychologist and family physician Leonard Sax, using twenty years of published research, offers a guide to the growing mountain of evidence that girls and boys really are different . . . This extremely readable book also includes shrewd advice on discipline, and on helping youngsters avoid drugs and early sexual activity. Sax's findings, insights, and provocative point-of-view should be of interest and help to many parents."   —*New York Post*

"Using studies as well as anecdotes from his practice and visits to classrooms, [Sax] offers advice on such topics as preventing drug abuse and motivating students . . . The book is thought-provoking, and Sax explains well the science behind his assertions . . . [*Why Gender Matters*] is a worthy read for those who care about how best to prepare children for the challenges they face on the path to adulthood."   —*Scientific American*

"*Why Gender Matters* is an instructive handbook for parents and teachers . . . to create ways to cope with the differences between boys and girls."   —*Boston Globe*

"*Why Gender Matters* pulls together wide-ranging findings on everything from how girls respond to stress, to how antidrug ads actually encourage teenage boys to use drugs, and how all of these differences are hardwired from birth."   —*The National Post* (Canada)

"A potent new book . . . [Dr. Sax] cites a cascade of research that shows the many ways boys and girls differ, from how their brains develop to how they handle stress."

—Margaret Wente, *The Globe and Mail* (Canada)

"[Sax] challenges parents and teachers to acknowledge the latest evidence of lifelong gender differences or risk their children's educational success and emotional health."

— Joanne Good, *Calgary Herald*

"Sax presents a reader-friendly, persuasive argument, challenging many basic assumptions by interspersing hard data with numerous case studies." —Mary Ward Menke, *January Magazine*

"Fascinating . . . This book takes an 'outside the box' position on gender. Paradoxically, Sax says, gender-neutral education favors the learning style of one sex or the other, and so only drives men and women into the usual stereotyped fields. The best way to raise your son to be a man who is caring and nurturing, says Sax, is to first of all let him be a boy. The best way to produce a female mathematician is to first of all let her be a girl . . . I think Sax is on to something. Mature men and women do draw on qualities that stereotypically belong to the opposite sex. But the easiest way to get them to that point is to first make them confident about being a man or a woman . . . Sax adds that children are less happy and confident nowadays because no one is teaching them how to be men and women. This is a powerful, even obvious insight, once you dare think it." —Stanley Kurtz, *National Review Online*

"As the principal of an elementary school, I am constantly on the lookout for outstanding articles and books about gender-specific learning differences. *Why Gender Matters* is the best I've read." —John Webster, Head of School, San Antonio Academy

"*Why Gender Matters* is an outstanding work of scholarship. I am going to make it our 'faculty read' this summer." —Paul Krieger, Headmaster, Christ School (North Carolina)

"Extremely interesting . . . Challenged many of my basic assumptions and helped me to think about gender in a new way." —Joan Ogilvy Holden, Head of School, St. Stephen's and St.Agnes School, Alexandria, Virginia

"*Why Gender Matters* is a fabulous resource for teachers and parents. Dr. Sax combines his extensive knowledge of the research on gender issues with practical advice in cogent, highly readable prose. I am eager to have my colleagues at school read this book and discuss it!" —Martha Cutts, Head of School, Agnes Irwin School, Rosemont, Pennsylvania

"In this reader-friendly book, Dr. Sax combines his comprehensive knowledge of the scientific literature with numerous interesting case studies to argue for his thesis that single-sex education is advantageous."

—Sandra Witelson, Ph.D., Albert Einstein Chair in Neuroscience, McMaster University

"I simply will never be able to express how eye-opening this book has been for me. Yes, me—even though I thought I was a boy-raising specialist. After all, I have produced four healthy, smart athletes. I must know what I'm doing. But many of my boy-raising days I thought I was going mad. I'd come home from some sports event trembling because of the way the coach yelled at my kid. I'd ask my husband and whichever son it happened to be that day how they could stand being yelled at like that. Almost every time husband and son would look at me and not have any recollection of being yelled at during the game. Now I understand!"

—Janet Phillips, mother, Potomac, Maryland

"As the father of a four-year-old daughter and now new twin boys, this particular book looked intriguing. Well, I couldn't put it down. Not only is it well written, with engaging anecdotes, but it presents the latest scientific findings in gender research (with lots of footnotes so you can read the studies yourself if you are so inclined) and relates [them] to the job of parenting. It helps that the author is a family doctor who has seen his share of dysfunctional situations that in hindsight might easily have been prevented with a little knowledge. The book is more than just informative about gender differences in children—he relates this information to such parenting topics as disciplining your child, gender specific education strategies, dealing with problem children, kids and drugs (both the legal and nonlegal kind), and teenage sex."

—Phillip Trubey, father, Rancho Santa Fe, California

"As a high school administrator, I am leading a book study on *Why Gender Matters* with my faculty this fall. As an aunt to a newborn, this was the shower gift to my sister. As a mother of two boys and one girl, I hung on every word. There is simply no category of individuals who are in contact with children of any age who should not read this book. I cannot recommend it strongly enough."

—Leone Langseth, Deer Park, Texas

Why GENDER *Matters*

What Parents and Teachers Need to Know
about the Emerging Science of Sex Differences

Leonard Sax, M.D., Ph.D.

Broadway Books • New York

BROADWAY

A hardcover edition of this book was originally published in 2005 by Doubleday, a division of Random House, Inc. It is here reprinted by arrangement with Doubleday.

Broadway Books titles may be purchased for business or promotional use or for special sales. For information, please write to: Special Markets Department, Random House, Inc., 1745 Broadway, New York, NY 10019.

PRINTED IN THE UNITED STATES OF AMERICA

BROADWAY BOOKS and its logo, a letter B bisected on the diagonal, are trademarks of Random House, Inc.

Visit our Web site at www.broadwaybooks.com

First Broadway Books trade paperback edition published 2006

Book design by Michael Collica

The Library of Congress has cataloged the hardcover edition as follows:
Sax, Leonard.
    Why gender matters : what parents and teachers need to know about the emerging science of sex differences / Leonard Sax.—1st ed.
        p. cm.
    Includes bibliographical references.
    1. Sex role. 2. Sex differences. 3. Child development.
    4. Child psychology. 5. Child rearing. I. Title.
    HQ1075.S28 2005
    305.3—dc22
                                                                        2004055149

ISBN 0-7679-1625-5

10   9   8

In Memory of David Reimer,
August 22, 1965–May 4, 2004

CONTENTS

Why
GENDER
Matters

1
DIFFERENCES

We're entering a new period in science, in which the rewards will come less from the breakthrough investigations of individual scientists than from fitting together the pieces of research to see what it all means . . . Social and biological insights are leaping together, part of a large and complex jigsaw puzzle to which the contributions of many sciences are essential.

—Shelley Taylor, professor of psychology, UCLA, 2002[1]

Matthew turned five years old the summer before kindergarten started. He was looking forward to it. From what he had heard, kindergarten sounded like just one long play date with friends. He could hardly wait. So his mother, Cindy, was surprised when, in October, Matthew started refusing to go to school, refusing even to get dressed in the morning. More than once, Cindy had to dress him, carry him writhing and thrashing into the car, and then drag him from the car into the school. She decided to investigate. She sat in on his kindergarten class. She spoke with the teacher. Everything seemed fine. The teacher—gentle, soft-spoken, and well-educated—reassured Mom that there was no cause for alarm. But Cindy remained concerned, and rightly so, because major problems were just around the corner.

Caitlyn was a shy child and just the slightest bit overweight all through elementary school. In middle school, she underwent a metamorphosis from chubby wallflower to outgoing socialite. She lost weight so quickly that her mother, Jill, worried she might be anorexic. For the next four years, though, everything seemed great—in a frantic and crazy sort of way. Caitlyn was juggling a heavy academic load, had lots of friends, and maintained a full schedule of after-school activities, staying up until midnight or later doing homework. But she seemed happy enough: often frenzied and frazzled, sure, but still happy. Or at least that's what everybody thought until the phone rang at 3 A.M. that awful, unforgettable November night. A nurse told Jill that Caitlyn was in the emergency room, unconscious, having tried to commit suicide with an overdose of Vicodin and Xanax.

These true stories[2] share a grim common element: each kid started out okay, then took a turn in the wrong direction. There is another element in common as well. In both cases the problem arose because the parents did not understand some basic differences between girls and boys. In each case, trouble might have been averted if the parents had known enough about gender differences to recognize what was really happening in their child's life. In each case, the parents could have taken specific action that might have prevented or solved the problem.

We will come back to both of these kids later in this book. Right now it may not be obvious to you how each of these stories illustrates a failure to understand sex differences in child development. That's okay. Later on, we'll hear more about Matthew and Caitlyn. Armed with some basic knowledge about hardwired gender differences, you'll be able to recognize where the parents made the wrong decision or failed to act, and you'll see how the story might have ended differently.

The Dubious Virtue of Gender-Neutral Child-Rearing

I enrolled in the Ph.D. program in psychology at the University of Pennsylvania in September 1980. Governor Ronald Reagan was challenging President Jimmy Carter for the Presidency. The original Apple computer had recently come on the market. "My typewriter is working fine," was the answer the department secretary gave me when I asked her whether she would be getting a word processor anytime soon. Nobody I knew had ever heard of Bill Gates, e-mail, or the Internet. The invention of the World Wide Web still lay ten years in the future.

Among the courses I took that fall was a graduate seminar in developmental psychology. "Why do girls and boys behave differently?" my professor, Justin Aronfreed, asked rhetorically. "Because we *expect* them to. Imagine a world in which we raised girls to play with tanks and trucks, in which we encouraged boys to play with dolls. Imagine a world in which we played rough-and-tumble games with girls while we cuddled and hugged the boys. In such a world, many of the differences we see in how girls and boys behave—maybe even *all* the differences—would vanish."

In another seminar my fellow graduate students and I learned about the extraordinary work of Professor John Money at Johns Hopkins. Professor Money had been consulted by the parents of an unfortunate little boy whose penis had literally been sizzled off during a botched circumcision. At Dr. Money's recommendation, the boy had been raised as a girl, with excellent results (according to Dr. Money). The child loved to play dress-up, enjoyed helping Mom in the kitchen, and disdained "boy toys" such as guns or trucks. "Dr. Money's work provides further evidence that most of the differences we observe between girls and boys are socially constructed," professor Henry Gleitman told us. "We reward children who follow the sex roles we create for them while we penalize or at least fail to reward children who don't conform. Parents create and reinforce the differences we observe between girls and boys."

We nodded sagely. In clinical rotations we often encountered parents who still clung to the quaint notion that girls and boys were different from birth. But we knew better.

Or so we thought.

When I left Philadelphia to begin my residency in family practice, I threw out most of the papers I had accumulated during my six years at the University of Pennsylvania. Stacks of photocopied scientific papers had to go out in the trash. But there was one manila folder I didn't throw out, a folder containing a series of studies done by Professor John Corso at Penn State during the 1950s and 1960s, demonstrating that females hear better than males.[3]

Four years later, after I finished my residency, my wife and I established a family practice in Montgomery County, Maryland, just outside of Washington, D.C. Years passed. I wasn't thinking much about gender differences. Then in the mid-1990s, I began to notice a parade of second- and third-grade boys marching into my office, their parents clutching a note from the school. The notes read: "We're concerned that Justin [or Juan or Michael or Tyrone] may have attention deficit disorder. Please evaluate."

In some of these cases I found that what these boys needed wasn't drugs for ADD, but rather a *teacher* who understood the hardwired differences in how girls and boys learn. Upon further inquiry, I found that nobody at the school was aware of gender differences in the ability to hear. I reread Professor Corso's papers, which documented that boys don't hear as well as girls. In the next chapter we'll look more closely at evidence for gender differences in hearing.

Think about the typical second-grade classroom. Imagine Justin, six years old, sitting at the back of the class. The teacher, a woman, is speaking in a tone of voice that seems about right to her. Justin barely hears her. Instead, he's staring out the window, or watching a fly crawl across the ceiling. The teacher notices that Justin isn't paying attention. Justin is demonstrating a deficit of attention. The teacher may reasonably wonder whether Justin perhaps has attention deficit disorder.

The teacher is absolutely right about Justin showing a deficit of attention. But his attention deficit isn't due to "attention deficit disorder," it's due to the fact that Justin can barely hear the soft-spoken teacher. The teacher is talking in a tone of voice that is comfortable to her and to the girls in the class, but some of the boys are practically falling asleep. In some cases we might be able to fix the problem simply by putting the boy in the front row.

Once, after I had done such an evaluation and made my recommendations, the parents told me that the school had advised them to seek a second opinion. "It's not that we don't trust you, Dr. Sax," Mom said. "It's just that the school really thinks we should get an opinion from an expert."

I soon learned that the only doctors that this particular school considered to be "experts" were doctors who always prescribed medication. Curious to know whether my experience was unique, I obtained funding from the American Academy of Family Physicians to survey all the doctors in the Washington area. Our survey basically asked one simple question: Who first suggests the diagnosis of ADD? The results: in the majority of cases the diagnosis of ADD is made by the teacher. Not by the parents, nor the neighbors, nor the doctor.[4]

There would be nothing wrong with teachers diagnosing their students as long as they had the training—and the resources, and adequate *time*—to distinguish the boy with ADD from the boy who just doesn't hear as well as most girls do. But after talking to dozens of teachers in our county, I didn't find one who was aware of the studies showing that girls hear better than boys.

"You should write a book, Dr. Sax," one of these parents told me. "Write a book so that teachers know about the differences in how girls and boys hear."

I allowed myself a patronizing smile. "I'm sure that there must already be dozens of such books for teachers, and for parents," I said.

"There aren't," she said.

"I'll find some for you," I said.

That conversation took place about seven years ago. Since then I've read lots of popular books about differences between girls and boys. And guess what. That mom was right.

Not only do most of the books currently in print about girls and boys fail to state the basic facts about innate differences between the sexes, many of them promote a bizarre form of political correctness, suggesting that it is somehow chauvinistic even to hint that any innate differences exist between female and male. A tenured professor at Brown University recently published a book in which she claims that the division of the human race into two sexes, female and male, is an artificial invention of our culture. "Nature really offers us more than two sexes," she claims, adding, "Our current notions of masculinity and femininity are cultural conceits." The decision to "label" a child as a girl or a boy is "a *social* decision," according to this expert. We should not label any child as being *either* a girl *or* a boy, this professor proclaimed. "There is no either/or. Rather, there are shades of difference."[5] This book received courteous mention in the *New York Times* and the *Washington Post*. America's most prestigious medical journal, the *New England Journal of Medicine*, praised the author for her "careful and insightful" approach to gender.[6]

I soon assembled a small library of best-selling books that counsel parents that the best child-rearing is *gender-neutral* child-rearing. These books tell parents that true virtue is to be found in training your child to play with toys traditionally associated with the opposite sex. You should buy dolls for your son, to teach him how to nurture.[7] You should buy an Erector set for your daughter. The underlying assumptions—that giving dolls to boys will cause boys to become more nurturing, or that giving girls Erector sets will improve girls' spatial relations skills—are never questioned. In fact, no scientific evidence exists to support the claim that gender-neutral child-rearing has any measurable benefit, regardless of which parameter you measure.[8]

On the same bookshelf you can find books that do affirm the

existence of innate differences in how girls and boys learn. But what books! Books with titles like *The Wonder of Boys* and *Girls Will Be Girls* promote antiquated and inaccurate gender stereotypes. "Girls are more emotional than boys." "Boys have a brain-based advantage when it comes to learning math." As we'll see, those familiar notions turn out to be false.

On one hand, you have books claiming that there are no innate differences between girls and boys, and that anybody who thinks otherwise is a reactionary stuck in the 1950s. On the other, you have books affirming innate differences between girls and boys—but these authors interpret these differences in a manner which reinforces gender stereotypes.

These books have only one thing in common. They are based less on fact, and more on their authors' personal beliefs or political agenda—either to deny innate sex differences, or to use sex differences in child development as a justification for maintaining traditional sex roles.

After waiting a few years for somebody else to write a book about girls and boys based on actual scientific research, I finally decided to write one myself. But I made myself a promise. Every time I make any statement about how girls and boys are different, I will also state the evidence on which my statement is based. Every statement I make about sex differences will be supported by good science published in peer-reviewed journals.

There is more at stake here than the old question of nature versus nurture. The failure to recognize and respect sex differences in child development has done substantial harm over the past thirty years—such will be my claim throughout this book. Children today face challenges that are substantially different from those you faced as a child or teenager, fifteen or twenty or thirty or forty years ago. Look at the statistics on drugs and alcohol, for starters. Teenage girls today are four times more likely to drink than their mothers were. They're *fifteen* times more likely to use drugs than their mothers were.[9] Traditionally, alcohol abuse has been more of a problem for teenage boys than for teenage girls. Not anymore. In a report published in 2004, the

National Research Council reported that young teenage girls are now *more* likely than boys to be drinking alcohol regularly—not because boys are drinking less, but because girls are drinking more.[10]

If girls have closed the gender gap with regard to alcohol abuse, boys are still more likely to be getting into trouble with drugs. According to FBI statistics, the number of boys under eighteen arrested for drug abuse offenses has increased by more than 50 percent in the past ten years; boys under eighteen are still five times more likely to be arrested for drug abuse violations than are girls under eighteen.[11] In chapter 7, I'll explore how the cultural and professional neglect of sex differences has compounded the drug problem.

But school, not drugs, is the "new" problem for boys. While today's girl is more likely to have problems with drugs and alcohol than her mother was, today's boy is much more likely to be struggling in school than his father was. Boys today are increasingly alienated from school. Recent investigations have shown a dramatic drop over the past twenty years in boys' academic performance in American schools.[12] According to the United States Department of Education, the average eleventh-grade American boy now writes at the same level as the average eighth-grade girl.[13] Similar gender gaps have been documented in the United Kingdom, Australia, New Zealand, and Canada.[14] And the percentage of boys going on to college, and graduating from college, is falling. The U.S. Department of Education now projects that in the year 2011, there will be 140 women graduating from college for every 100 men—very nearly a 60/40 female-to-male ratio.[15]

The future may already have arrived. Several major U.S. colleges and universities, such as New York University and the University of North Carolina, already report that their student body is more than 60 percent female.[16] I'm all in favor of women's colleges, but you have to ask the question: Why are nominally coed schools looking more and more like all-women's colleges? The proportion of boys going on to college is dropping steadily, as is the proportion of young men who are sticking around long enough to graduate. The high school dropout rate in the United States is now close to 30 percent, and the great majority of dropouts are boys.[17] More and more boys, discouraged by years of failure in elementary school, middle school, and high school, are asking: "Why should I stick around for any more of this?" Later in the book we'll hear from teachers who know how to *use* gender differences to kindle real enthusiasm for learning in both girls and boys.

Still, many educators and policymakers stubbornly cling to the dogma of "social constructionism," the belief that differences between girls and boys derive exclusively from social expectations with no input from biology. Stuck in a mentality that refuses to recognize innate, biologically programmed differences between girls and boys, many administrators and teachers don't fully appreciate that girls and boys enter the classroom with different needs, different abilities, and different goals.

In 2001, Republican Senator Kay Bailey Hutchison joined with Democratic Senator Hillary Clinton to craft new legislation legalizing single-sex education in American public schools. Their statute passed the Senate by a unanimous vote and is now law. Since the passage of their amendment, the number of public schools in the United States offering single-sex educational options has more than tripled.[18] Single-sex education is enjoying surging popularity in Australia, New Zealand, the United Kingdom, and Ireland.[19] At various points throughout the book we will consider the pros and cons of single-sex schools and single-sex activities, such as the Girl Scouts. I will suggest that for at least some children in some circumstances, single-sex activities offer unique opportunities and may even serve to "inoculate" girls and boys against some of the societal ailments that now threaten children and teenagers.

For the past three years I've been invited to schools around the United States and Canada to speak to teachers about differences in how girls and boys learn. I've been struck by the similarities between good teachers and good parents. They both stay up late at night agonizing how best to help a child. They both may shed tears when they tell me how they've struggled with a particular child. Good teachers and good parents both understand that every child is unique. Both want to help every child achieve his or her full potential. Teachers and parents are *partners* in helping each child grow up to be the woman or man that child was meant to be.

As you read through the book you'll find that I speak to you sometimes as though you're a parent, sometimes as though you're a teacher. In chapter 7, for example, I'll suggest how you might talk with your daughter or son about drugs. In chapter 5, I'll share some tips on teaching math to girls in a way that gets girls excited about learning math, and also some ideas for keeping boys interested in art. I hope you'll read chapter 5 as well as chapter 7, even if you're not a teacher. Because when you get right down to it, every parent *is* a teacher, and education begins at home.

FEMALE BRAINS, MALE BRAINS 2

There is increasing evidence to suggest that the brain is a sexual organ, that brain sex [i.e., the sex of the brain] is paramount in determining human gender identity.

—pediatric endocrinologists Dr. Gaya Aranoff and
Dr. Jennifer Bell, Columbia University, 2004[1]

Left Brain Verbal, Right Brain Spatial?

In the late 1800s, French neurologist Charles Edouard Brown-Séquard and British neurologist Henry Charlton Bastian independently discovered that the left side of the brain seems to be specialized for language. A man who suffers a stroke affecting the left side of the brain is much more likely to lose language functions than a man who suffers a stroke on the right side of the brain. The right side of a man's brain seems to be specialized for spatial functions such as navigation or mental imagery. But does this rule—left brain verbal, right brain spatial—apply to women as well as it applies to men?[2]

The modern era of research in gender differences may be said to have begun in 1964, when Herbert Lansdell reported the existence of anatomic sex differences in the organization of female and male brains.[3] Over the next two decades, a series of studies demonstrated that while the left hemisphere of the brain is clearly specialized for language functions in *men*, that asymmetry is much less noticeable in *women*.[4] Research with people who have suffered a stroke provided further support for the notion that male brains and female brains are organized differently, with functions more compartmentalized in male brains and more globally distributed in female brains. For example, men who suffer a stroke involving their brain's left hemisphere suffer a drop in verbal IQ of, on average, about 20 percent (from 111.5 to 88.7); men who suffer a stroke which affects their brain's *right* hemisphere suffer virtually no drop at all in their verbal IQ. If you damage a man's left hemisphere, he loses a big chunk of his language abilities; damage a man's right hemisphere, and his language ability is not affected. That sort of information provides strong evidence that the left hemisphere of a man's brain is very important for language, while the right hemisphere of a man's brain is not.

Women are different. Women who suffer a stroke affecting their brain's left hemisphere suffer a drop in their verbal IQ, on average, of about 9 percent (from 113.9 to 103.6); women who suffer a stroke affecting their brain's right hemisphere suffer a similar drop in verbal IQ, about 11 percent (from 113.9 to 101.0).[5] Women use both hemispheres of their brain for language. Men don't.

By the mid-1980s it was clear that the hemispheric compartmentalization of function that is so obvious in men's brains—left brain verbal, right brain spatial—applies less well or not at all to female brains. At that time most scientists believed that these differences in the brain derived from hormonal differences. Harvard neurologist Norm Geschwind and others suggested that male hormones were responsible for the hemispheric specialization seen in male brains.[6]

The belief that hormones are responsible for sex differences in the brain led many scientists to believe that sex differences must be small in the brains of children. After all, prepubescent children don't manufacture sex hormones in large quantities.

Were those scientists right?

Probably not. Research in laboratory animals, for starters, has demonstrated large, innate, genetically determined sex differences in the brain. One striking illustration of this principle was published in 2004 by scientists at UCLA. They examined a bird that was a lateral gynandromorphic hermaphrodite: in other words, a bird that was half-female and half-male. Every cell on the right side of this bird's body was male; every cell on the left side of this bird's body was female. This bird had a testicle on the right and an ovary on the left. If you look at a picture of this

Hermaphrodite bird provides a clue to the importance of hardwired sex differences.

bird, you will notice that it has male plumage on the right and female plumage on the left. This bird's blood contains a mix of female and male hormones: female hormones manufactured by the ovary and male hormones from the testicle.

Now let's take a look at this bird's brain. If the theory popular in the 1970s and 1980s were correct, we shouldn't see big differences between the left and right sides of this bird's brain. The brain of this bird is nourished with blood that contains an equal mix of female and male hormones. So, if hormones are responsible for sexual differentiation of the brain, then the left and right sides of the brain should look the same.

But they don't. The left and right sides of this bird's brain are

male   female

Male brain tissue is intrinsically different
from female brain tissue.

dramatically different. Scientists who have studied this bird have concluded that female brain tissue and male brain tissue are "intrinsically different,"[7] as a result of females and males having a different complement of sex chromosomes—and regardless of the mix of hormones in the blood.

Maybe that's true for birds, but what about humans? In fact, recent research suggests that female brain tissue is "intrinsically different" from male brain tissue in our species just as in other animals. In 2004 an all-star team of fourteen neuroscientists from the University of California, the University of Michigan, and Stanford University published their findings demonstrating a dramatically different expression of proteins derived from the X chromosome and the Y chromosome in human female and male brains. In men, many areas of the brain are rich in proteins that are coded directly by the Y chromosome. Those proteins are absent in women's brain tissue. Conversely, women's brain tissue is rich in material coded directly by the X chromosome; these particular transcripts of the X chromosome are absent from men's brain tissue.[8] These sex differences, then, are *genetically programmed*, not mediated by hormonal differences.

These scientists analyzed thirty samples of human brain tissue collected from different areas of the brain and different individuals. The scientists were not told the sex of the individuals from whom the specimens were taken. But just by analyzing the expression of two different genes in the brain tissue, they were able to correctly identify the sex of every one of the thirty specimens, female versus male. Female brain tissue and male brain tissue are intrinsically different.

Stop and think about this for a moment. This new research shows that females get more from their X chromosomes than males do,[9] and that the Y chromosome in men is directly responsible for differences in the brain. Differences. Not one better than the other. Not one worse than the other. Just different.

Scientists continue to recognize that sex hormones do affect the brain. However, this recent research has also demonstrated that the direct effect of the sex chromosomes on brain tissue need not be mediated by hormones. It's genetically programmed. It's present at birth.

Sex differences in brain anatomy are all well and good, but do they matter? Do those sex differences in brain anatomy mean that there are sex differences in brain *function*? Are there significant differences in how girls and boys hear, or how they see, or how they learn? And if so, are those differences present at birth? Or not?

Lessons from the Nursery

Janel Caine, a graduate student at Florida State University in the late 1980s, was interested in studying the effects of music therapy on premature babies. Some researchers believed that playing soft music in a baby's crib might help relax the baby, which might improve the baby's appetite, so the baby would grow faster. Janel Caine wanted to test that hypothesis. She obtained permission from parents of twenty-six premature babies to play soft music in the babies' cribs. She also enrolled twenty-six other premature babies, matched in age and weight to the first set, but those babies didn't get to hear any music. Sure enough, she found that babies who had music played in their crib grew faster, had fewer complications, and were able to be discharged home from the hospital about five days earlier on average than babies who didn't receive music therapy.

Janel Caine's master's thesis is still on file deep in the stacks of Florida State University's Robert Manning Strozier Library. Go to that library and ask to borrow her thesis. Flip to the back and you'll see the results broken down by gender. When you review those data tables, you'll find something unexpected. Girl babies who received music therapy left the hospital nine and a half days earlier on average than girl babies who did not. But *boy* babies who received music therapy did not leave the hospital *any* earlier than boys who did not! Music therapy was very beneficial for the girls, but not at all beneficial for the boys. Curiously, Ms. Caine never mentioned this gender difference in her results, neither in her thesis[10] nor in her subsequent publication.[11]

A more recent study with even younger, more premature babies, confirmed both Ms. Caine's overall findings as well as the gender difference in the results. In this later study, young women hummed the Brahms lullaby over and over to some premature babies, but not others. Overall, babies who had women humming to them were discharged on average six days earlier than babies who didn't. This time the gender difference in the results was even larger. Premature girl babies who were hummed to left the hospital *twelve days earlier* on average than girl babies who weren't. But premature boy babies who were hummed to didn't leave the hospital any earlier than boy babies who weren't.[12]

Why the difference? Why did music therapy work so well for the girls and not at all for the boys? The most plausible explanation is simply that boy babies don't hear the music as well, or in the same way that girl babies do.

There's good evidence now, from several different sources, that newborn baby girls really do hear better than newborn baby boys. Pediatric audiologists Barbara Cone-Wesson, Glendy Ramirez, and Yvonne Sininger have done careful studies of the hearing of newborn babies. When any baby or child (or adult for that matter) hears a sound, there's an immediate reaction, called an acoustic brain response. Cone-Wesson and her colleagues decided to measure the acoustic brain response of more than sixty newborn girls and boys. For a 1,500 Hz tone played to the right ear, they found that the average girl baby had an acoustic brain response about 80 percent greater than the response of the average baby boy.[13] (The range of sounds around 1,500 Hz is especially important, because that range of sound is critical for understanding speech.)[14]

This finding—that newborn baby girls hear differently than boys, especially at higher frequencies—was recently confirmed by Jane Cassidy, a professor at Louisiana State University. Professor Cassidy used a different technique than Cone-Wesson, Sininger, and Ramirez had used to evaluate hearing in newborns: specifically, Professor Cassidy used a technique known as transient evoked otoacoustic emissions.* Professor Cassidy, studying 350 newborn baby girls and boys, found that the girls' hearing was substantially more sensitive than the boys', especially in the 1,000- to 4,000-Hz range, which is so important for speech discrimination.[15] Other studies have demonstrated that teenage girls (for example) do in fact hear better than boys do.[16] The female-male difference in hearing only gets bigger as kids get older.[17]

These built-in gender differences in hearing have real consequences. As we've seen, music therapy works for girl babies but not for boy babies—although perhaps it might work for baby boys if the volume was adjusted or if other characteristics of the music were altered. Janel Caine used the Brahms lullaby, "Rock-

---

*We humans, like all mammals, hear because little "hairs" on cells in our inner ear are very sensitive to sound. Those "hair cells" wiggle when they detect a sound. That wiggling generates a subtle acoustic response, which is the transient evoked otoacoustic emission.

a-Bye Baby," "Twinkle Twinkle Little Star," and similar songs. The later study, as we saw, used only the Brahms lullaby. Maybe boys would do better with Wagner's "Ride of the Valkyries" or Gregorian chant or Bruce Springsteen or Snoop Dogg. We just don't know.

The difference in how girls and boys hear also has major implications for how you should talk to your children. I can't count the number of times a father has told me, "My daughter says I yell at her. I've never yelled at her. I just speak to her in a normal tone of voice, and she says I'm yelling." If a forty-three-year-old man speaks in what he thinks is a "normal tone of voice" to a seventeen-year-old girl, that girl is going to experience his voice as being about ten times louder than what the man is hearing.[18] He *is* yelling at her, but he doesn't realize it. The father and his daughter are experiencing the same sound in two different ways.

The gender difference in hearing also suggests different strategies for the classroom. More than thirty years ago, psychologist Colin Elliot demonstrated that eleven-year-old girls are distracted by noise levels about *ten times* softer than noise levels that boys find distracting.[19] That boy who's *tap-tap-tapping* his fingers on the desk might not be bothering the other boys, but he *is* bothering the girls—as well as the (female) teacher. One reason for that difference, of course, is that eleven-year-old girls *hear* better. If you're teaching girls, don't raise your voice—and try to keep the classroom free of extraneous noise. Girls won't learn as well in a loud, noisy classroom. When we come back to this topic later in the book, we'll discover that the rules are different when you're teaching boys.

The Eye of the Beholder

Most girls and women interpret facial expressions better than most boys and men can.[20] Researchers at Cambridge University wondered whether female superiority in understanding facial expressions was innate or whether it developed as a result of social factors such as parents encouraging girls to interact with other girls while the boys shoot each other with ray guns. These researchers decided to study newborn babies *on the day they were born.*

Their plan was to give babies a choice between looking at a simple dangling mobile or at a young woman's face—more precisely, a live young woman, right there with the baby. The young woman smiled at the baby but didn't say anything. The mobile dangled and twisted but made no noise.

Was there a gender difference in what the babies preferred to look at? All 102 babies in the study were videotaped and their eye motions analyzed by researchers who didn't know the sex of the baby. The boy babies were much more interested in the mobile than in the young woman's face. The girl babies were more likely to look at the face. The differences were large: the boys were more than twice as likely to prefer the mobile. The researchers concluded that they had proven "beyond reasonable doubt" that sex differences in social interest "are, in part, biological in origin."[21]

The results of this experiment suggest that girls are born prewired to be interested in faces while boys are prewired to be more interested in moving objects. The reason for that difference has to do with sex differences in the anatomy of the eye.

The retina is that part of the eye that converts light into a neurological signal. The retina is divided into layers. One layer contains the photoreceptors, the rods and the cones. Rods are sensitive to black and white. Rods are color-blind. Cones are sensitive to color.

The rods and cones send their signals to the next layer, the ganglion cells. Scientists have known for many decades that some ganglion cells are very large (magnocellular), while others are small (parvocellular). Most papers on this topic just refer to them as M and P ganglion cells.

P cells and M cells have very different jobs. M cells are wired primarily to rods, with little input from cones; they are essentially simple motion detectors. M cells are distributed all across

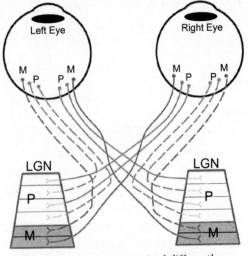

The visual system is organized differently
in girls and boys.

the retina, so they can track objects anywhere in the visual field. You can think of the M cells as being wired to answer the questions "Where is it now and where is it going?" P cells are wired (in our species) to all three varieties of cones, but have much less input from the rods. P cells are concentrated in and around the fovea, the center of the field of vision. You can think of the P cells as answering the question "What is it?" P cells compile information about texture and color; M cells compile information about movement and direction.[22]

The P cells send information via their own special division of the thalamus to a particular region of the cerebral cortex that appears to be specialized for analysis of texture and color. The M cells send their information via a separate pathway to a different region of the cerebral cortex, a region that is specialized for analysis of spatial relationships and object motion. And guess what? *Every step in each pathway, from the retina to the cerebral cortex, is different in females and males.*[23]

The real surprises have come from microscopic analyses of

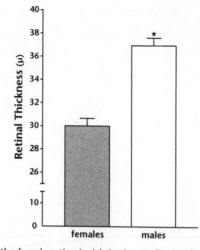

Because the female retina is rich in the smaller P cells, while the larger M cells predominate in the male retina, the male retina is much thicker than the female retina. Note the small variation within the sexes and the large difference between the sexes.

the eye performed in the past five years. Using recently developed techniques, scientists have found that the human retina is full of receptors for sex hormones.[24] Anatomist Edwin Lephart and his associates have found that the male retina is substantially thicker than the female retina.[25] That's because the male retina has mostly the larger, thicker M cells while the female retina has predominantly the smaller, thinner P ganglion cells.

We're not talking about small differences between the sexes, with lots of overlap. We're talking about large differences between the sexes, with no overlap at all. Every male animal had a thicker retina than any female retina, due to the males having more M cells (see the accompanying graph).

Suppose you give crayons and a blank sheet of paper to young girls and young boys. Let them draw whatever they like. You'll find that girls will prefer colors like red, orange, green, and beige, because those are the colors that P cells are prewired to be most sensitive to. Boys prefer to simulate motion in their

Summary of Differences between P Cells and M Cells

	P CELLS	M CELLS
Are wired predominantly to . . .	Cones	Rods
Are located mostly in . . .	The center of the retina (center of the field of vision)	All throughout the retina (entire field of vision, peripheral and central)
Are best adapted to detect . . .	Color and texture	Location, direction, and speed
Answer the question:	"What is it?"	"Where is it now? Where is it going? How fast is it moving?"
Ultimately project to:	Inferior temporal cortex	Posterior parietal cortex
Predominate in:	**Females** (more P cells than M cells)	**Males** (more M cells than P cells)

pictures. Boys prefer colors such as black, gray, silver, and blue because that's the way the M cells are wired.[26]

Studies in young children have demonstrated that girls are better at tasks involving object discrimination—answering the question "What is it?"—whereas boys are better at tasks involving object location—"Where is it?" Similar sex differences in abilities have recently been demonstrated in young monkeys as well.[27]

Sex differences in toy preferences start to make more sense once you understand this research. A richly textured doll will be more appealing than a moving truck if your system favors the P cells, as is the case in females. So we shouldn't be surprised that young females—whether human or monkey—prefer dolls over trucks, while young males, human and monkey, prefer trucks over dolls.[28] Nor should we be surprised when—in the Cambridge study referenced above—the girl babies look at the young woman's face, while boy babies look at the mobile.

Girls Draw Nouns, Boys Draw Verbs

Ms. Kanovsky teaches kindergarten. She's given each of her students a blank sheet of paper and told them to draw anything they like, using the colored crayons available to all the children. The teacher walks around the room encouraging each child. She stops by five-year-old Anita. Anita has about a dozen crayons spread out around her picture of three people. The people are facing the viewer, all smiling. Anita's picture is rich in reds, browns, oranges, and flesh tones. "That's wonderful, Anita," Ms. Kanovsky says. "Who are those people in the picture?"

"That's me," Anita says, pointing to one of the figures. "That's my brother Carlos, and that's my Mommy."

"That's really great, Anita," Ms. Kanovsky says. "Good job."

Five-year-old Matthew—the same Matthew we met in chapter 1—is frantically scribbling with a black crayon. "What's that?" Ms. Kanovsky says.

"It's a rocket about to smash into the Earth," Matthew says gleefully. "See! There's the rocket! There's the Earth!"

Ms. Kanovsky sees that Matthew has used only one crayon, the black crayon, for both the rocket and the Earth. There's no color, no people, no trace of any human anywhere. "That's nice, Matthew," Ms. Kanovsky says without conviction (despite her best efforts). "How about adding a little color? And is there anyone in the rocket?"

There is one thing that five-year-olds, both girls and boys, are very good at: figuring out what the grown-ups like. In this situation, I guarantee you that Matthew understands that his picture doesn't please Ms. Kanovsky the way Anita's picture does. In her defense, Ms. Kanovsky is applying the criteria she was taught. "Encourage children to draw people-centered pictures, using lots of colors." That's what Ms. Kanovsky learned when she was earning her bachelor's degree in early elementary education. But that old recommendation doesn't take into account what's been learned in the last twenty years about differences in the way girls and boys see the world.

Researchers who have studied the pictures drawn by young

girls and young boys have found that girls typically draw pictures of people (or pets or flowers or trees), arranged more or less symmetrically, facing the viewer. Girls usually use ten or more colors in their pictures (remember all the crayons Anita had strewn around her picture?), and they are more likely to use the colors that researcher Yasumasa Arai calls "warm" colors—red, green, beige, and brown.[29] Boys typically draw *action*: a rocket hitting its target, an alien about to eat somebody, a car about to hit another car. Boys typically use at most six colors and they prefer what Yasumasa Arai calls "cold" colors such as blue, gray, silver, and black. Boys are also much more likely to employ a third-person perspective, looking at the action from a remote vantage point rather than from a perspective facing the vehicle or the animal actually doing the action.[30] Psychologist Donna Tuman summarizes the difference this way: girls draw nouns, boys draw verbs.[31]

If we consider what we know about P cells and M cells, these differences aren't surprising. Of course boys draw action, using black, gray, silver, and blue. That's the way the M cells are wired. Of course girls draw more richly colored subjects with a preponderance of red, orange, beige, yellow, and so on. That's the way P cells are wired.

At least 95 percent of kindergarten teachers are women. Most are not aware of these differences . . . because nobody has ever told them. Instead, the teachers often act like Ms. Kanovsky, encouraging children to draw pictures of people, using lots of colors. Five-year-olds like Anita and Matthew quickly figure out that Anita is doing it "right" and Matthew is doing it "wrong." Matthew will soon discover that he's not very good at trying to copy Anita, that is, trying to draw pictures of people, using lots of colors. Matthew will quickly decide that he's no good at art. Only five years old, Matthew has decided that "art is for girls." Other experiences he will have (which we will get to later in the book) will teach him that he's no good at anything else that's going on in a twenty-first-century "gender-neutral" kindergarten. The teacher wants him to sit still and be quiet and listen, while he wants to run around and jump and yell. After a few weeks he's not going to see the point of going to school at all. That's when the tantrums begin.

Ms. Kanovsky wasn't aware of the hardwired differences between the visual world of girls and the visual world of boys. Ironically, the result of her lack of awareness of gender differences is a reinforcement of traditional gender stereotypes. "Art is for girls." A more informed, gender-aware approach might have broken that stereotype.

Ask for Directions?

Let's look at another difference in how girls' and boys' brains work: geometry and navigation. Researchers have found that females and males use fundamentally different strategies for those tasks. Ask a woman how to get to a friend's house and she may tell you something like, "Go down King Street till you see the McDonald's. Then make a left, go past the hardware store and the Exxon station until you see the elementary school. Make a right just past the elementary school and go down Scottsdale Boulevard. Their house is the fourth from the intersection, on the left. It's a split-level house painted *lime green*. You won't believe that house. The shutters and trim are painted *fuchsia*. Lime green and fuchsia. It looks like a gingerbread house after some kind of glow-in-the-dark *mold* has started to grow on it. That's their house. Just *please* don't tell them what I said about it. About the gingerbread and the mold, I mean."

A man giving directions to the same house might say, "Go south on King Street about two miles, then turn so you're heading east on Duke Street. After about a mile on Duke Street, turn south again onto Scottsdale Road. Their house is half a block down Scottsdale, on the east side of the road. They just painted it. Green and pink, I think."

Women typically navigate using landmarks that can be seen or heard or smelled. Men are more likely to use absolute direction such as north and south or absolute distance such as miles or city blocks.[32] A study published in 2003 demonstrated that this gender difference in navigation is well established by five years of age.[33] Those different strategies correlate with different brain regions. Neuroscientists have found that young women and young men use different areas in the brain when they navigate: young women use the cerebral cortex while young men use the hippocampus, a nucleus deep inside the brain that is not activated in women's brains during navigational tasks.[34]

These sex differences may actually be *more* pronounced in children and adolescents than in adults. Later on we'll see how these differences affect best practices for teaching subjects like geometry and number theory to girls and boys.

Trucks, Rockets, Dolls, and Crayons

Over the past twenty years the scientific foundation underlying the belief that all children are androgynous at birth has crumbled away. Dr. John Money's claim that a boy could be raised as a girl has been shown to be fabrication pure and simple, indeed just the opposite of what really happened . . . as related eloquently by the child himself, David Reimer, just a few years before he committed suicide in May 2004 at the age of thirty-eight.[35]

Another good example of how these old ideas have collapsed has to do with the kinds of toys girls and boys choose to play with. During the "Dark Ages"—that period from the mid-1960s to the mid-1990s during which it was politically incorrect to suggest that there were innate differences in how girls and boys learn and play—most experts insisted that children's toy preferences are socially constructed. The experts believed that a two-year-old boy prefers to play with trucks rather than dolls because (they believed) the boy's behavior is governed by the following syllogism, which they called a *gender schema*:

1) I am a boy.
2) Boys are supposed to play with trucks, and not with dolls.
3) Therefore I will play with trucks and not with dolls.

There are several major problems with the social learning/ gender schema theory, the biggest being that it doesn't fit the facts. Child psychologist Lisa Serbin and colleagues at Concordia University studied 77 one-and-a-half-year-old toddlers, girls and boys. They found that these little children—boys especially— had not a clue which gender they belonged to, even when the psychologists used the simplest nonverbal prompts. Kids this age just cannot reliably assign themselves to the correct gender, and they score only slightly above chance in assigning other kids to the correct gender. Nevertheless, Serbin's group found that children's toy preferences are firmly in place by this age, especially among boys. When the experimenter offered a boy a truck or a doll, the boy chose the truck. In fact, the boys preferred trucks over dolls more strongly than girls preferred dolls over trucks.[36] That ought to be surprising if you buy into social learning/ gender schema theories, because eighteen-month-old girls were more likely than boys to be able to classify themselves and other children by gender. If the social learning/gender schema theories were correct, the girls should show a stronger preference for gender-typical toys, because girls this age have a more mature understanding of gender. But the reality is just the opposite.

Another group, led by child psychologist Anne Campbell, looked at toddlers as young as *nine months* of age—and they found the same results. Nine-month-old boys strongly preferred "boy toys" such as balls, trains, and cars.[37] Nine-month-old girls preferred "girl toys" such as dolls and baby carriages, although the girls' preference was (again) not quite as strong as the boys' preference. Campbell's study is especially striking because she showed very clearly that kids this age have no clue what gender they belong to. Boys and girls show gender-typical toy preferences long before they understand gender. Dr. Campbell has recently said, politely, that "the impact of cognitive variables may have been overestimated."[38] In other words, eighteen-month-old boys don't choose to play with trucks rather than dolls because they know they're "supposed" to. They choose trucks because they'd rather play with trucks.

Gerianne Alexander, a psychologist with the Yale Child Study Center, recently showed that male monkeys prefer to play with toy cars while female monkeys prefer to play with dolls.[39] Again, if you recall our earlier discussion of the differences between M cells and P cells, this shouldn't come as a surprise.

In fact, gender differences in play behavior are present in just about every mammal that's been studied.[40] More than twenty years ago, scientists knew that young male rats engage in much more rough-and-tumble play than do young female rats. In one study, scientists damaged the amygdala of young rats. (The amygdala, a small nucleus at the base of the brain, plays an important role in emotion and affect.) That damage dramatically decreased rough-and-tumble play among the males but had no effect on females, suggesting that the gender difference in play behavior was due at least in part to sex differences in the amygdala.[41] The fact that gender differences in play behavior are found in so many other species is another nail in the coffin for the idea that similar preferences in human children are entirely due to culture.

Today we know that innate differences between girls and boys are profound. Of course, not all girls are alike and not all boys are alike. But girls and boys do differ from one another in systematic ways that should be understood and made use of, not covered up or ignored.

Girls and boys play differently. They learn differently. They fight differently. They see the world differently. They hear differently. When I started graduate school in 1980, most psychologists were insisting that those differences came about because parents raised girls and boys in different ways. Today we know that the truth is the other way around: parents raise girls and boys differently because girls and boys are so different from birth. Girls and boys behave differently because their brains are wired differently.

Feelings

Deborah Yurgelun-Todd and her associates at Harvard have used sophisticated MRI imaging to examine how emotion is processed in the brains of children from the ages of seven through seventeen. In young children, these researchers found that negative emotional activity in response to unpleasant or disturbing visual images seems to be localized in phylogenetically primitive areas deep in the brain, specifically in the amygdala. (A phylogenetically primitive area of the brain is one that hasn't changed much in the course of evolution: it looks pretty much the same in humans as it does in mice.) That may be one reason why it doesn't make much sense to ask a seven-year-old to tell you why she is feeling sad or distressed. The part of the brain that does the talking, up in the cerebral cortex, has few direct connections to the part of the brain where the emotion is occurring, down in the amygdala.

In adolescence, a larger fraction of the brain activity associated with negative emotion moves up to the cerebral cortex. That's the same division of the brain associated with our higher cognitive functions—reflection, reasoning, language, and the like. So, the seventeen-year-old is able to explain why she is feeling sad in great detail and without much difficulty (if she wants to).

But that change occurs *only in girls*. In boys the locus of brain activity associated with negative emotion remains stuck in the amygdala.[42] In boys there is no change associated with maturation. Asking a seventeen-year-old boy to talk about why he's feeling glum may be about as productive as asking a six-year-old boy the same question. A recent study from a team of German researchers duplicated this finding in young adults: in young women, brain activity associated with negative emotion was mostly up in the cerebral cortex, whereas in young men it remained stuck down in the amygdala.[43]

Emotions—both positive and negative—are processed differently in girls' brains than in boys'.[44] We'll talk about this partic-

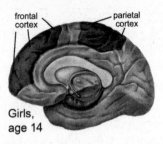

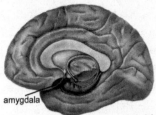

As girls mature, brain activity associated with emotion moves out of the amygdala and into the cerebral cortex.

As boys mature, brain activity associated with emotion remains in the amygdala.

ular sex difference at greater length later on in the book. For now, let's pause to think about the implications of this difference. In boys, as in men, the part of the brain where emotions happen is not well connected to the part of the brain where verbal processing and speech happens—unlike the situation in teenage girls and in women. There's been much talk in recent years about the need to increase the "emotional literacy" of boys.[45] Such people maintain that boys would be better off if we encouraged them to talk more about their feelings. That sort of talk betrays (in my judgment) a lack of awareness of basic sex differences in the underlying wiring of the brain. Asking a teenage boy to talk about how he *feels* is a question guaranteed to make most boys uncomfortable. You're asking him to make connections between two parts of his brain that don't normally communicate. This is a very different task for a boy than for a girl. As one thirteen-year-old boy said, "My English teacher wants me to write about my 'feelings.' I don't know what my 'feelings' are, and I can't write about them. Anyway, my feelings are none of their business! I hate school!"[46]

The Sorry Burden of the Past

There's a long history of people misinterpreting scientific research and misusing that research to reinforce gender stereotypes . . . usually at the expense of girls and women. One hundred years ago, German physician Paul Julius Möbius wrote a bestseller entitled *Regarding the Physiological Weak-Mindedness of Women*. Möbius compared the cranial capacity of women and men of the same height. He showed that if you examined the skull of a five-foot-nine-inch-tall woman and compared it to the skull of a man the same height, you would find, on average, that the volume capacity of her skull—and hence the size of her brain—was about 8 to 10 percent smaller than the man's.[47]

Women do have slightly smaller brains than men, on average, even after controlling for body size. To Möbius, that fact seemed irrefutable evidence that women are "physiologically weak-minded." Möbius assumed that intellect was a simple function of brain size: the bigger the brain, the greater the intellect. He was not aware of other differences that distinguish female and male brains from each other. All these differences are roughly as robust, statistically, as the difference in average brain size:

- Women have higher brain blood flow per gram of tissue than men have.[48]
- In some critical areas of the brain, women have larger brain cells that receive more inputs than are found in corresponding areas in men's brains.[49]
- For many tasks, brain imaging studies show that women use the most advanced areas of the brain, the cerebral cortex, whereas men doing the same task use more "primitive" areas of the brain such as the globus pallidus, the amygdala, or the hippocampus.[50]

Even Dr. Möbius's most basic assumption—that brain size correlates with intelligence—applies differently to women and men. In men that assumption has some validity. Men with high

IQs do, on average, have slightly larger brains (after adjusting for body size) than do men who score lower on IQ tests. But that correspondence may not hold true for women. Studies suggest that women with high IQs do not have larger brains than women with low IQs.[51] In a recent Harvard Medical School study of teenagers, there was a positive correlation between brain size and intelligence for teenage boys, but there was no correlation between brain size and intelligence for teenage girls.[52]

"The more you use it, the bigger it will be." One widely held belief about brain anatomy is that the more you use a particular area of the brain, the larger that area of the brain will be. (Dr. Möbius's assumption that overall brain size correlates with overall intelligence is a corollary of this belief.) For men that assumption appears to have some validity. Consider the area of the brain involved in music, for instance. In men, the "music" area of the brain is larger in musicians than in nonmusicians. But in women there is no such association: the brains of women musicians are not demonstrably different from the brains of women who are not musicians, according to a 2003 study from Harvard Medical School.[53]

The bottom line is that the brain is just organized *differently* in females and males. The tired argument about which sex is more intelligent or which sex has the "better" brain is about as meaningful as arguing about which utensil is "better," a knife or a spoon. The only correct answer to such a question is: "Better for what?" A knife is better than a spoon if you want to cut through a piece of meat, while a spoon is better if you're facing a bowl of chicken broth.

Let's pursue that analogy for a moment. You can offer the same nutrients in different forms. You can accomplish similar nutritional aims with meat loaf and with beef stew. If your child has a spoon but no knife, then you'll want to give your child some beef stew. If your child has a knife but no spoon, then you'll give your child some meat loaf.

Likewise, the differences between what girls and boys can do are not large. But the differences in how they do it can be very large indeed. For example, as we'll see later, you can teach the same math course in different ways. You can make math appealing to girls by teaching it one way, or you can make it appealing to boys by teaching it in another way. Girls and boys can both learn math equally well if you understand those gender differences.

Gender Differences vs. Gender Stereotypes: Barbie Liberation!

It's Christmas morning. Seven-year-old Zachariah Zelin rips the gift wrap off a present and squeals with delight when he sees a Talking G.I. Joe action figure. But this G.I. Joe is a little bit different. Standing in army fatigues, machine gun and hand grenades at the ready, this G.I. Joe exclaims in a high-pitched, girly voice, "Math is hard!" and "Want to go shopping?" and "Will we ever have enough clothes?"

The Barbie Liberation Organization (BLO) had struck again. The BLO is a group of activists dedicated to proving the inanity of prevailing gender stereotypes. These activists infiltrated toy stores and surreptitiously switched the voice boxes of G.I. Joe with the Talking Teen Barbie. So somewhere in Zachariah Zelin's town, there must have been a girl whose Barbie yelled—in a deep, gruff voice—"Vengeance is mine!" and "Dead men tell no lies."[54]

I don't condone the vandalism of the BLO. But I think the image of a G.I. Joe saying "Math is hard!" in a sweet feminine voice should make us reconsider our own beliefs about gender. In our culture you'll often encounter widespread assumptions about differences between boys and girls, such as the belief that math is harder for girls than for boys. Many of those assumptions are wrong—by which I mean that there is good science to refute them. Here are some examples of false beliefs about gender differences:

- Boys are "naturally" better at math and science than girls are.

- Girls are "naturally" more emotional than boys are.
- Girls are "naturally" collaborative, while boys are competitive.

Each of these statements is false. (We'll consider evidence supporting this assertion at appropriate points throughout the book.) These prevalent stereotypes often confuse parents and teachers when they come to hear me speak. Parents often assume that I endorse these inaccurate gender stereotypes just because my topic is innate gender differences.

One parent approached me after one of my presentations and told me about her children. Her son Noah loves to sew and also does macramé. He's very careful about his appearance. He doesn't like to get his clothes messed. Her daughter Stephanie on the other hand is a real tomboy. Stephanie plays soccer, climbs trees, and doesn't mind rolling in the mud. How do children like Stephanie and Noah affect the arguments I'm making here?

Girls and boys who show gender-atypical behaviors and preferences deserve special consideration. We'll devote much of chapter 9 to such children. But the bottom line is that essentially all of the differences I will tell you about apply equally to such children.

The differences we've considered in how girls and boys hear and see appear to apply to all children, regardless of whether they play with dolls or trucks or both. One illustration of that principle comes from our discussion earlier in this chapter of differences in the visual systems of girls and boys. In girls, the P system predominates, giving girls more sensitivity to small differences in color. It's easy to understand, then, why teenage girls will describe a shirt as being lime green or forest green or emerald or jade, while teenage boys will just say the shirt is . . . green. Researchers at Auburn University wondered whether more feminine girls would make more subtle color distinctions than less feminine girls. Is it blue, or is it navy blue or sky blue or periwinkle?

These researchers interviewed and tested each girl in their study to see where she scored on a scale of femininity. They then looked to see whether there was a correlation between a girl's femininity and the subtlety of her color distinctions. They found no correlation. Girls make more elaborate and more subtle color distinctions than boys do, *regardless of whether the girls are very feminine or not feminine at all.*[55] Tomboys have more in common with very feminine girls than they have with boys, at least when it comes to how they see the world.

Every child is unique. I'm *not* saying that all boys are the same or that all girls are the same. But the fact that each child is unique and complex should not blind us to the fact that gender is one of the two great organizing principles in child development—the other principle being age. Trying to understand a child without understanding the role of gender in child development is like trying to understand a child's behavior without knowing the child's age. Pick up a book with a title like *What to Expect from Your Two-Year-Old.* That book is very different from *What to Expect from Your Eight-Year-Old.* Of course, nobody is saying that all two-year-olds are alike or that all eight-year-olds are alike. While recognizing diversity among two-year-olds, we can still have a meaningful discussion of the ways in which two-year-olds and eight-year-olds differ, categorically, in terms of what they can do, what they're interested in, how they relate to their parents, and so on.

At least with regard to how children hear and speak, gender may be even more fundamental to learning than age is. When noted linguist and Georgetown University professor Deborah Tannen compared how girls and boys of different ages use language, she "was overwhelmed by the differences that separated the females and males at each age, and the striking similarities that linked the females, on one hand, and the males, on the other, across the vast expanse of age. In many ways, the second-grade girls were more like the twenty-five-year-old women than like the second-grade boys."[56]

Brain research bears out Professor Tannen's findings. In a recent study of human brain development, scientists found that differences in the brain associated with biological sex—female compared with male—were substantially more significant than differences in the brain associated with age—younger compared with older.[57]

The analogy to age differences provides a good way to think about sex differences. No two girls are alike, just as no two boys are alike. Stephanie who likes to roll in the mud and play soccer is very different from seven-year-old Zoe. Zoe's favorite hobby is playing with her Barbies. Zoe also insisted on joining the Junior Poms (a sort of cheerleading group). Zoe was asking for lipstick at age five. Her mother, Barbara, a sincere old-school feminist, was horrified. "Where is this coming from?" she asked me, bewildered. "I only own one lipstick and I haven't used it in six months. And I loathe and despise Barbies. I've never even bought one for Zoe. She gets all that trash as gifts from her aunts and uncles."

Despite the superficial differences, Stephanie may share more with Zoe than you might imagine. In their ability to listen, in their willingness to affiliate with adults, and in their emotional development, Stephanie probably has more in common with Zoe than she has in common with her brother or with any boy.

Sex Differences vs. Sexual Orientation

How about gay versus straight? Does what I say about boys apply to gay boys as well as straight boys? How about lesbian girls and straight girls? We're going to talk at length about lesbian, gay, bisexual, and transgender individuals in chapter 9. Basically, I will argue that sex differences—female compared with male—are far more profound than any differences attributable to sexual orientation. For example: the superior hearing of girls compared with boys still holds true regardless of whether you're talking about gay boys or straight boys, or lesbian girls or straight girls.[58] Likewise, sex differences in how children relate to parents don't appear to be influenced significantly by sexual orientation.

My bottom line is that *sex, female or male*, is more fundamental than sexual orientation, gay or straight. A lesbian girl and a straight girl have much more in common with each other, as a rule, than a lesbian girl has in common with a gay boy—in terms of how they learn, how they play, how they fight, and how they relate to their friends, to their parents, and to the world in general.

Recent studies suggest that male-female differences are more fundamental than gay-straight differences even when we're talking about sexual attraction and sexual behavior. UCLA psychologist Anne Peplau recently reviewed the published research on human sexuality in gay and straight women and men.[59] She found that for both gay and straight women, "Women's sexuality tends to be strongly linked to a close relationship. For women, an important goal of sex is intimacy; the best context for pleasurable sex is a committed relationship. This is less true for men," whether they are gay or straight. Straight men often buy pornography. Gay men often buy pornography. But few women, whether lesbian or straight, buy pornography. Few women will spend eight dollars to purchase a magazine featuring photographs of the genitals of strangers. You can't have a committed relationship with a picture in a magazine.

In addition, Peplau found that most men's sexual self-concept has an aggressive dimension, whether that man is gay or straight. There is no corresponding element of aggression in women's sexual self-concepts, according to Peplau, either in lesbian women or in straight women. Rape is a crime committed almost exclusively by men—both by straight men (against women) and by gay men (against other men). Women seldom rape, regardless of their sexual orientation.

An international consortium of psychologists recently published a survey of over 16,000 individuals from 52 countries, including Eastern and Western Europe, North and South America,

Africa, Australia, South Asia, East Asia, and Japan. Comparing women and men across all cultures and continents, these psychologists found "universal" sex differences in sexual motivation and sexual interest. To give just one example, they asked women and men, gay and straight, whether they would like to have more than one sexual partner in the next month. Among heterosexual men, 25 percent said yes, they would like to have more than one sexual partner in the next month. Among homosexual men, 29 percent answered yes. Among heterosexual women, just 4 percent answered yes; among lesbian women, just 5 percent answered yes. These authors concluded that men "desire larger numbers of sexual partners than women in every major region of the world regardless of relationship status, *sexual orientation*, or whether the person is actively seeking [a partner]."[60]

We'll come back to this topic at greater length in chapter 9. But as a general rule, male-female differences are more consistent and more fundamental than differences in sexual orientation or sexual identity.

3
RISK

The secret to getting the most fun out of life is: to live dangerously. Build your cities on the slopes of Vesuvius! Send your ships into unknown seas! Live at war with your peers and with yourself!
—Friedrich Nietzsche, 1887[1]

Tossing the Ring

Let's suppose you're a college freshman taking introductory psychology. One of the course requirements includes "volunteering" as a subject in a study. You choose the ringtoss study, because the course guide says it will take only twenty minutes and no needles are involved.

You show up for the study. The technician shows you what you're supposed to do. There's a one-foot pole standing upright on the floor. You are given six rubber rings, each about the size of a horseshoe. The technician tells you to toss the rings at the pole, one ring at a time. The object of the game is to land the ring right on the pole.

"Where do I stand?" you ask, noticing that the floor is marked off one foot from the target, two feet, five feet, ten feet, fifteen feet, and twenty feet.

"Anywhere you like," the assistant says.

"You mean I could do all the tosses from one foot away?" you ask.

The technician nods.

"Do I have to hit the target a certain percentage of times?"

"No," the technician answers. "Just toss the six rings, and we'll move on to the next part of the experiment. I'll step out of the room, to give you some privacy."

"Privacy?" you ask, but the technician is already gone.

What do you do now? Most young women will stand one or two feet away from the target, toss the rings, and move on. Most young men stand five or ten feet away from the target, even though doing so greatly increases their risk of failure.[2]

You toss the rings.

"Okay, now we move on to the next part of the experiment," the assistant says. A door opens and in step two of your classmates. You nod and say hello. The sex of the two classmates is the same as yours. If you're a woman, they're female. The two classmates are asked to sit in chairs along the wall, facing you.

"Okay, now we do it again," the assistant says, handing you the rings again.

Most young women will toss the rings just the same when other women are present as they do when they are by themselves. But most young men behave differently. When other young men are watching, most young men will demonstrate what psychologists call a "risky shift."[3] If the man tossed the rings from two feet when he was alone, he'll back up to five feet when other men are in the room. If he tossed the rings from five feet when he was alone, he'll back up to ten feet when other men are watching—even if he's never met the men before and never expects to see them again. "I guess I didn't want them to think I was a wuss," is the way one explained the change in his behavior.

Living Dangerously

Many boys enjoy taking risks. And most boys are impressed by other boys who take risks, especially if the risk-taker succeeds. Girls are less likely to enjoy risk-taking for its own sake and are much less likely to be impressed by risk-taking behavior in others. Girls may be *willing* to take risks, but they are less likely to *seek out* risky situations just for the sake of living dangerously.

Imagine yourself back in middle school. Suppose you heard about a friend who rode a bicycle off of a twelve-foot-high boardwalk and landed on a sandy beach. All on purpose, just for fun. Boys who engage in that kind of risk-taking behavior raise their status in the eyes of their peers. "Did you hear what Brett did! Rode his bike off the top of the boardwalk! Awesome!" Even if they fail, those boys are likely to earn the respect of other boys for trying.

If girls heard about another girl who rode her bike on purpose off the top of a twelve-foot-high boardwalk, they would be less likely to ooh and ahh and more likely to be critical. "She must be totally nuts to do something like that. What a weirdo," the other girls might say.

Another example, this time with high school kids. Suppose a twelfth-grade boy goes to a party Friday night and has unprotected sex with a college woman he's just met, and then on Saturday night he goes to another party and has unprotected sex with a different young woman. His buddies will be impressed, especially if the two women were pretty. "You da *man*," they might say, and give him a high-five.

Suppose now that the same thing happens, but with genders reversed. A twelfth-grade girl goes to a party Friday night and has unprotected sex with a college man she's just met, and then on Saturday night she goes to another party and has unprotected sex with a different man. If her girlfriends find out about her exploits, they are *not* likely to be favorably impressed, regardless of whether the men in question are good-looking or not: they are more likely to think she's a slut, or insane, or both.[4]

Girls and boys assess risk differently, and they differ in their likelihood of engaging in risky behaviors. As soon as kids are old enough to toddle across the floor, boys are significantly more likely to do something dangerous: put their fingers in a socket, try to stand on a basketball, jump off a chair onto the floor.[5] And when parents try to stop their child from doing something risky, boys are less likely to comply. Studies in the United States and around the world universally find that boys are more likely to engage in physically risky activities.[6] Boys are more likely than girls to be seriously injured or killed in accidents such as drowning, misuse of firearms, or head injury related to riding a bicycle.[7]

Psychologist Barbara Morrongiello interviewed children ages six through ten who had been injured or who had been in "close calls." She found that compared to the girls, the boys:

- were more likely to attribute their injuries *erroneously* to "bad luck" rather than to any lack of skill or foresight on their part;
- were less likely to tell their parents about the injury;
- were more likely to be around other boys at the time the injury occurred.[8]

A boy is much more likely to do something dangerous or stupid when he's in a group of boys than when he's by himself.

Why are boys more likely to engage in risky and dangerous activities? One reason derives from gender differences in the autonomic nervous system, which we'll discuss at length in the next chapter. Risky and dangerous activities trigger a "fight or flight" response that gives a tingle, a charge, an excitement that many boys find irresistible. "The secret to getting the most fun out of life is: to live dangerously," Nietzsche advised his readers. Nietzsche wasn't saying that you should live dangerously in order to achieve some great goal, or because risk-taking is necessary in order to arrive at some other objective. He insisted that risk-taking is fun for its *own* sake, for the thrill of taking the risk. That's a very male thing to say. As we'll see in the next chapter, the hardwired response to risk and danger is different in girls.

Lizette Peterson and her associates at the University of

Missouri wanted to study sex differences in children's responses to risky situations. They set up a video game in which kids rode a stationary bicycle while watching an interactive video screen. The simulation was so realistic that when the bicycle on the screen went under the branch of a tree, some kids ducked their heads. Then the kids suddenly confronted a hazard: in some cases just a coiled garden hose blocking the path; in other cases, an extremely dangerous situation such as an oncoming car swerving suddenly from the opposing lane so that the car is about to hit the kid head-on. The bike was wired so that Peterson and her colleagues could measure how quickly the kids stepped on the brake to avoid a collision.

Let me tell you one thing: I wouldn't want to be sitting on the back of a bike if one of those boys was riding it. The boys were much slower to brake than the girls were. If the simulation had been real, many of the boys would have sustained life-threatening injuries. The boys were also more likely to report feeling *exhilarated* by the simulated collision, whereas girls were far more likely to report feeling *fearful*.[9]

So: one reason many boys engage in physically dangerous activities may be that *the danger itself* gives the activity a pleasant tingle. That's a tough concept for some women to grasp. A mother who warns her son, "Don't ride your bike off the boardwalk. You might get hurt," has missed the point. Her son knows it's dangerous. He's riding his bike off the boardwalk *because* it's dangerous.

But there's another basic reason why boys are more likely to engage in physically risky activities. Boys systematically *overestimate* their own ability, while girls are more likely to *underestimate* their abilities. For example, psychologists at Boston University asked a simple question: Why are almost all drowning victims male? They concluded that a major contributor was that the men consistently overestimate their ability to swim.[10] "I'm strong enough to outswim the current," a teenage boy may think. By the time he discovers his error, it may be too late. Likewise, epidemiologists at the University of Pittsburgh have found that males are much more likely to die in thunderstorms than females are. Many of those deaths occur when a flash flood blocks a road. A female driver, encountering a stretch of road under water, is likely to do the sensible thing: turn around and find another way. Male drivers, on the other hand, are more likely than female drivers to drive right into the water—and die.[11]

Gender stereotypes may be playing a role here. When kids are asked which child—a girl or a boy—is most likely to get hurt when riding a bike, climbing a tree, etc., girls and boys agree that the girl is more likely to get hurt. In fact, the reality is just the opposite: *boys* are more likely to get hurt.[12] Most of our entertainment, most of our television and movies and novels and stories, and most of our video games show the boy saving the girl or the man saving the woman. That kind of cultural programming may be partly to blame for boys' overestimation of their abilities.

But we should be careful before we march down the same road as those 1970s-era scholars who believed that sex differences derive primarily from cultural influences. For one thing, a similar phenomenon—the male taking greater risks—has been observed in primates such as monkeys, baboons, and chimpanzees. Anthropologists Linda Marie Fedigan and Sandra Zohar wanted to find out why there are so many more adult female Japanese macaque monkeys than male monkeys. Although the ratio of female to male monkeys is roughly 1:1 at birth, by adulthood there are as many as *five* females for every one surviving male. What happens to all the other male monkeys? And why isn't a similarly imbalanced sex ratio seen in zoos? Fedigan and Zohar considered many possible explanations, such as:

- The "fragile male" hypothesis: maybe the males are just more susceptible to illness and disease;
- The predator hypothesis: maybe the males are not as good at escaping predators;
- The risk hypothesis: maybe the males engage in more dangerous behaviors;

- The mutant hypothesis: maybe the males are more likely to carry harmful mutations (this is actually a variation on the "fragile male" hypothesis).

After carefully reviewing twenty-one years of data, Fedigan and Zohar found support only for the risk hypothesis. "Males are mainly lost to the population because of their risk-taking behaviors." Male monkeys do wild and crazy things, just like teenage boys. For example, these researchers found that male monkeys take stupid risks around highways: they try to scamper across a highway, only to be crushed by an oncoming truck. Female monkeys are much less likely to take the same risks. They tend to avoid highways.[13]

These differences appear to be inborn. It's hard to claim that male monkeys overestimate their abilities because they've been watching too many James Bond films. We have to consider the possibility that the tendency for male primates (including humans) to do insanely dangerous things may be innate rather than culturally programmed.

Learned Helplessness

If you have a son, it's obvious that you need to understand his motivations, so you'll be able to keep him from riding his bike off a cliff. Parents of daughters need to understand this issue, too, from another perspective. Most young girls need some encouragement to take risks, the right kind of risks, and to raise their estimation of their own abilities.

Many gender-based inequities persist in our society. Men remain far more likely to be CEOs of major corporations despite the fact that there is now a substantial cohort of equally well-trained women.[14] Men are more likely to start their own businesses. Men are still more likely to be leading politicians, although women are gaining ground.

Consider the gender gap in income. The average woman in the United States working full-time still earns only about 73 percent of what the average man earns.[15] Some of that difference is explained by differences in occupation. The average software engineer with a master's degree in software engineering earns more than the average elementary school teacher with a master's degree in elementary education. Most software engineers are men. Most elementary school teachers are women.

But even when you control for occupation, education, and hours worked, a significant gender gap in pay persists. Men still get paid somewhat more than women do for doing the same work, on average, both in the United States and around the world.[16] What especially troubled economist Linda Babcock was the finding that the trend toward gender equity in pay has reached a plateau. Women made gains from the 1960s through the 1980s, but there was no significant progress made in the United States in the gender gap in pay between 1990 and 2000.

Professor Babcock studied students graduating from Carnegie Mellon University with a master's degree in a business-related field. She found that the starting salaries of the men were about 8 percent higher on average than those of the women: the men were paid about $4,000 more. Babcock then looked to see who had *asked* for more money during the job-finding process. It turned out that only 7 percent of the female students had asked, compared with 57 percent of the men. Controlling for gender, Babcock found that students who asked for more money received a starting salary that was $4,053 higher on average than students who didn't ask. In other words, the gender gap could be explained by the fact that the women *hadn't asked* for more money.[17]

Asking for more money when you've just received a job offer is taking a risk. You might give offense to a prospective employer. You might give the impression of being greedy. You might conceivably lose the job or start off in your new job on the wrong foot. So most women don't ask. And those that don't ask, don't get.

To be successful, *really* successful in business or politics, you have to be willing to take those kinds of risks. You want your daughter to be able to do that. To take a risk when the moment is right. How can you empower her to have that kind of self-confidence?

When I was a graduate student in psychology at the University of Pennsylvania twenty years ago, I had the privilege of taking several seminars with Martin Seligman, who is best known for developing the theory of *learned helplessness*. Here's a simple experiment that illustrates his theory: Suppose you take a mouse and give it a really fun environment to explore. The mouse gets to burrow through dirt and sand, squiggle through narrow tunnels, and jump around in the branches of little plastic trees. Dr. Seligman refers to such a mouse as a "master mouse" because that mouse has become a master of its environment.

Let's suppose you're not so nice to a second mouse. The second mouse doesn't get to play in the fun environment. Instead, you just squeeze it tight. You hold it. The mouse might try to wriggle away, but you don't let it. You keep holding it tight. You do this over and over again, several sessions a day, day after day. The mouse learns that no matter what it does, it can't get out of your grip. Dr. Seligman called that mouse a "helpless" mouse.

Now comes the test. You toss each mouse in a bathtub filled with water. The "master" mouse immediately paddles to the side of the bathtub (mice actually can swim, a little), scrambles up and out of the bathtub on the little rope ladder you've hung on the side of the tub, and shakes itself off.

The situation is dramatically different when you toss the "helpless" mouse into the same bathtub. The helpless mouse makes only pathetic and feeble attempts to swim out of the bathtub. It flounders for a moment, then sinks. If you don't reach in and pull it out, it will drown.

Moral of the story: if you have had plenty of experiences exploring new situations, facing your fears and mastering them, then you can face new challenges and conquer them as well. If you don't have that experience of taking a risk and succeeding, then you won't be able to summon up your strength when it really counts. That appears to be at least as true for people as it is for mice.

Some scholars have suggested that the way we raise girls in our society may promote the learned helplessness that Dr. Seligman documented in laboratory animals. Parents in North America and Europe are more likely to shield their girls from risks and less likely to praise them for engaging in risky activities such as climbing trees or riding a bike hands-free. I myself have observed enormous differences in the way parents respond when their child is injured. Let's say fourteen-year-old Jason injures his back playing JV football. He can barely walk. Dad helps his wounded warrior stagger in to my office. Dad is concerned, of course, but I also detect a subtle note of pride. "It was a goal line stand. They had the ball on our two-yard line. Fourth down. Fourth quarter. Jason just threw himself at the running back. Sacrificed his body totally. Stopped the other guy cold. We took over on downs and won the game." I check the X rays: everything is fine. Neurological exam is normal. I reassure Dad that Jason just has a bad muscle spasm from the injury. I recommend rest, hot baths, and a muscle relaxant. Dad's first question: "So when can Jason get back on the field?"

I saw a very similar injury last year in a fourteen-year-old girl playing field hockey. Let's call her Tracy. Tracy also could barely walk. *Both* Mom and Dad accompanied Tracy to my office. Once again the X rays were normal. The neurological exam was normal. I reassured the parents that Tracy just had a muscle spasm. I recommended rest, hot baths, and a muscle relaxant medication, just as I did for Jason. Parents' first question: "Do you think Tracy should give up field hockey? Maybe she's just not cut out for it. Or at least she should take the rest of the season off?"

The difference in the parents' reaction is striking. It's so remarkable, I've begun calling parents' attention to it. "Suppose Tracy were a boy, with the exact same injury. Would you be thinking about taking your child out of the sport?" I ask them.

"No, you wouldn't," I say, while they're still hesitating. "You'd be saying things like, 'Walk it out. Work it out. You can do it.' "

What are good ways to get girls to be more comfortable with risk-taking? Margrét Pála Ólafsdóttir, an educator in Iceland, has developed a program for kindergarten-age girls that she calls "dare training." The idea first occurred to her during a field trip for girls only. It was a warm day, and some of the girls took off their shoes and socks. On an impulse, she encouraged all the girls to take off their shoes and socks and run around on the stones and pebbles in the park (you have to wonder whether a teacher in our more litigious society would have had the courage). Then she dared them to dance. One girl moaned when a stone hurt her foot. "What can we do instead of complaining when it hurts?" Ólafsdóttir asked the girls. "Sing," suggested one of the girls. "And so we did," Ólafsdóttir says. "Sang and danced all the way [back to the school]—barefooted. We felt like superwomen."[18]

The girls were "joyful and proud that they had discovered a new world," Ólafsdóttir wrote. Inspired, Ólafsdóttir hauled mattresses into the girls' kindergarten. She stacked the mattresses on the floor, put a table next to the mattresses, and encouraged the girls to jump from the table onto the mattresses, with an invitation to scream as they jumped. Because "an important part of the [stereotypical] female role is to keep quiet and because noise is not integrated into girls' play, it became obvious that training in making noise and using the voice should be part of the 'daring' exercises," Ólafsdóttir wrote. Soon the girls' room was almost as loud as the boys' room. When the girls said it was too easy to jump from a table onto a mattress, "we just put another table on top of the first one—and at last a chair on top of everything."

Once the girls understood that they had a teacher who *wanted* them to take risks, they started creating their own challenges. They tossed raw eggs high in the air and caught them without breaking them (sometimes). They squirted each other with water pistols. One girl built a high wall out of sponge-foam bricks. "What are you going to do?" Ólafsdóttir asked the girl. "Jump over the wall!" the girl shouted back. The wall was obviously too high. But: "How could I destroy her faith after months of developing a new self-image?" Ólafsdóttir asked herself.

> [The little girl] climbed up, took a deep breath and jumped directly on to the wall, which collapsed. The whole group laughed but our heroine was not sure how she should react and looked to me for help.
>
> Suddenly I remembered everything I had heard about "learned helplessness of girls" and how they give up every time they fail. I thought of my own experience of not feeling good enough no matter how hard we try, until at last we stop trying, lose our confidence and stop taking risks . . . That is how we are kept in the old role of passivity and stopped from trying new things . . . [That little girl] had found the perfect way. We have to train away the old fear of mistakes that holds us back . . . I gave the girls exactly this speech though in different words.

This story highlights a problem with this approach. If a girl takes a risk and fails, she may end up being *more* risk-averse, not less. Ólafsdóttir acknowledges this hazard. "The feeling of weakness and inability and the tendency to low self-esteem are so integrated into girls' thinking, that [this] training can be counter-productive if we do not know exactly what we are doing." Start with something the girls know they can do, then gradually let them build up that wall, stretch their abilities to the limit. Don't throw the mouse in the bathtub until it's had plenty of experience climbing the little trees and squiggling through the tunnels. And when the girls fail and they fall, you have to be there to catch them, dust them off, encourage them to try again.

It's also important, Ólafsdóttir found, for other girls to be supportive. That's one reason why she insists on a girls-only classroom for her "dare training." "The sexes not only monopolize space, objects, and roles," she writes, "they also constantly monopolize particular behavior and qualities. Children always gravitate toward familiar actions and roles . . . [In a class with both girls and boys,] the boys take over the equipment and the playground. The boys take over [any activity that involves] action, motion, and noise." By insisting on a girls-only classroom for "dare training," Ólafsdóttir makes it easier for girls to take risks without fear of the boys making fun of them or belittling their achievements.

The Blessing of a Skinned Knee?

Let's go back to Lizette Peterson's study, where she rigged up a stationary bike so kids could "ride" through a hazardous environment. Peterson then asked all the *parents* whether their kids had ever been injured riding a bike, injured badly enough to require medical attention. She found that kids who had been injured were *less* fearful doing the simulation than kids who had never been injured—even after controlling for the degree of confidence kids felt riding bicycles. She calls this the "invulnerability" effect. When a kid has fallen and (let's say) scraped a knee or gotten a cut, they recover. One week later that kid is thinking, "Hey, that wasn't so bad. I got hurt and now I'm fine."

Child psychologist Wendy Mogel has written a charming book called *The Blessing of a Skinned Knee*. Without mentioning the theory of learned helplessness, she points out that shielding children from injury makes them more risk-averse. And, letting them explore their world—at the cost of a few scrapes and cuts—builds their character and gives them self-confidence, resilience, and self-reliance.[19] "What doesn't kill me, makes me stronger," Nietzsche wrote.

I agree that a skinned knee can be a blessing. Girls in particular benefit from "dare training," to use Ólafsdóttir's term once again. Trying to jump over the wall, and failing, and getting bruised, and then discovering that you can *get over it* is a great way to build your daughter's courage and inner strength.

I'm not so sure when it comes to boys, though. Many boys are already prewired to take risks and *enjoy* taking risks. Those boys need to be *more* risk-averse, not less.

You have to know your child. When it comes to risk-taking, individual differences can be huge. I've met a girl who rides her ATV down a steep, rugged, heavily wooded mountain about five miles north of my office. I know a little boy who doesn't want to finger-paint because he's worried the paint won't come off his fingers. Those kids are exceptions (and we'll come back to them in chapter 9). But if your kid doesn't fit gender-typical roles, then you need to modify your parenting accordingly. The girl on the ATV could use some of the "hazard precautions" we'll describe momentarily. The boy who doesn't want to finger-paint could use some "dare training."

Hazard Precautions

What about the boy who gets a thrill out of taking risks? He skateboards down a banister. He rides his bike off a brick ledge onto the sidewalk. When the family goes to the swimming pool, all he wants to do is run at top speed off the highest diving board. You've already taken him to the emergency room once, or twice, or three times with injuries. Now he's doing aerial skateboard tricks and asking for skydiving lessons. Each year he wants to do something even more hazardous. You have nightmares about spinal cord injuries. What to do?

There are at least three basic principles involved in decreasing the risk of your child experiencing a severe injury. The first principle is: remember the "risky shift." Boys in groups do stupid things. Your boy wants a thrill. Great. Take the whole family skiing or snowboarding. Insist on everybody having a lesson first, no matter what their level of expertise. Taking a lesson from an expert will keep your boy in touch with reality and give him a more accurate assessment of his skills. He may think he's ready to tackle the black diamond "expert" slopes. The teacher can show him how he'll actually have more fun and be able to do more on slopes that are better suited to his skill level. A family trip to the ski slopes is a much safer undertaking than a group of teenage boys going to the same mountain.

The second principle is: supervised is better than unsupervised. I've seen parents who refuse to let their boy play football because they think it's too dangerous, but they allow him to practice his skateboarding with his buddies in the parking lot. I've got news for those parents: your son is at much greater risk of injury in an unsupervised setting with other boys than in any setting where there's a responsible adult in charge. Boys who enjoy taking risks will take risks. Yes, there is a risk involved when your son runs out onto a football field. He's going to collide with players who are bigger and stronger than he is. But that risk can be managed. A football practice supervised by a competent coach is a much lower risk environment for *serious* injury than a parking lot. Your boy will be safer on a football field than he would be roaming the streets with a group of other boys.

The third principle is: assert your authority. A few years back, Dallas Cowboys cornerback Deion Sanders suffered a concussion during a game with the Washington Redskins. The team doctor correctly advised Sanders to stay out for the rest of that game. When you've suffered a concussion, the brain swells just a bit. You may feel okay an hour later. But if you're hit in the head again, the swelling can be massive, leading to death in minutes via a process called uncal herniation in which the increased pressure causes a piece of the brain to squirt down into the spinal column. You need to avoid all sports for at least twenty-four hours.

Sanders disregarded the doctor's advice. When he felt better, he went back out on the field. When Sanders returned to the sideline, the doctor didn't scream or yell. He simply took Sanders's helmet and walked away. The doctor kept Sanders's helmet tucked under his arm for the rest of the game.

That's a good example of how to assert your authority with a boy who likes to take risks. Don't argue. Don't negotiate. Just do what you need to do. If you've told your boy that he's not allowed to ride his mountain bike without your permission, and he's broken that rule, don't tell him again. Don't ask him to "promise." When his friends come by and ask him to go riding, he'll look like a wimp if he says, "I can't go because I promised my father I wouldn't." In the "boy code," honoring a promise made to a *parent* is a sign of weakness. But the "boy code" respects a heavy-duty woven-steel cable lock.

So, go to the hardware store and buy a sturdy lock. That way, when his friends come by and ask him to go riding, he can say, quite honestly, "*I can't.* My dad put this monster lock on my bike." When you've decided that your son can ride his bike again—and you know when, where, and *with whom* he'll be riding—then unlock it.

AGGRESSION

Real men like to fight.

—Gen. George S. Patton, 1944[1]

I enjoy hitting people.

—Bill Romanowski, linebacker, Oakland Raiders, 2003[2]

The surface of a girl fight can be as silent and smooth as a marble.

—Rachel Simmons, 2002[3]

Jeffrey

Jeffrey, age fourteen, was moody, irritable, and depressed. School annoyed him. Sports didn't really interest him. He didn't have many close friends. The psychiatrist had prescribed an antidepressant plus Ritalin for attention deficit disorder. Even with the medication, Jeffrey was still withdrawn and despondent. Getting through the school day was a struggle, even though his parents had enrolled him in a private academy where the classes were small and the teachers were caring and attentive.

That summer, Jeffrey's father arranged for him to spend two months in Zimbabwe. (This happened seven years ago, just before Zimbabwe self-destructed.) Jeffrey had been hired as an assistant to Cliff, a professional hunter. Cliff makes his living taking American and European men into remote areas of Africa to hunt wild game. Jeffrey's parents packed enough medication to last Jeffrey all summer.

After three days with Jeffrey, Cliff told him to stop taking the pills. "You don't need them," Cliff said. And he was right—at least as far as hunting in the African bush was concerned. Jeffrey could sit for hours, motionless in the tall grass, waiting for prey to appear.

The local Ndebele tribesmen took a liking to Jeffrey. They could see that he was different from other American and European tourists. Jeffrey was comfortable with the locals, and the locals were comfortable with him. More than anything else, Jeffrey wanted to learn to hunt as they did. So they taught him to use their hunting javelin.

Have you ever tried to hit an archery target using a bow and arrow? Imagine that you are trying to hit that target, but instead of a bow and arrow you have only a wooden spear—twice as long as a baseball bat—and you have to *throw* it at the target from a distance of thirty yards.

After an hour of practicing, Jeffrey told the tribesmen that he was ready to hunt. They chuckled and pointed at a grouse about thirty yards away. Jeffrey stared at the bird, nodded to himself, then hurled the javelin with all his might. The bird, transfixed by the spear, was killed instantly. Everyone was amazed—except for Jeffrey.

Cliff snapped a picture of Jeffrey standing on a pile of rocks, his arms raised in triumph, holding the dead bird in one hand and the javelin in the other. Jeffrey gave me a copy of that picture when he came back home.

"That summer was a turning point," his mother, Jane, told me later. Jeffrey still had to take medication in order to function well in school. But his whole attitude had changed and his depression lifted. He no longer saw himself as a failure. "That summer gave him confidence," Jane said.

Now suppose Jeffrey's parents had not sent him to Zimbabwe. Suppose they had sent him instead to "Camp ADD," a summer

Jeffrey

camp where boys diagnosed with attention deficit disorder spend their summer working on reading and writing skills. There are many such camps today. They're springing up like weeds. Six weeks indoors in July and August. Then you go right back to school in September for more of the same. If Jeffrey's parents had done that, I doubt that he would have grown up to be the outgoing and amiable man he now is.

"Our greatest moment comes when we find the courage to rechristen our 'evil' as the best within us," Friedrich Nietzsche once wrote.[4] The same hidden intensity and impulsiveness that had been liabilities for Jeffrey at school in Maryland became advantages when he was hunting in the wilds of Zimbabwe. The experience of feeling himself to be a genuinely gifted and talented hunter changed his whole outlook on life. After nailing a grouse at thirty yards when nobody thought he could do it, schoolwork didn't seem so hopelessly difficult anymore.

Here's the part that many women have real problems with: if Jeffrey had just hit a target on a wall, it wouldn't have had the same effect. Hitting a target on a wall wouldn't have changed his life. The fact that he had *killed a living thing* was crucial. Most women (and some men) recoil from that idea. And I'm not endorsing it. But the reality is that girls and women relate to violence very differently than boys and men do.

Lessons from the Playground

Ever watch kids playing on a playground? Psychologist Janet Lever spent a whole year at elementary school playgrounds, watching girls and boys play. Boys fight a lot, she noticed: about twenty times as often as girls do. To her surprise, though, she found that boys who fight each other usually end up being *better* friends after the fight.[5] They are more likely to play together in the days after the fight than they were in the days before.

Girls seldom fight, but when they do—often with words rather than fists—the bad feelings last. "I hate you! I'm never ever *ever* going to play with you again!" Katie says to Amy, and the older she is, the more likely that she will be true to her word. After a big fight between Katie and Amy, "Amy's group" may not play with "Katie's group" again for the rest of the school year.

Lever's reports are similar to what scientists have found with chimpanzees. Male chimpanzees are about twenty times as likely to fight as females are, but the fights don't last more than a few minutes and rarely result in major injury. Two male chimps who fight each other this morning may be grooming each other this afternoon. According to Frans de Waal, a primatologist at the Yerkes Primate Research Center in Atlanta, "Picking a fight can actually be a way for [male chimps] to relate to one another, check each other out, and take a first step toward friendship." Female chimps rarely fight, but when they do, their friendship is over. The hostility that results can last for years. Serious injury is also *more* likely to occur when female chimpanzees fight. Female chimps who have fought one another are "vindictive and irreconcilable," according to Dr. de Waal.[6]

In our species these differences are apparent as soon as children can talk. Boys as young as two years of age, given a choice

between violent fairy tales and warm and fuzzy fairy tales, usually choose the violent stories. Girls as young as two years of age
consistently choose the warm and fuzzy stories.[7] In another
study, psychologists found that five- and seven-year-old girls
who prefer violent stories are more likely to have significant
behavior problems than girls who prefer warm, nurturing stories. However, among boys, preference for violent stories is *not*
an indicator of underlying psychiatric problems.[8] A preference
for violent stories seems to be normal for five- to seven-year-old
boys, while the same preference in five- to seven-year-old girls
suggests a psychiatric disorder.

Psychologists Louise and David Perry interviewed girls and
boys (average age ten years), asking them how they might respond to certain situations.[9] For example [they asked the chil-
dren], suppose you're playing soccer with your friends, and
some other kid comes and grabs the ball from you. Would you
hit the other kid? If you did hit the other kid, do you think hitting the kid would get you the ball back? And how would you
feel afterward? Most boys said that they would hit the kid who
tried to steal the ball. The older the boy, the more confident he
was that he would succeed in getting the ball back by hitting the
other kid. And the boys who said that they would hit the other
kid also said that they would feel absolutely no guilt about hitting him. "Why should *I* feel guilty? He took my ball!" They
were confident that other boys would approve of their action.
For good reason: Boys who act aggressively usually *raise* their
standing in the eyes of other boys, as long as their action is provoked, that is, as long as it's not bullying.

Girls respond differently. Not only were girls less likely to respond aggressively to the kid who stole the soccer ball, they
were also more likely to have misgivings about responding aggressively and less confident of a successful outcome. They were
more likely to anticipate feelings of guilt and emotional upset
about hitting someone else, even in response to the provocation
of someone taking away their soccer ball. And, they did not ex-

pect other girls to approve of their action, even though it was provoked. Girls who act aggressively may *lower* their standing in the eyes of their peers.

There's good evidence that at least some of these differences are biologically programmed. Some of that evidence comes from studies of girls with congenital adrenal hyperplasia (CAH). Owing to a genetic defect in the adrenal glands, the adrenal tissues of girls with CAH produce high levels of male hormone while the girl is still in her mother's womb. That male hormone partially masculinizes the girl's brain. When young girls who have CAH are offered a toy—given the choice of an airplane, a ball, military action figures, Barbie and Ken dolls, or Magic Markers—CAH girls are more likely to choose an airplane or a ball or the fighting action figures and less likely to choose the Barbie and Ken dolls or Magic Markers, compared with normal girls. When CAH girls are tested at age four, they are found to have story preferences about halfway between those of normal girls and normal boys: CAH girls are more likely to choose violent stories than normal girls are, but less likely to choose violent stories than normal boys are.[10] In fact, the masculinity of a CAH girl's choice of toy is directly proportional to the severity of that girl's CAH. The more severe her CAH—that is, the more male hormone her brain was exposed to before birth—the more masculine her behavior and her toy preferences will be.[11] These researchers also found no evidence of parental influence on their child's play behavior. Parents who encouraged their daughters to play with more "feminine" toys had zero effect on their child's play behavior.

Studies with laboratory animals show the same pattern. Among most higher mammals, and especially among our closest relatives, the primates, juvenile males are more likely to engage in rough-and-tumble play than females are.[12] In one study of long-tailed macaques, for example, the "boy" monkeys were six times more likely to engage in rough-and-tumble play than the "girl" monkeys were.[13] "Girl" monkeys on the other hand are more likely to engage in what primatologists call *alloparent-*

ing. They're babysitting.[14] Young female monkeys are far more likely than young males to look after a baby monkey, allowing the baby's mother time off to forage. The mother returns to retrieve the baby from the "babysitter" when it's time for the baby to breastfeed.

Wherever you look among the primates, you'll find that young females show much more interest than young males do in taking care of babies. That's certainly true for baboons,[15] rhesus monkeys,[16] marmosets,[17] and vervet monkeys.[18] It's also true for humans: girls, on average, are much more likely to embrace little babies and be interested in babies than boys are.[19] That sex difference is not affected by parents' attitudes toward their child's behavior. Sons whose parents encourage them to nurture babies are no more nurturing than sons of parents who make no such efforts.[20]

One essential premise of evolutionary biology is that if you find a behavior that is conserved across many different species within an order (in this case, the primate order), then that behavior probably serves some biologically useful purpose. It's not hard to see a biologically useful purpose for young female primates to feel drawn to caring for little babies. Formal studies have demonstrated that the more practice a young female monkey has taking care of a little baby, the better she will be at doing it.[21]

But what about rough-and-tumble play? What evolutionary purpose is served when young males chase each other and wrestle, sometimes for hours on end? Primatologists have suggested two reasons why young males, and not young females, spend so much time engaged in rough-and-tumble play. One reason is that in many primate species—including our closest relative, the chimpanzee—the male is much more likely to pursue and kill moderate-size prey. The adult male chimpanzee commonly hunts, kills, and eats medium-size animals such as monkeys while the adult female chimpanzee very rarely hunts such prey, instead preferring nuts, berries, and invertebrate species such as termites. Adolescent male chimpanzees often kill monkeys; adolescent female chimpanzees never do.[22] If males and females eat differently, then they may benefit from different activities in childhood. If you are going to be chasing and killing monkeys for your supper, then you can use all the practice you can get chasing and wrestling.

But there's another reason, primatologists say, why it's useful for young males to engage in play-fighting. Wrestling and fighting with other males teaches them the rules of the game. If young male primates are deprived of the opportunity to fight with other males, those males grow up to be *more* violent as adults, not less.[23] They've never learned how to get along with other males in a playful, aggressive way. The rage seems to get bottled up inside until it explodes. And if it's true for our cousins, it may be true for us. In just a moment we'll discuss proposals offered by well-intentioned reformers to ban dodgeball and even snowball-throwing on the grounds that such activities are "violent" and "aggressive." The irony is that if our sons are anything like their primate cousins, such measures may not decrease the likelihood of serious violent acts: indeed, it may increase the likelihood of exactly the kind of violent outburst the reformers are trying to prevent.

Affirm the Knight

Aggression has a different meaning for girls than it has for boys. For many boys, aggressive sports—such as football, boxing, wrestling—may not only be fun, they may actually form the basis for a lasting friendship. The concept "aggression = fun" doesn't come naturally to most girls. Aggression between girls doesn't build friendships, it destroys them. So it's hard for girls to imagine any positive consequences from aggressive play.

These differences also affect how children *talk* with each other, especially with same-sex peers. Put a tape recorder in a boys' locker room and listen to the banter.

"Your Momma's so dumb, she thinks Taco Bell is a phone company in Mexico."

"Your Momma's so old, I told her to act her age and she died!"

"Your Momma's so stupid, she thinks Fleetwood Mac is a hamburger at McDonald's."

When girls and boys interact, styles often clash. A classic example comes from the children's book *Anne of Green Gables*. Remember how Gilbert teases Anne Shirley, calling her "Carrots," making fun of her red hair? If Anne were a boy, she'd know that the right response would be to make fun of Gilbert. Instead, she misinterprets Gilbert's friendly teasing as being hostile and she keeps silent. She gets angrier and angrier until finally she smashes her slate over his head. Having made that violent gesture, she doesn't speak to him again for the rest of the year.

Incidentally, this example illustrates an important principle: Putting girls together with boys creates special risks. Boys often employ aggressive behaviors playfully, as a way of making friends. Girls, especially young girls, very seldom do that. The proverbial boy pulling on a girl's pigtail is a boy who is trying to make friends with that girl. But his message is misunderstood. Sally doesn't appreciate having her hair yanked. As far as Sally is concerned, Damian is acting like a bully. Explanations don't help much. "Well, Sally, when Damian yanks on your hair, that means he likes you." Sally may not believe you. She may still regard Damian's behavior as hostile and ill-intentioned. If she *does* believe what you say, then she may conclude that Damian is a creature from another planet. What a stupid way to behave! If you like somebody, why would you yank on their hair?

Differences between girls and boys are natural. Those differences should be acknowledged, accepted, and exploited for educational purposes. Instead, many educators today seek to eradicate gender-specific behaviors. In particular, they don't like "aggressive" play. In the past ten years, many school districts—including my home district of Montgomery County, Maryland—have banned kids from playing dodgeball on school playgrounds in the belief that dodgeball encourages violent behavior.[24]

Some schools are taking these prohibitions to the extreme,

banning even games like tag. "Body contact is inappropriate for recess activities," explains Doris Jennings, principal of Woodlin Elementary School in Silver Spring, Maryland.[25] Other school districts threaten expulsion for kids who throw snowballs.[26]

The basic premise underlying the arguments against dodgeball and throwing snowballs is: if you prevent kids from playing aggressive games, then kids will *be* less aggressive. In fact, there is no evidence that preventing kids from acting out their aggression in healthy ways will diminish or eliminate their aggressive impulses. Instead, prohibiting these activities may actually increase the likelihood that the suppressed aggression will manifest itself in less healthy ways. "You can try to drive out nature with a pitchfork, yet nature will always return," according to the old Latin proverb.[27] Research bears this out. According to psychologist and criminologist Edwin McGargee, three-quarters of all murders are committed not by overtly aggressive people, but by quiet, seemingly well-behaved men who have never found a safe or appropriate outlet for their aggression.[28]

The solution to taming a boy's aggressive drive is NOT to squelch the drive every time it appears. Banning dodgeball from the schoolyard makes as much sense as Prohibition. Instead, you want to *transform* the boy's aggressive drive. Sublimate it into something constructive. Julie Collins, a counselor at a high school I visited, explains it this way: "You can't turn a bully into a flower child. But you *can* turn a bully into a knight."

Her motto: Affirm the knight.

Here is a true story that exemplifies Julie Collins's principle. A small town in rural Illinois was being terrorized by a local gang of teenage thugs. Storekeepers who refused to pay tribute in the form of free drinks or other goodies saw their stores vandalized. One storekeeper made a wager that his clerk could beat the gang leader in a fight. The gang leader accepted the challenge.

Most of the town turned out to watch the fight. The store-keeper's clerk and the gang leader fought each other, hitting and grunting and shoving, for what seemed like hours. Finally the clerk backed away and proposed that they call it a draw. "The fight ended in friendship," we are told, and the clerk "not only earned the group's respect but became their informal leader." The name of the storekeeper's clerk was Abraham Lincoln.[29]

In 1831 the town organized a militia to fight in the Black Hawk War. The militia, comprised mainly of the young gang members, elected Lincoln to be their captain. They remained loyal to him throughout the next thirty years as he rose from storekeeper's clerk to president of the United States.[30]

This archetypal-but-true story of the young Abe Lincoln resonates with ancient traditions of male friendship. "The youthful leader often establishes his authority by besting the strongest young tough in the neighborhood," one writer observes. "King Arthur beats the undefeated Lancelot, and Robin Hood knocks Little John off a bridge with a blow from his staff."[31] I would add that this tradition is even more ancient than King Arthur and Robin Hood. It goes back to the very roots of the recorded history. The Epic of Gilgamesh, dating back roughly five thousand years, begins with a similar fight between Gilgamesh and Enkidu. As in all these stories, the two protagonists become close friends after the fight. Indeed, the fight somehow consecrates the friendship and makes it lifelong.

The PainStation

Two German college students, both young men, recently attracted media attention for inventing a modified video game they call the PainStation. The video game portion of the device is fairly simple: it's a version of the old video game Pong, a sort of computerized table tennis. When you play the game on the PainStation, though, the machine itself will inflict pain on you. The machine can hurt you in three ways: it can give you a jolt of electricity, or slash your hand with a little whip, or blast your hand with intense heat. If you withdraw your hand from the PainStation, you're safe from the pain—but you lose the game.

"It's fun," explained coinventor Volker Morawe in an interview with National Public Radio, "because you play against your opponent, and you will see him suffering, and the next time you will suffer."[32]

A British firm expressed interest in marketing the game until they learned that the little whip can actually draw blood. "If you dropped the whip and you kept the shock and the heat, do you think you could get a big-time marketer for this product?" asked the (female) interviewer.

"If you take away the pain, where is the concept?" responded coinventor Tilman Reiff. "If the PainStation does not force you to quit playing, the whole game gets stupid."

The female interviewer was baffled by the appeal of the game. "Are you targeting your game to sadomasochists?" she asked. "I mean, who's interested in doing this?"

"A lot of people!" Reiff answered.

"Is this an acquired taste, or do you think you can really sit down and have fun getting hurt?" she asked.

"Some people play it once and never play it again," said Reiff. "Other people, they play it once and they can't stop playing. They come back even though their hand looks really bad already. They still keep playing."

"Why?" she asked, perplexed.

"If there's danger involved, it's way more fun. It's a big thrill," Reiff explained. "Also winning is way more fun if it's *combined with pain.*"

Some boys will actually spend money to play a game in which a computer zaps them with electricity, whips their hand, or blasts them with heat. Very few girls will seek to play the same game. One reason for that sex difference may simply be that boys don't feel pain in the same way that girls do.

Twenty years ago, psychologists knew that girls and women appeared to be more sensitive to pain than boys and men are.

Back then, though, most psychologists believed that the apparently greater female sensitivity to pain was a product of societal expectations. Men and boys claimed not to feel pain because they wanted to look tough, these psychologists thought. "We teach boys not to cry. We tell them it's not manly to show pain. So, of course, men are less willing to acknowledge pain than women are," these psychologists said. "They feel the pain just the same as women do. They're just less willing to admit it." Psychologists assumed that there were no fundamental sex differences in the perception of pain.

That assumption was wrong. In the past twenty years it's become clear that there *are* fundamental sex differences in the perception of pain: not just in humans, but in laboratory animals as well. The difference is especially large with regard to what scientists call stress-induced analgesia. Scientists have found that when you stress an animal in the laboratory—say, by immobilizing it—and then you subsequently test that animal's sensitivity to pain, you will find that the animal is much less sensitive. But that phenomenon is seen *primarily in males*. Females of all mammalian species studied so far show this effect to a much lesser extent. In some cases, exposure to stress actually makes females *more* sensitive to pain.[33]

Human females as well as female laboratory animals do demonstrate *pregnancy*-induced analgesia. If you test a woman's sensitivity to pain late in her pregnancy, you will find that she is significantly less sensitive to pain than when she is not pregnant. For example, a mild electrical shock that she might find very painful when she is not pregnant may be barely perceptible when she's in her third trimester.[34] That numbing of pain is nature's way of making pregnancy and the birthing process a little more bearable. And, it may explain the action of one pain medication—alphaxalone—which is "for women only." Alphaxalone is a non-narcotic pain reliever based on the female hormone progesterone. It's four times more effective in females than in males.[35]

In 2003, two different groups of researchers—one at the University of Texas at Austin, the other at the University of

California at San Francisco—identified another factor underlying sex differences in pain perception: the cellular mechanism that mediates pain sensation is structurally different in males compared with females.[36] Dr. Igor Mitrovic, the lead author of one of the two studies, suggested that these sex differences may lead to the development of other pain relievers specifically for women.[37] These pills might have the potential to be more effective than current "one-pill-fits-both-sexes" pain medications.

The same jolt of electricity, the same blast of heat, will be experienced differently by girls and boys. The girl will experience more pain. This fundamental sex difference in sensory perception, mediated at the cellular level, may conceivably play some role in boys' greater willingness to risk pain. If you're a boy, the PainStation just isn't as painful.

Fight or Flight?

Seventy years ago, physiologist Walter Cannon studied the hormonal response of animals to stress and confrontation. He didn't want to bother with the hormonal fluctuations of female estrus and menstrual cycles, so he studied only male animals. Cannon described the cascade of hormonal responses to stress: increased heart rate, dilated pupils, a surge of adrenaline in the blood, all mediated by that division of the autonomic nervous system known as the *sympathetic* nervous system. Because these responses prepare the animal to fight or run away, Cannon named this cascade the "fight or flight" response.

Incredibly, researchers who followed up on Cannon's work continued to study only *male* animals. UCLA professor Shelley Taylor has estimated that roughly 90 percent of all scholarly work on hormonal responses to stress has been done exclusively on male animals (including humans).[38] Scientists assumed that males and females were wired the same way. It never occurred to those (male) scientists that females might be different. Nobody studied women.

We now know that females are wired to respond to stress in a different way than males are. Dozens of studies over the past twenty years have consistently shown dramatic sex differences in the biobehavioral response to stress. The female autonomic nervous system has been shown to be influenced more by the *para*sympathetic nervous system, which is energized by acetylcholine rather than adrenaline and which causes an unpleasant, nauseated feeling rather than the "thrill" of the sympathetic nervous system.[39]

When most young boys are exposed to threat and confrontation, their senses sharpen and they feel an exciting tingle. (In chapter 9, we'll consider boys who are exceptions to this rule.) When most young girls are exposed to threat and confrontation, they feel dizzy and "yucky." They may have unaccustomed trouble expressing themselves with just the right words. They may experience nausea or an urge to use the bathroom.

Bottom line: many young boys get a thrill from violent or quasi-violent confrontation. Most young girls don't. Some ten-year-old boys will spend their last nickel to play video arcade games in which enemies are shooting at them. Few ten-year-old girls find simulated combat worth spending their last nickels on.

I'm not saying that girls are never violent, just that girls seldom *enjoy* physical violence the way boys do. Girls are violent in their own way. We'll get to that in a minute.

Fight Club

Reporters recently have picked up on a popular phenomenon sweeping the United States: backyard wrestling. Teenage boys assemble a wrestling ring with rope and plywood and mattresses. Like-minded boys meet to pummel each other. There are now over a thousand such organizations in the United States, with names like the Backyard Brawlers (New York), Backyard Hardcore Wrestling (Crawford, Colorado), and the Real Wrestling Federation (Ventura, California). "Yeah, sure, we're getting hit in the head with chairs and getting cut and everything, and bleeding, but . . . we're still having fun," said Chris Jackson.

"The pain they inflict actually bonds them to one another," remarked NPR reporter Alix Spiegel with a touch of amazement in her voice. As you might expect, these impromptu wrestling matches do build friendships between boys. "Some of the kids are like brothers almost, you know?" said one participant. "I've become very close to some of them," he continued. "It's like that movie *Fight Club*. What can you say about yourself if you've never been in a fight?"[40]

I'm not endorsing backyard wrestling. It's unsupervised and dangerous. But it's also exactly what you can expect some boys to do when other venues for aggressive sports are closed. I've already mentioned the fact that many schools now prohibit activities such as dodgeball and throwing snowballs. Across the United States the physical education curriculum is shifting away from traditional sports in favor of aerobic activities such as riding a stationary bicycle or jogging.[41] Advocates of this shift point out that competitive sports have winners and losers, and often involve an aggressive component. Nobody's a loser if you're just riding a stationary bike. But people who make that argument don't understand that many boys *need* the aggressive element found in sports such as basketball and soccer. The result of the shift away from competitive sports to aerobics is that boys who aren't athletic enough to make the team now have *no* socially acceptable outlet for their aggressive impulses.

Grand Theft Auto

What do you do if your son wants to energize his sympathetic nervous system, to get his fix of tingles, by playing a violent video game? *Grand Theft Auto*, referred to by teenage boys as *GTA*, is one of the most popular games in the ultraviolent genre. You play the part of an excon who has to reestablish his reputation as a tough guy. You steal cars, run over pedestrians, and kill people. You can have sex with a prostitute, then shoot her in the head and take your money back while blood oozes from her head and she moans in agony. Police officers are the enemy. The more police you kill, the better—if you can get away with it.

The most successful installment of *GTA*, entitled "Vice City," sold 1.4 million copies—at $50 each!—in its first week alone, and $400 million worth of product in its first year. That's roughly the same amount of money that the movie *Titanic* earned in its first year.

Do not buy this game for your son. Don't buy any video game that employs what I call a "moral inversion"—where good is bad and bad is good. Playing those games for hours on end can warp your mind. If your son absolutely has to play violent video games, choose something like *SpyHunter* instead. In *SpyHunter*, you're a James Bond sort of character, assigned missions such as escorting diplomats to embassies while various enemies try to shoot you and the diplomat you're escorting. In other missions, you're trying to destroy interballistic missiles in their silos or save a crowd at a stadium by disarming a hidden explosive device before it goes off—all while the bad guys are shooting at you and you're shooting back. You lose points if you kill or injure a civilian. You can't just fire your weapon blindly. You have to avoid the civilians (who become more numerous as you advance in the game) and make sure you're right on top of the bad guy before you fire. I've played both *SpyHunter* and *GTA* "Vice City" and I can tell you, those two games leave a very different residual in your head. After playing *GTA* "Vice City," when you see a real police car, you really do feel a momentary impulse to shoot or run away.

Stay involved. Your son needs to know that you're aware of every video game he's playing. Sit down and play with him. If the violence and gore turns your stomach, tell your son that you're going to toss that game in the garbage can.

Better yet, get your son away from video games altogether and toward *real-life* aggressive games such as football and ice hockey. Playing a violent sport like football or lacrosse can build

many virtues in a boy: courage, physical endurance, and camaraderie, among others. No video game can do that.

Boys who need an aggressive outlet need an aggressive outlet.
That's not as obvious as it might seem. Parents—mothers in particular—may find it hard to understand how any human being
could get a thrill out of shooting someone in the head at close
range, even if only in a computer simulation. But many boys do
get a thrill out of simulated violence. If your son is one of those
"real boys" who needs some kind of aggressive outlet, does he
have one? Have you ever encouraged him to try out for football
or ice hockey? If not, why not? Do you think those activities are
too dangerous or violent? On the contrary, the greatest health
risk facing American children today seems to be *inactivity*.
According to the Centers for Disease Control, boys today are
four times more likely to be overweight than thirty years ago.[42]
Thirty years ago there was no Internet, there were no video
games, and most of the fun things to do were outdoors.
Channeling your young son's aggressive impulses into football
and soccer may be a better choice—just in terms of his physical
health—than almost any indoor recreational activity you can
name.

Violence, Girl Style

Mary is the mother of fifteen-year-old Julie. Mary recently
told me how Julie came home from her riding lesson with a
funny look on her face. Over supper, Mary asked what was
wrong.

"Nothing," Julie said.

"Come on. You're upset. Tell me."

Julie looked as though she might cry. "It's all the girls at the
barn. They *hate* me."

"That's silly. They're some of your best friends," Mom said.

Julie said nothing. She gripped her spoon and looked at her
soup.

"You all went out together last Saturday, to the horse show

and then to dinner afterward," Mary reminded her. "You told me you all had a great time. That was just five days ago. What makes you think they don't like you all of a sudden?"

"The moment I walked in the barn. They were all talking about me. As soon as they saw me they stopped," Julie said.

"How do you know they were talking about you?" Mom asked.

Julie rolled her eyes. "It's obvious," she said. She stirred her still-untasted soup. "They *all* hate me now. I said hi to Lisa and she acted like I wasn't even there. Lisa, of all people! Can you believe that? If it weren't for me, Lisa wouldn't have a single friend at the barn. She wouldn't even be *at* the barn." Tears welled in Julie's eyes. "It's all Karen's fault. Karen hates me. She's *always* hated me. She's jealous of me because I'm a better rider and I have a nicer horse. And now she's gotten the other girls to be mean to me."

Next morning, Julie announced she didn't want to ride any-more. She'd been riding since she was six years old. "Don't make me go back to that barn," she begged her mother.

Many parents in this situation might make the mistake of as-suming that the problem is all in their daughter's head. They think that because the signs of aggression are absent, nothing is really going on. Don't be deceived. Odds are your daughter is right.

Girls and boys fight differently. Boys can be mean to one an-other, but the meanness is usually right there on the surface. Riley puts a wad of sticky used chewing gum on Mike's seat at the cafeteria table when Mike isn't looking. Mike sits down, re-alizes he's got somebody else's chewing gum on his butt, and looks around to see who did it. Somebody points at Riley. Mike hauls off and slugs him. The two boys roll on the floor, hitting and kicking, until Mike pins Riley down. The teachers pull them apart and send both of them to the principal's office. One day later, Mike and Riley may be sitting together at lunch—better friends than they were before.

Provocation, leading to a violent response, followed by reso-lution. That's the pattern with many boys. But that simple pattern is rare among girls. "The surface of a girl fight can be silent and smooth as a marble," observes Rachel Simmons.[43] Tension can arise so subtly that even the girls themselves sometimes can't honestly tell you how it started. A violent response is seldom appropriate and seldom made, because the provocation may be hard to define:

- She ignored me in the hall even after I said hello to her.
- She sat with Karen instead of me at lunch, and she knows Karen hates me.
- She sighed when I spoke up in English class, like I had said something stupid.

Tensions can simmer and build for weeks or months, corroding a friendship until there is no friendship left.

Simmons uses the phrase "alternative aggression" to describe these ongoing wars among adolescent girls. It's a useful term because it reminds us that these ongoing tensions *are* a form of aggression. Parents sometimes don't recognize the damage that alternative aggression can cause. For one thing, the perpetrator is often a "good girl," polite to adults and clever at hiding her traces. A girl who victimizes other girls in this manner is often the *most* socially skilled and may even be one of the most popular girls—just the opposite of the typical boy bully.

Girl bullies are different from boy bullies. Boys who bully are often pathetic characters themselves. The male bully may have few friends, may be socially inept, may not be doing well in school. He picks on his victim as a way of improving his own status, at least in his own eyes. "I can't be the most contemptible person in the school if Tyler is terrified of me," he thinks. But he probably doesn't know Tyler very well. His bullying is motivated not so much by anything Tyler has done or said, but by his *own* insecurities, his vague hope that he will feel better by making someone else miserable. He may also hope to ingratiate himself with other boys by picking on the victim. "When an unpopular kid is harassed by someone from a popular crowd, wanna-bes and posers may take the incident as a signal that their own status can be improved by going after that victim," observes Professor John Bishop of Cornell University.[44]

The situation is almost completely reversed for girls. Whereas boys typically bully kids they barely know, girls almost always bully girls within their social group. These girls are intimate enemies. They know each other. They know where it hurts most.[45]

Here's a summary:

GIRLS who bully typically . . .	BOYS who bully typically . . .
have many friends	have few friends
are socially skilled	are socially inept
act in groups to isolate a single girl	act alone
are doing well in school	are doing poorly in school
know the girls they are bullying	don't know the boys (or girls) they bully

So what do you do if you discover that your daughter is the "odd girl out," the girl who's being ignored and ostracized by other girls? Start by taking the problem seriously. Don't dismiss or minimize it by telling her she's just imagining things. Maybe she is being oversensitive, but it pays to make sure. When did the problems begin? Who are your daughter's "enemies"—who's taking part in the campaign against her? What might be motivating those girls? Remember that other girls might ostracize your daughter not because of something *bad* she's done, but because she prompts other girls' envy. As Simmons observes, "The girls who get ostracized are usually the ones who have what most girls are expected to want: looks, the guy, money, and cool clothes." Make an appointment to talk face-to-face with the guidance counselor at the school—this is too important for a phone call. Sometimes the counselor really knows the situation at the school. Sometimes, unfortunately, the counselor is clueless. Either way, you need to be sure that the counselor understands your level of concern.

Consider signing your daughter up for after-school activities that would involve her with a different group of girls. Team sports are one option, if she is so inclined. Dance or drama may be a good choice. Or horseback riding, or swimming. Of course, girls in these other activities can be just as prone to cliques and rivalries as the girls at her school. But girls need connection with other girls. By showing your daughter that you understand her situation and that you're taking the problem seriously and doing your best to help—instead of trying to talk her out of it—you're already helping her feel better.

In extreme cases you may need to talk with your daughter about other options. Ask her how she would feel about transferring to another school. If you're in the public school system, the guidance counselor can often facilitate this transfer. That's another reason why you'll want to be in touch with the guidance counselor throughout the process. Sometimes a transfer can be accomplished seamlessly over a semester break.

Watch for signs of clinical depression. If your daughter is crying uncontrollably, if she's lost interest in doing the things she used to enjoy, or if (God forbid) she starts talking about suicide, then you should seek professional help. The experience of being shunned by other girls *can* precipitate full-blown clinical depression, with the associated risk of suicide. Don't hesitate to schedule a consultation with a qualified psychologist or psychiatrist if you have any doubt.

SCHOOL

Girls don't receive their fair share of education. Teachers of good intention respond to boys and teach them more actively, but . . . while the teachers are spending time with boys, the girls are being ignored and shortchanged.

—Myra and David Sadker, 1994[1]

A review of the facts shows boys, not girls, on the weak side of an educational gender gap. Boys, on average, are a year and a half behind girls in reading and writing; they are less committed to school and less likely to go to college.

—Christina Hoff Sommers, 2000[2]

Both girls and boys are being shortchanged.

—Jackie Woods, president, American Association of University Women, 2002[3]

Melanie

Melanie was an academic superstar all through high school. In eleventh grade she took Advanced Placement (AP) English, AP Spanish, AP American history, and AP biology as well as trigonometry. Not only did she get straight A's that year, she also really seemed to enjoy each class. She was especially interested in the environmental science unit of her biology class. Her biology teacher, Ms. Griffith, recognized Melanie's talent and encouraged her. With Ms. Griffith's help, Melanie devised a science project to test and correlate levels of pollutants in samples of water taken from the Potomac River at different points, from Harpers Ferry in West Virginia all the way down to Georgetown and Anacostia in Washington, D.C. Her project won second place at an environmental science fair. "You're more than just smart," Ms. Griffith told Melanie after the fair. "Lots of scientists are smart. The great scientists are those who have imagination." Melanie beamed.

At Ms. Griffith's suggestion, Melanie signed up to take AP physics in her senior year. Ms. Griffith assured her she wouldn't have any problem. "Physics will come naturally to you," Ms. Griffith said. "You have an analytical mind."

The first day of physics class seemed to go okay. The instructor, Mr. Wallace, plunged right in, presenting formulas and equations relating distance, velocity, and acceleration. At the end of class, as students were standing up and gathering their books to leave, he called out, "First seven problems in chapter 1, due tomorrow" (the class groaned), "in writing, show your work, make it neat, hand them in at the start of class!"

Melanie looked at the problems that evening. The first five weren't too difficult. The last two were harder. They didn't seem to fit any of the formulas in the book.

That semester, Melanie was also taking AP Spanish, AP English, AP European history, and AP calculus. She had homework assignments in each of those subjects already as well. She wrote out the answers to the first five physics problems. Then, rather than waste time trying to figure out the two remaining problems, she decided to do her homework in her other subjects, and to meet with Mr. Wallace for help during her morning study period.

She didn't have any trouble finding Mr. Wallace during second period the next morning. He was in the physics lab, checking the equipment for the first experiment. She introduced herself, and then asked: "About the homework assignment, I had a question. The first five problems were pretty easy, but I had trouble with the last two. They didn't fit any of the problems that were solved in the chapter. Like the problem where the boy is trying to catch the bus. The bus is pulling away from the bus stop, it's accelerating at a constant rate, which means that its speed is increasing, and we're supposed to figure out whether the boy can catch the bus, and if so how long it will take him to catch up with the bus . . ." She paused to give Mr. Wallace a chance to say something, to suggest how to solve the problem.

Mr. Wallace said nothing. He glanced at her, then looked out the window. It was almost as though he hadn't heard anything she had said.

"Would you like me to show you the problem?" she asked, taking her book out and flipping to the page.

He shook his head.

"It's right here on page twenty-two," she began.

Mr. Wallace interrupted. "I think maybe you're in the wrong class," he said.

"What?" Melanie asked.

"Physics isn't for everybody," Mr. Wallace said. "Ms. Griffith told me what a hardworking student you are. In subjects like biology, students who work hard will do well. But physics is different. Either you have the right kind of mind for it or you don't."

"But you don't even know me," Melanie protested. "How do you know what kind of mind I have?"

"I just don't want you to hurt your grade point average," Mr. Wallace said. "Ms. Griffith told me that you're a straight-A student, that you might be the class valedictorian. I'd hate for you to lose that by staying in this class."

"You're saying I should drop this class?" Melanie said in disbelief. "After one day? One homework assignment? Which we haven't even discussed yet?"

Mr. Wallace nodded. "I'm sorry," he said.

Melanie slammed her book shut and left the room without another word. She wanted to go to Ms. Griffith and ask: What is *wrong* with this guy? Or maybe she would go to the school counselor and complain.

But she did neither. Instead, she dropped the course. "If he doesn't want me in his class, then I don't want to be in his class," Melanie told me later. "I mean, what if he gives me a lower grade just because he doesn't like me? I have to think about my college transcript. I don't want a B on my transcript in the last semester that colleges will see."

Some people would say that this incident illustrates the way in which sexist male teachers drive well-qualified girls out of physics classes. Those critics would point to the fact that Melanie was one of only six girls in a class of twenty-three students as evidence that the school was biased against girls taking physics. Those critics might also mention the fact that the homework problems in this particular textbook refer to boys, almost never girls, chasing after buses, hitting baseballs, driving race cars, and so on.

That analysis has some merit, but I don't think it's the whole story, in part because I know Melanie. Melanie was a victim, yes, but not primarily a victim of sexism. She was more a victim of Mr. Wallace's lack of understanding of the differences in how girls and boys learn. Here's my assessment of what happened and why.

First, here's the "why": girls and boys have different educational styles, and different expectations for the teacher-student relationship. Because teachers are often unaware of those differences, male teachers especially often misunderstand and misinterpret the behavior of their female students. Most girls will naturally seek to affiliate with the teacher. They expect the teacher to be on their side, to be their ally. Most girls won't hesitate to ask the teacher for help when they need it. Educational researchers have consistently found that girls are more concerned than boys are with pleasing the teacher and more likely than boys to follow the teacher's example.[4] Remarkably, a similar finding has recently been described in our closest genetic relative, the chimpanzee. In 2004, anthropologists who had spent three years observing chimpanzees in the wilds of Tanzania reported sex differences in learning similar to what we see in human children. Girl chimps follow their teacher's example—in this case, regarding the proper way to dig for termites—while boy chimps completely disregard the teacher, preferring to do it their own way—or they ignore the teacher's example altogether and go off to swing from a nearby tree or wrestle with another male chimp. The boy chimps are consequently much slower to master the task than the girls are.[5]

Sex differences in how students relate to their teacher give rise to sex differences in motivation to study and in the weight that students give to their teacher's opinions. As a result, according to educational psychologist Eva Pomerantz, girls are at greater risk of being harmed by a negative assessment from a teacher:

> Girls generalize the meaning of their failures because they interpret them as indicating that they have disappointed adults, and thus they are of little worth. Boys, in contrast, appear to see their failures as relevant only to the specific subject area in which they have failed; this may be due to their relative lack of concern with pleasing adults.[6]

Girls are more likely to do their homework even if the particular assignment doesn't interest them. Girls want the teacher to think well of them. Boys on the other hand will be less motivated to study unless they find the material intrinsically interesting. Likewise, most boys will consult the teacher for help only as a last resort, after all other options have been exhausted.

Mr. Wallace was a student himself once, of course. When he was a student, he probably had the typical male study pattern. Most likely he studied alone, asking the teacher for help rarely and only after he had agonized for hours over a problem. When Melanie asked him for help on the second day of class, he probably assumed that she had been working on the problem for hours. He knew from Ms. Griffith that Melanie was a smart, hardworking student. He thought: If this smart, hardworking student has worked on this problem for hours and she still can't figure it out, then she probably doesn't belong in my class. When he suggested that she drop the class, he was sincerely trying to act in her best interests.

If Mr. Wallace had taken a few minutes to ask Melanie how much effort she had put into solving the problems on her own, he would have realized his mistake. She hadn't spent even five minutes on those problems. However, Mr. Wallace and Melanie would still have had to reconcile their conflicting educational styles. If she had explained to Mr. Wallace that she was asking him for help *before* making a sustained effort to solve the problem on her own, he would have been surprised, even annoyed. He might conclude that maybe she wasn't such a hard worker after all. Melanie would most likely have sensed his annoyance and been irked by his response. "Why *shouldn't* I ask the teacher for help? Isn't that what the teacher is there for? Why should I waste hours working on the problem the wrong way, when the teacher can show me the right way?" That's what other girls have told me in similar situations.

Melanie went on to get straight A's again that semester. She was accepted at her first-choice school, the University of Maryland. I hear from her mother that Melanie is majoring in marketing. There's nothing wrong with marketing, except that Melanie never expressed any interest in it when she was in high school. She was really on fire in that biology class. I can't help wondering whether she might have gone on to become the great scientist Ms. Griffith predicted she could be, if only her high school physics teacher had known more about the different educational styles of girls and boys—if he had encouraged her instead of pushing her out the door.

Face-To-Face, Shoulder-To-Shoulder

Friendships between girls are different from friendships between boys. Girls' friendships are about being together, spending time together, talking together, going places together. Friendships between boys on the other hand usually develop out of a shared interest in a game or an activity. We might characterize the difference this way: girls' friendships are *face-to-face,* two or three girls talking with one another. Boys' friendships are *shoulder-to-shoulder,* a group of boys looking out at some common interest.[7]

Conversation is central to girls' friendships at every age. Girlfriends love to talk with each other. When they start having trouble talking, the friendship is in trouble. The mark of a truly close friendship between two girls or two women is that they tell each other secrets they don't tell anyone else. They confide in each other about their most personal doubts and difficulties. *Self-disclosure* is the most precious badge of friendship between females. When she tells you a secret she's never told anyone else, then you know that you are truly her dear friend.

Boys are different. Most boys don't really want to hear each other's innermost secrets.[8] With boys the focus is on the activity, not on the conversation. Four boys can spend hours playing a video game without exchanging a single complete sentence. You'll hear screams of agony and shouts of exultation, but you may not hear much that qualifies as conversation.

Girls' friendships then are more intimate and more personal than most boys' friendships. That has advantages and disadvantages. The advantage of course is that each girl derives strength from the intimacy of the friendship. When a girl is under stress, she looks to other girls for support and comfort. When girls are under stress, they want to be with their friends *more.* When boys are under stress, they usually just want to be left alone.[9] (Many mothers don't know about these differences. When a mother sees that her son is under stress, she often tries to comfort him. Almost invariably she will be rebuffed.) Psychologist Shelley

Taylor, who has specialized in the study of gender differences in the response to stress, summarizes her findings this way: "Women maintain more same-sex close relationships than do men, they mobilize more social support in times of stress than do men, they turn to female friends more often, and they report more benefits from contact with their female friends and relatives."[10]

Girls' Friendships Have Distinct Values and Exhibit Different Dynamics Compared with Boys' Friendships

	Girls	Boys
Friendships form among . . .	Two or three girls	Two to twelve boys
Friendships focus on . . .	Each other	A shared interest in a game or activity
Games and sports are . . .	An excuse to get together	Central to the relationship
Conversation is . . .	Central to the relationship	Often unnecessary
Hierarchies . . .	Destroy the friendship	Build and organize camaraderie
Self-revelation is . . .	A precious badge of friendship	To be avoided if possible

These differences are relevant to education for many reasons, chief of which is that girls and boys relate to teachers differently. For most boys, being friends with a teacher is a sure sign of geekdom.* Professor Bishop at Cornell University writes:

> In the eyes of most students, the nerds exemplify the "I trust my teachers to help me learn" attitude that prevails in most elementary school classrooms. The dominant middle school crowd is telling them that trusting teachers is baby stuff. It is "us" [the boys] versus "them" [the teachers].

*The coach is an exception to this rule. It's okay for boys to be friends with the coach—as long as the coach himself is a real jock, not a dork or a geek.

Friendships with teachers make you a target for harassment by peers. . . . Boys are not supposed to suck up to teachers. You avoid being perceived as a suck-up by avoiding eye contact with teachers, not raising one's hand in class too frequently, and [by] talking or passing notes to friends during class (this demonstrates that you value relationships with friends more than your reputation with the teacher).[11]

Girls are less likely to think friendship with teachers equals geekiness. On the contrary, a girl student may actually raise her status in the eyes of her friends if she has a close relationship with a teacher—especially if the teacher is young, "cool," and female. I know of a young teacher at an all-girls school who occasionally invites two or three girls in her class to go to the movies with her. Being invited to see a movie with that teacher is a major status booster. (Being friends with a teacher is less likely to boost a girl's status if the teacher is male, as other girls may suspect that she is using her sexuality to get a better grade.) With boys, it's different. A boy who is buddy-buddy with the teacher does not thereby raise his stature in the eyes of his peers. On the contrary, being friends with the teacher can *lower* a boy's status in the eyes of other boys.

Girls are more likely to assume that the teacher is an ally and a friend. Boys are less likely to make that assumption. So, when encountering difficulties, girls are more likely to consult the teacher early. Boys, as I said a moment ago, usually consult the teacher only as a last resort. And girls are much more likely than boys are to ask a teacher for advice about personal matters, totally unrelated to the academic material.

Continuing with our discussion of friendship: girls' friendships work best when the friendship is between equals. If you're a girl or a woman and you think your friend believes herself to be "better" than you, then your friendship with her is not likely to last. Boys on the other hand are comfortable in an unequal relationship, even if they are the lesser party. The third-string linebacker may enjoy being the best buddy of the star quarterback. He may not resent the quarterback's higher status. He may even try to magnify his friend's status in the eyes of others. This male characteristic has roots that go very deep. If you know the stories of Gilgamesh and Enkidu, Achilles and Patroclus, David son of Jesse and Jonathan son of Saul, or for that matter Don Quixote and Sancho Panza, then you've heard this story before. Those friendships were not less strong because of the difference in status between the friends. On the contrary, the hierarchical character of the relationship defined and even ennobled the friendship. "Jonathan and David made a pact because *Jonathan loved David*," we read in 1 Samuel. Not because David loved Jonathan. "Jonathan took off the cloak and tunic he was wearing and gave them to David, along with his sword, bow, and belt . . ." Jonathan said to David, "You are going to be king over Israel and *I shall be second to you*."[12] Jonathan's dream was a world in which his hero, David, would be king and he, Jonathan, would be the king's right-hand man.

These differences explain a useful tip that several teachers have shared with me. If you're working with a girl, *smile and look her in the eye* when you're helping her with a subject. That gives her nonverbal reassurance that you like her and you're her friend. Too many teachers (especially men) don't make eye contact with their female students. "I asked him a question, and he answered it, but he just seemed to be talking into empty space. He didn't even look at me," said one girl. "He didn't care about *me*. It was almost like I wasn't even there."

If you're working with a boy, sit down *next* to him and spread out the materials in front of you, so you're both looking at the materials, shoulder-to-shoulder. Don't hold an eye-to-eye stare with a boy unless you're trying to discipline him or reprimand him. Don't smile. "Whenever that old witch smiles, it gives me the creeps," one boy told me. "When she smiles, she looks like the evil lady in *101 Dalmatians*. She looks at me like I'm one of those Dalmatians."

Another application of these differences is that *small group*

Handwritten margin notes: *Small group bad for boys ??* *group assignments* — *goes against everything we believe in !!*

learning is a good teaching strategy for girls, but seldom for boys. How come?

First reason: Girls are more comfortable asking the teacher for help when they need it. If you give four girls a group assignment, you can be confident that if they get stuck, at least one of them will come to you for help.

Not so with boys. If four boys get stuck, there's no guarantee that any of them will ask the teacher for help, unless one of the boys is a geek, and even geeks know that asking the teacher for help lowers their status in the eyes of the other boys. If the boys get stuck, they may just throw spitballs and get rowdy instead of asking for help.

That leads us to a second reason why small-group self-directed learning works for girls but not for boys. Boys can raise their status in the eyes of other boys by disrupting the teacher's program. If the teacher breaks the class into small groups and two boys in a group of four start being disruptive, those boys raise their status in the eyes of at least some of the other boys in the room, no matter how puerile their behavior. (Incidentally, the word *puerile* is derived from the Latin word *puer*, meaning young boy. There is no pejorative word corresponding to the Latin *puella*, young girl.) That's what education writer Elinor Burkitt was trying to communicate when she wrote that "teen culture celebrates public displays of contempt for education and authority," which if unchecked will cause the class to disintegrate into "total anarchy."[13]

Hearing the Difference

In chapter 2 we noted that girls hear better than boys. Anytime you have a teacher of one sex teaching children of the opposite sex, there's a potential for a mismatch, if only in decibel level. If a male teacher speaks in a tone of voice that seems normal to him, a girl in the front row may feel that he is yelling at her.

I talked with Melanie around Thanksgiving of her senior year. That's when she told me the story about Mr. Wallace advising her to drop the course on the second day of school. I asked her how she felt about a teacher telling her to drop a class for no good reason.

"No big deal," she said. "I don't think I could have put up with Mr. Wallace for very long, anyhow," she added.

Why not, I asked.

"He was a shouter," she said, "That one day I was in his class, he was shouting right in my face. I wanted to put my hands over my ears."

Recall our discussion in chapter 1 of the misdiagnosis of attention deficit disorder. Some boys diagnosed with ADD may just need the teacher to raise her voice a bit. This fundamental fact is not taught in most schools of education. When I speak to teachers, they are fascinated to learn that girls and boys do indeed differ in their ability to hear. Experienced teachers often figure this out on their own—after five or ten years of teaching. One veteran teacher told me that she puts the boys in the front of the class and the girls in back. That's pretty much the opposite of how girls and boys normally seat themselves. In most classes you'll have two or three academically talented boys sitting in the front row, the rest of the boys at the back, and the girls in the middle. That's the "natural" way for kids to seat themselves, because most girls like to affiliate with the teacher and most boys don't. (In chapter 9 we'll talk about the two or three boys who do.)

The Teacher's Guilty Secret

The differences in girls' and boys' ability to hear is one hardwired reason why both girls and boys are shortchanged by gender-neutral education. Another reason has to do with differences in the way girls and boys respond to threat and confrontation.

"I really yelled at one of my students one day," middle school teacher Tina Spencer confessed to me. "I was just so frustrated with him, because Sam is a smart boy, but he just wasn't doing the work. He never did the homework. So one day I just lost it. I really let him have it. I yelled at him, in class, in front of the other students. I didn't mean to but I did.

"Right afterward, I was worried he'd never speak to me again," Tina said. "I expected to get an angry phone call from the parents. But the next day, Sam turned in his homework perfect and on time, for the first time ever. He even asked me whether I would like to look at his collection of baseball cards. Those baseball cards are his most prized possession. He'd never shown them to me before.

"Then three weeks later, the parents finally did call," Tina told me. "I was so nervous! I was sure they were going to be angry with me for screaming at their son. But they weren't. They were calling to thank me. They didn't seem to know anything about that episode. They wanted to know what magic I had used to get Sam so energized about his schoolwork. I didn't know what to say. I didn't feel I could tell them what really happened."

That kind of confrontational, in-your-face approach would be precisely the *wrong* approach to use with most girls. "If I had done that with a girl, I'm sure she wouldn't have spoken to me for the rest of the semester, at the very least," adds Ms. Spencer. Teachers report more success with girls when they use a supportive, nonconfrontational approach.

Laboratory animals also exhibit sex differences in learning under stressful situations. Professor Tracey Shors and her colleagues at Rutgers, Princeton, and Rockefeller University have demonstrated that stress improves learning in males while it impairs learning in females.[14] "Exposure to the stressor had diametrically opposed effects" on learning in females compared with males, Professor Shors has reported.[15] She has also shown that exposure to stress enhances the growth of neural connections in the male hippocampus while it inhibits growth of connections in the female hippocampus. Shors has conclusively demonstrated that the beneficial effect of stress on learning in males depends on *prenatal* masculinization of the male brain.[16]

Reports like these prove that there are innate differences in how females and males respond to stress. I still hear educators insist that if we just raised girls to play with trucks and boys to play with dolls, then most differences in how girls and boys learn would just go away. Laboratory animals don't get to play with trucks or with Barbies, so it's hard to use that argument to explain Professor Shors's findings. And if female laboratory animals learn differently than male laboratory animals do, isn't it reasonable to look for sex differences in how human children learn?

Professor Shors's work also ties into what we discussed earlier about gender differences in response to stress. Many young boys are energized by confrontation and by time-constrained tasks. Few young girls will flourish in high-pressure, do-it-in-five-seconds-or-you-lose formats. What application does that have for the schoolroom?

Recently I had the privilege of sitting in on Trent Anderson's seventh-grade English class at Stuart Hall for Boys, an all-boys school in San Francisco. Mr. Anderson had divided the class into teams. They had to answer questions about John Steinbeck's *The Pearl*.

"What did the doctor give Coyotito after Coyotito began convulsing? Team A!"

The boys in Team A huddled, whispering frantically. "Some white powder?" one boy said at last.

"NO!" Mr. Anderson said. "Team B!"

The boys in Team B whispered to one another. "A capsule? A capsule of medicine?" another boy ventured.

"NO!" Mr. Anderson said. "Team C!"

The boys in Team C talked with one another for a few seconds. "A few drops of ammonia, diluted in water," a boy said.

"YES!" Mr. Anderson said. All the boys in Team C high-fived each other and cheered. Then Mr. Anderson began calling on a particular boy from each team in turn. The team's score goes up or down depending on whether the boy knows the answer. All the boys are called on at least once. That means it's not enough to have just one guy on your team who knows the book well. *Everybody* has to know the book or your team will lose. So the boys work together. They collaborate as a team to win the competition.

I've seen similar tactics used in other all-boys classrooms. Sometimes the teacher will put a ticking timer at the front of the class, allowing just ten or fifteen seconds for each answer before the timer emits a loud buzz. Sometimes Mr. Anderson will award certificates for a free pizza to the winning team. Other times he may announce that the winning team doesn't have to take the quiz on the book; all members of the winning team get an automatic A. The boys will study the material just because they don't want to let their teammates down.

This approach is not as useful for girls. Fewer young girls will get excited about the opportunity to shout out answers to questions in a time-constrained way. Girls are more likely to regard such an exercise as silly. Older girls will complain that the exercise forces them to focus on small details from the book when they'd rather talk about larger themes.

Amy Van Dragt—who teaches at an all-girls school, also in San Francisco—told me about her routine on test days. "I have the girls start by taking their shoes off, relaxing," she said. "We sit in a circle and just help each other chill for a few minutes. Then I pass out the tests. But I *never* use timed tests," Ms. Van Dragt said. "I let each girl have as long as she needs."

"What happens if all the other girls have finished, and one girl still needs more time?"

"Then I give her more time," Ms. Van Dragt said.

I think that makes sense. After all, in real life very few tasks are truly time-constrained in the sense that a few minutes matter. Unless you're a professional athlete or a soldier or a pilot, in most adult jobs if you need five or ten or fifteen more minutes to figure out the answer to a question, you can take that time. Ms. Van Dragt is de-stressing her classroom, by removing the time constraints and having the girls kick off their shoes. That's a good way to keep stress from impairing the girls' test performance.

Rule of thumb: moderate stress improves boys' performance on tests—the boys do *better* than you might expect—whereas the same stress *degrades* young girls' performance on tests (this effect may be smaller in adult women than it is in school-age girls).[17] Differences in the effect of stress on test performance may explain one of the most robust findings in educational testing: namely, that girls on average don't do quite as well as you might expect on standardized tests such as the SAT, based on their grades in school. The girl who gets straight A's in school doesn't necessarily get a perfect score on the SAT or even a score above the ninetieth percentile. Conversely, boys often do better than you would expect on time-constrained, stressful standardized tests such as the SAT. "That boy is so smart when he takes those standardized tests, but he just doesn't apply himself in class or when he's supposed to be doing his homework. He rarely gets anything better than a B."

A Different Sequence

In chapter 1, I related how—ten years ago—I started seeing a wave of young boys flooding my office. Each boy's parent carried a note from somebody at the school (teacher, guidance counselor, reading specialist) suggesting that Justin or Brett or Carlos or Simon might have ADD. I evaluated each of these kids to determine whether each one met the criteria for ADD. Some kids did meet the criteria; others did not. I've already mentioned how some of the boys who were sent to my office with a presumed diagnosis of ADD actually were normal boys who were sitting in the back of a class in which the teacher was a young woman who didn't talk very loud.

But there was another important difference that the school was overlooking. Girls and boys differ in their developmental timetables. Those differences in brain maturation are detectable while the baby is still in its mother's womb.[18]

The differences are larger and more complex than you might expect. Researchers at Virginia Tech examined brain activity in 508 normal children—224 girls and 284 boys—ranging in age from two months to sixteen years. This study, the largest and most carefully executed of its type, demonstrated that various regions of the brain develop in a different *sequence* in girls compared with boys. It's not correct to say, "Boys develop along the same lines as girls, only slower." The truth is more nuanced. These researchers found that while the areas of the brain involved in language and fine motor skills mature about six years earlier in girls than in boys, the areas of the brain involved in targeting and spatial memory mature about four years earlier in boys than in girls. These researchers concluded that the areas of the brain involved in language, in spatial memory, in motor coordination, and in getting along with other people develop in a "different order, time, and rate" in girls compared with boys.[19]

Their conclusion—that different areas of the brain develop in a different sequence in girls compared with boys—is supported by other studies looking at specific skills in young children. Researchers in France watched two-year-olds building bridges out of blocks. At that young age, they found that a boy is about three times more likely than a girl to be able to build a bridge out of blocks.[20] On the other hand, researchers at Wellesley College found that three-and-a-half-year-old girls could interpret facial expressions as well as or better than five-year-old boys could.[21] So it's too simple to say that boys mature more slowly than girls do. Boys mature faster than girls in some areas, slower in others.

This leads us to another important point. *Sex differences in childhood are larger and more important than sex differences in adulthood.* By thirty years of age, both females and males have reached full maturity of all areas of the brain. When people over thirty years of age think about their own experience as adults,

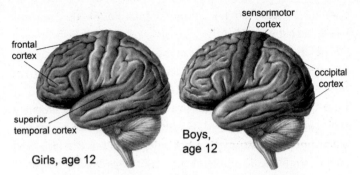

In girls, the superior temporal cortex and the frontal
cortex mature earlier than areas involved in visuospatial
processing and targeting. In boys, the areas of the brain
involved in visuospatial processing and targeting develop
earlier than other areas of the brain.

they may not see enormous sex differences in how women and
men learn new material or master new tasks. So some adults assume that if they're not seeing big differences in how adult
women and men learn to do new things, then there probably
aren't big sex differences in how six-year-old girls and boys
learn. That assumption is wrong.

Thirty years ago, when kindergarten was all about finger-
painting and singing together and playing duck-duck-goose, sex
differences in brain maturation didn't matter as much. Thirty
years ago, kindergartners weren't expected to sit in chairs and
do pencil-and-paper exercises all day long. First-graders had to
do that, but kindergarten was more about socialization, about
learning to get along with other kids. Thirty years ago, the primary mission of kindergarten was to acclimate the kid to school,
not to get a jump start on academics.

No more. Today, educators throughout North America make
no apologies for the academic character of the twenty-first-
century kindergarten. The curriculum of kindergarten today is
essentially the first-grade curriculum of thirty years ago.[22] The
objective of kindergarten today is simple: achieving literacy and
numeracy. While that sounds good, there's a problem. Many

five-year-old boys just don't have the fine motor skills necessary to write the letters of the alphabet. Remember that the Virginia Tech researchers found that boys are *years* behind girls in the development of the area of the brain responsible for fine motor skills. In the jargon of educational psychology, the objectives of today's academically oriented kindergarten are not *developmentally appropriate* for many kindergarten boys.

hold back

The unspoken assumption behind the push to teach reading and writing in kindergarten is that earlier exposure will guarantee improved performance. But that assumption is valid only if what you're teaching is developmentally appropriate for your students. If you try to teach your seven-year-old kid to drive a car, you won't end up with a better driver. Starting kids reading before they're ready to read can actually boomerang and turn them *off* to reading.

When I share this with kindergarten teachers, they often respond, "Oh, we understand that! We understand that not every five-year-old is ready for reading, not ready for paper-and-pencil exercises and all that. We customize what we do to each child's individual needs."

That sounds nice. But what does it really mean in practice? What it actually means is that many modern kindergartens are divided in two. Over here, with the teacher, are the kids who can handle the academic curriculum of today's accelerated kindergarten. These kids are sounding out words, writing short sentences, remembering to put a capital letter at the start of the sentence and a period at the end. This group is mostly girls with a few precocious boys.

Over there are the kids who aren't ready to handle the accelerated academic curriculum. Those kids are playing with blocks or putting together puzzles—activities most of us recognize as traditional kindergarten activities from our own childhood.

A five-year-old boy may not be very good at fine motor skills such as writing the letters of the alphabet, and he may not be developmentally ready to learn about vowels and consonants. But there's one thing most five-year-old boys are very good at:

figuring out that they've been put in the "dumb group." And they don't like it.

That's what happened to Matthew, the boy whose story opens chapter 1. Before starting kindergarten, Matthew had always been the star, the leading player in the drama of his life. "He was always ready to try anything," his mother told me. "Last July, I suggested to my husband that we paddle a canoe across the Potomac, at White's Ferry. My husband didn't want to. But Matthew did, so we rented a canoe, just me and five-year-old Matthew, and we had a great time. The rental place gave him this little plastic paddle. He loved it. He talked about it for days afterward. But now it's different. It's like he's turned into a completely different kid. He never used to throw temper tantrums before, but he's throwing a tantrum almost every morning now, for no reason, refusing to get dressed, refusing to go to school. I have to carry him kicking and screaming into the car, and then drag him from the car into the school. You'd think they were torturing him or doing something horrible. But they're not. I've sat in on his kindergarten and there's nothing wrong with it. The teacher is wonderful, in fact. She's very gentle, very patient. I've talked with her many times now, and she's reassured me that this is nothing unusual. She keeps saying I shouldn't worry. But I'm still concerned. Matthew's starting to hate school."

While Matthew's reaction was extreme, many studies now have shown that when the main emphasis in kindergarten is on learning to read at the expense of other less structured and more developmentally appropriate activities, many boys tune out and turn off. Those boys develop negative feelings toward school that are likely to persist and color the child's entire academic career.[23] Deborah Stipek, now dean of the School of Education at Stanford University, has shown that boys who fail to do well in kindergarten develop "negative perceptions of competence," and those negative attitudes are "difficult to reverse as [they] progress through school."[24]

When Matthew's mother, Cindy, told me how her son was

throwing a tantrum every morning, I advised her to take him out of kindergarten and put him back in preschool. This is the educational equivalent of a medical emergency, I told her. One more month in that kindergarten and his whole attitude toward school might be irreparably damaged.

Cindy refused. She kept saying, "But he's bright. Who's ever heard of a bright child flunking out of kindergarten?"

He's not flunking out, I said. This kindergarten is just not developmentally appropriate for him.

Cindy insisted on keeping Matthew in kindergarten. A month later she told me that the problem had been solved: Matthew wasn't throwing tantrums anymore. The teacher said that he was behaving better in class.

One year later Mom was back with Matthew, now in first grade. This time Cindy had one of those papers from the school. "Matthew is inattentive and easily distracted in class . . . Would you please evaluate to determine whether Matthew might meet criteria for ADHD [attention deficit hyperactivity disorder] . . ." And of course the teacher was absolutely right. Matthew *was* inattentive and easily distracted in class. He was now firmly convinced that school was just one big bore, an annoyance to be endured for a few hours each day until that wonderful moment when school let out and he could go home and do all the fun things he enjoyed. As far as Matthew was concerned, each day really began only when school ended.

"What's your favorite thing to do at school?" I asked.

"Recess," he said.

"What's your next favorite thing at school?" I asked.

"Lunch," he said.

There are no good choices for parents at this point. "Retention in grade," holding Matthew back a year, won't solve the problem at this stage. You've already missed your best chance. There's a big difference between *delaying* a child's entry to kindergarten versus his *repeating* first grade a year later. Studies have shown that if you delay entry into kindergarten for a boy like Matthew, he'll do much better than if you start him at age five; but if you let him start kindergarten when he's not ready for it, and then you make him repeat first grade when the time comes, he may do *worse* than if you didn't make him repeat.[25] The stigmatizing effect of having to repeat a year of school has a long-lasting effect that is not easily purged. The boy labels himself as "dumb," and he believes that label, and no amount of talking on your part will change his mind.

Mom and I weren't getting along at this point, so I referred Matthew to a child psychiatrist. The psychiatrist said that Matthew had ADHD *and* depression. He prescribed Ritalin and Prozac. When that didn't help, the specialist switched Matthew to Adderall and Wellbutrin. That didn't work either. The following month Matthew slapped a student in his first-grade class, resulting in a two-day suspension. When the psychiatrist heard about that, he added clonidine, a sedative, assuring Mom that the new medication would prevent Matthew from acting out. So now six-year-old Matthew was on *three* medications.

Matthew's story is all too common today. A report published in 2003 found that the proportion of young children on antidepressant medications has more than tripled in the past ten years.[26] We're not talking now about medications for ADHD such as Ritalin and Adderall, we're talking about medications for *depression*, such as Prozac, Zoloft, Paxil, Celexa, Lexapro, Wellbutrin, Pamelor, Elavil, and so forth. I have to wonder how many of these young children, boys especially, are depressed because they're trapped in a school that just is not geared to their needs. And they have no way out.

Girls Are Shortchanged, Too

When I speak to groups about differences in how girls and boys learn, I talk so forcefully about the harm done to boys in an overly academic kindergarten that I am often pegged as a "boys' advocate." But girls are being shortchanged as well, although the effects show up differently. The failure of schools to recognize differences in how girls and boys learn affects each sex at different ages. Boys are harmed most in kindergarten and the early elementary years.

For girls, the negative effects of gender-blind education become manifest in the middle school and high school years. Gender-blind education leads paradoxically to a strengthening of gender stereotypes, with the result that fewer girls take courses in physics, computer science, trigonometry, and calculus.

Why is gender-blind education harmful to girls? To understand the answer you have to know more about the differences in how girls and boys learn. Sex differences in learning aren't confined to differences in hearing, or differences in responses to confrontation, or differences in developmental timetables. There are consistent and significant brain-based sex differences in how girls and boys learn geometry and how they understand literature. Let's look more closely now at gender differences in how girls and boys learn geometry and number theory.

Recall our discussion of gender differences in how females and males give directions. In chapter 2 we learned that girls are more likely to use visible landmarks whereas boys are more likely to use compass directions: north, south, east, west. Psychologist Deborah Saucier and her colleagues wanted to see whether females could use the male-typical strategy (compass directions), and whether males could use the female-typical strategy (landmarks). They recruited students and divided them randomly into two groups. Both groups had the same task: to find an unknown location on campus, using directions provided by Dr. Saucier. In one group, both the females and the males were given directions in terms of landmarks. "Go straight down this road until you get to the small house with the green door. Then turn right and walk down the sidewalk until you get to College Avenue. Make a left onto College Avenue," and so forth. In the other group, both the women and the men were given compass directions: "Go north one block, then turn east and walk two blocks, then turn north," and so forth.

The results were dramatically different. When women and

men were both required to use compass directions, the women made many more errors than the men did, and the women took substantially longer to get to the target than the men. But when the volunteers were given visible landmarks rather than compass directions, the women did much better: the women made fewer errors than the men did and reached the target faster. When the researchers assigned a similar task using a video game, the differences were even more dramatic: women did much better using landmarks rather than compass directions whereas men did better using compass directions instead of landmarks.[27]

What's going on in the brain during these tasks? Georg Grön and his colleagues at the University of Ulm in Germany rigged up a nifty video game apparatus to answer that question. They created virtual reality goggles that allowed volunteers to play a video game while lying in an MRI brain scanner. In the video game the volunteer was trying to find a way out of a maze.

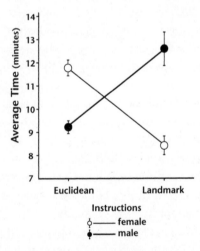

Males outperform females on spatial tasks when the task is framed in Euclidean terms (north, south, east, west); females outperform males when the task is geared to landmarks. Note the large differences between the sexes and the small variation within the sexes (from Saucier et al., 2002).

Their findings: females and males use completely different areas of the brain for the spatial task. Women use the cerebral cortex to solve the maze. You'll recall that the cerebral cortex is the most advanced area of the brain. We use our cerebral cortex for talking, for understanding, indeed for most of our interactions with the outside world. Men, on the other hand, do not use the cerebral cortex during the spatial task. Instead, they use the hippocampus, a phylogenetically primitive area of the brain that is prewired for spatial navigation.[28]

The unique function of the hippocampus was first demonstrated in the 1970s by John O'Keefe and Lynn Nadel. These neuroscientists demonstrated that the hippocampus functions as a *cognitive map*.[29] They found they could map an animal's environment right onto the animal's hippocampus. When the animal moved in a straight line north to south across a room, the locus of activity in the hippocampus moved "north to south" as well, so to speak, tracking the animal's movement. Research over the subsequent three decades has confirmed O'Keefe and Nadel's hypothesis: The hippocampus is prewired to function as a dedicated microprocessor for spatial geometry, at least in males. O'Keefe and Nadel studied only *male* laboratory animals.

Remarkably, scientists have found sex differences in the performance of laboratory animals on spatial tasks that are similar to sex differences found in humans. Female laboratory animals use landmark cues while males use Euclidean cues ("compass directions").[30] Scientists have even proven that female laboratory animals use the cerebral cortex for spatial tasks while male laboratory animals use the hippocampus[31]—just as Dr. Grön's group showed to be the case in humans. Again, in view of the sex differences in how female and male laboratory animals navigate mazes, it's hard to argue that similar sex differences in humans are created by human culture. These differences are genetically programmed, not culturally constructed.

These differences also have major implications for teaching, especially for math and geometry. As I said, the hippocampus is an ancient nucleus buried deep in the brain, with no direct connections to the cerebral cortex. And that's the nucleus boys use for math problems. That may help explain why boys are comfortable with math "for its own sake" at a much earlier age than girls are. You can fascinate a group of twelve-year-old boys by getting them to think about transcendental numbers such as Φ (pronounced "Fie," not to be confused with π). Here's a good way to introduce Φ to twelve-year-old boys.

I'm thinking of a number between 1 and 2.

The reciprocal of that number is equal to that same number minus 1.

We can write that statement in equation form, like this:

$1/x = x - 1$

Can you tell me what number I'm thinking of?

Some boys may think this is an easy problem. They'll call out answers. "It's 1½," one boy might say. But that's not the right answer. The reciprocal of 1½ is ⅔, and ⅔ does not equal ½ (which is 1½ minus 1).

After a couple of minutes, one of the boys will figure out that the equation above can be simplified if you multiply both sides by x, yielding:

$1 = x^2 - x$

Subtracting 1 from both sides yields:

$x^2 - x - 1 = 0$

You can then use the quadratic formula to solve for x:

$x = (1 \pm\sqrt{5})/2$

We're looking for a number between 1 and 2, so we choose the positive solution:

$= (1 +\sqrt{5})/2$

$= 0.5 + 1.11803398874989 \ldots$

$= 1.61803398874989 \ldots$

You can tell the boys that mathematicians refer to this number as Φ. Sure enough, this number Φ has the characteristic we were looking for: the reciprocal of this number exactly equals this number minus 1:

$$1/1.61803398874989\ldots = 0.61803398874989\ldots$$

Now you change the subject (or appear to change the subject). You tell them about the Fibonacci series. A Fibonacci series is formed by adding two numbers to yield a third number, and reiterating the process to form a sequence. The simplest Fibonacci sequence is:

$$1 + 1 = 2$$
$$1 + 2 = 3$$
$$2 + 3 = 5$$
$$3 + 5 = 8$$
$$5 + 8 = 13$$
$$8 + 13 = 21$$
$$13 + 21 = 34$$

This yields the series: 1, 1, 2, 3, 5, 8, 13, 21, 34, 55, 89, 144 . . .

Now, ask your boys to take each number in the Fibonacci series and divide it by the number before it, starting with 3, and list their answers.

$$3/2 = 1.5$$
$$5/3 = 1.666\ldots$$
$$8/5 = 1.6$$
$$13/8 = 1.625$$
$$21/13 = 1.61538\ldots$$
$$34/21 = 1.61905\ldots$$
$$55/34 = 1.61764\ldots$$
$$89/55 = 1.61818\ldots$$
$$144/89 = 1.617977\ldots$$
$$233/144 = 1.61805\ldots$$

Now you can point out to the boys (if they haven't noticed already) that this process seems to be converging on Φ. Why is that? you ask them. While they're thinking about that, show them a pentagon with a triangle inscribed in it. Have them look at the triangle. Let them know that the side of the triangle is exactly equal to Φ times the length of the base. Why is that? Why does Φ keep popping up where you don't expect it?

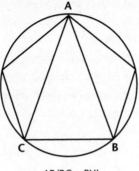

AB/BC = PHI

While the boys are pondering this question, you can step over to the girls' classroom to cover the same material. But to get girls the same age* excited about "pure" math and geometry, you need to connect it with the real world. Remember that in girls, geometry and "pure" math functions appear to be localized in the cerebral cortex, the same division of the brain that mediates language and higher cognitive function. So you need to tie the math into other higher cognitive functions. Here's how you might teach the same lesson about Φ and Fibonacci numbers to girls. You'd begin by explaining how a Fibonacci series is formed:

$$1 + 1 = 2$$
$$1 + 2 = 3$$
$$2 + 3 = 5$$
$$3 + 5 = 8$$
$$5 + 8 = 13$$
$$8 + 13 = 21$$
$$13 + 21 = 34$$

And so forth. You write down the first twelve numbers in the Fibonacci series: 1, 1, 2, 3, 5, 8, 13, 21, 34, 55, 89, 144 . . . In preparation for this session, you've already asked your girls to

---

*College women may be just as interested in "pure numbers" as college men are. But few twelve-year-old girls are interested in disembodied numbers for their own sake. Remember the Virginia Tech study on sex differences in how the brain develops (see note 19).

bring in any of the following: artichokes, sunflowers, pineapples, pinecones, delphiniums, black-eyed susans, field daisies, African daisies, and Michaelmas daisies. Start with the flowers. (We start with flowers not because flowers are "feminine" but because it's easier to count the number of petals on a flower than it is to count the rows of bracts on a pinecone.) Count the number of petals. You'll find that the number of petals is almost always a number in the Fibonacci series: 8 petals for delphiniums, 13 for double delphiniums, 21 for black-eyed susans, 34 for field daisies, 55 for African daisies and Michaelmas daisies.[32]

Then you can move on to the artichokes, sunflowers, pinecones, and pineapples. These are more complicated. In these, you're studying the number of rows, or bracts, rather than the number of petals. The number of rows counted vertically or obliquely will, again, be a number in the Fibonacci series. You can get more examples like these from the book *Fascinating Fibonaccis* by Trudi Hammel Garland. Older girls may enjoy *The Golden Ratio: The Story of PHI, the World's Most Astonishing Number* by Mario Livio. Or you might even let them read Dan Brown's suspense thriller *The Da Vinci Code* and challenge them to verify or invalidate each of the many claims made in that book about Φ and the Fibonacci series. Show them examples of natural phenomena that manifest Φ, such as a dying leaf or a spiral nebula. At this point you might also mention the fact that

$$\Phi - 1 = 1/\Phi$$

But don't expect the girls to ooh and aah over that fact the way the boys do. Twelve-year-old girls are likely to be more interested in the real-world applications of number theory than in remote abstractions. That difference reflects the fact that the girls are using the cerebral cortex while the boys are using the hippocampus. The girls are also more likely to be interested in the beliefs of the ancient Pythagoreans regarding the magical and mystical properties of Φ.

Now these girls will start asking questions. Why do numbers in the Fibonacci series keep showing up when you count the petals on a delphinium or the bracts on a pinecone? Why is it that a dying poinsettia leaf and a spiral nebula share similar structural features? How can abstract number theory explain these similarities? And you will have accomplished something that some of the gender experts we discussed in chapter 1 have deemed impossible: you've got a classroom of twelve-year-old girls excited about number theory.

I like this example because it illustrates the basic point I'm trying to make. *There are no differences in what girls and boys can learn. But there are big differences in the best ways to teach them.* At the end of the day you will have taught both girls and boys about the properties of Φ, using the Fibonacci series as an introduction to number theory. Girls and boys are equally capable of learning that material. But if you teach that material the way it's usually taught (the way we taught it to the boys in my example above), then many of the girls will tune out and be bored. Conversely, if you bring in pinecones for the boys, many of the boys will snicker and start throwing the pinecones around like hand grenades. "Incoming!"

Facts, Fiction, and Feelings

In chapter 2 we discussed brain imaging of emotion in girls and boys. We reviewed research done at Harvard University showing that activity in the brain of the teenage girl associated with negative emotion is localized to the cerebral cortex, the same part of the brain we use to comprehend and generate language. In teenage boys, brain activity associated with negative emotion is localized in the amygdala, a phylogenetically primitive nucleus at the base of the brain that makes few direct connections with the cerebral cortex.

That gender difference in brain organization has clear implications for education. In particular, questions of the form "How would you *feel* if . . ." don't work well for most boys. That question requires boys to link *emotional* information in the amygdala with *language* information in the cerebral cortex. It's like trying to recite poetry and juggle bowling pins at the same time. You have to use two different parts of the brain that don't normally work together. When most teenage boys experience intense feelings, they talk *less*.

So how does this affect how teachers should teach literature to girls and boys? Girls and boys like to read different things, for starters. That's one of the most consistent findings in education research. Most girls prefer fiction: short stories and novels. Boys are more likely to choose nonfiction: descriptions of real events—battles or adventures—or illustrated accounts of the way things work, like spaceships, bombs, or volcanoes.[33] "Girls tend to prefer books where they can be analytical about a character's motives and behaviors. Boys tend to prefer action," says Victoria Ehrhardt, an English teacher in Lewis County, New York. "Boys and girls have different reading interests," agrees Judy Hayn, professor of education at Loyola University in Chicago. She adds that "girls like stories about experiences that might happen over one summer and the emotional agonies that a character endures. Boys want stories with male protagonists that are exciting." "War stories and books about struggles really resonate with boys," adds Ehrhardt. "They see life as a battle, and war stories appeal to that side of their nature."[34]

Good teachers do their best to split the difference in educational style. They look for books that are halfway between *Are you There, God? It's Me, Margaret* (for girls) and, say, *The Jackie Robinson Story* (for boys). They're looking for books that appeal equally to both girls and boys. Problem: there are very few such books, especially for children in the early elementary school years. William McDonald, assistant superintendent for curriculum in Montgomery County, Maryland, told me that at least 80 percent of books targeted for early readers fall into the category of "girls' fiction." This preference for "girls' fiction" in the early reading curriculum has arisen not because girls' fiction is the best thing for all young children to read, McDonald says, but because girls' fiction is what appeals to the women who teach young children. Over 95 percent of teachers in kindergarten through third grade are women, McDonald told me. Nonfiction books targeted toward boys, geared toward early readers, "just aren't available," according to McDonald. "And when they are available, they often go out of print as soon as we start to use them."[35]

The difference lies not only in what books you choose to teach, but in how you teach them. Think about role-playing exercises, to consider one example. These sorts of exercises are popular in middle schools and high schools. Role-playing exercises work well for girls. For example, if you're teaching *Are You There, God? It's Me, Margaret*, one girl could be Margaret, another could be Margaret's mother, another could be Margaret's father, and another could be Margaret's grandmother. They could then discuss the pros and cons of moving from Manhattan to New Jersey, each girl talking in the voice of the assigned character. Or how about the fact that Margaret's mother was raised Protestant and her father was raised Jewish? "How would you feel if you were Margaret's mother and Margaret asked you whether she should join the JCC [Jewish Community Center] or the YMCA?" Let "Margaret's mother" answer, and then let's hear from Margaret's maternal grandmother (who is a devout Christian) and paternal grandmother (who is Jewish and proud of it), with different girls playing each role. Eleven- and twelve-year-old girls will take this very seriously and really gain a deeper level of understanding, not only of the book, but of their own feelings about religious heritage, relatives who don't get along with each other, and similar situations.

"How would you feel if you were this character?" That sort of role-playing exercise works for most girls. It gets them into the story. But that type of exercise doesn't work for most boys. They'll tell you it's dumb. "I'm not a grandmother, I'm never gonna be a grandmother, I'm not gonna pretend I'm a grandmother." So what *does* work to get boys into literature?

Three years ago I had the privilege of sitting in on Ben Williams's English class at the Georgetown Preparatory School. "G Prep" is a boys' school in Bethesda, Maryland. Mr. Williams is chairman of the English Department there. He had assigned *Lord of the Flies*.

I myself had to read *Lord of the Flies* when I was in Mrs. Buehler's English class thirty years ago at Shaker Heights High School, just outside of Cleveland. One of my assignments was to write an essay describing "How would you feel if you were Piggy?" (the outcast boy, stranded with other boys on a tropical island). I expected Mr. Williams to assign a similar topic to his boys. After all, that's the way *Lord of the Flies* is usually taught, according to the many study guides available for this book.

But that's not what Mr. Williams did. "Let's see your maps," he said. Mr. Williams had given the boys a very different assignment: prepare a three-dimensional map of the island.

Making a map of the island is not an easy assignment. There's no map in the book. The island does have many unique features, but how to make a map?

As these boys learned firsthand, you can use the book to construct an accurate map, but only if you read the text with care. For instance, in the closing chapter you'll find the sentence, "The sunlight was slanting now into the palms by the wrecked shelter." You know that the wrecked shelter is near the beach. It's late in the evening. Knowing that the sun sets in the west, you deduce that if the beach were on the east side of the island, it wouldn't be possible for sunlight to be slanting into the palms late in the evening because the forest would block the sunlight. The beach can't be on the south side of the island; if it were, the mountain would block the sunlight. Nor can it be on the north side of the island, or the forest would block the sunlight. The beach has to be on the west side of the island.

Once you've figured that out, you can use other clues in the book to triangulate the location of the mountain, the lagoon, the Castle Rock, and so forth. The boys had each made three-dimensional maps using papier-mâché, cardboard, and paint. The maps were similar, but there were a few points of difference. The boys had to hammer out the differences, looking up clues again in the book. "On page 23, it says that Ralph followed the outline of the crags up the mountain, so that part of the beach has to be right next to the mountain."

"Yeah, but on page 14 it says that the beach was 'miles in length.' So you don't really know exactly where those crags are." And so forth.

At this point I wanted to interrupt and say, "Mr. Williams, are you out of your mind? *Lord of the Flies* is not a travel guide or a set of clues to buried treasure. It's a book about the dark recesses of the soul! What does all this geometry and mapmaking have to do with that? You're missing the whole point of the book!"

But I noticed that the boys were really involved in the assignment. Mr. Williams was building on these boys' natural interests and their strengths: spatial relations, mapmaking. He was keeping the assignment objective. He wasn't asking them, "How would you feel *if* . . ."

And the skills these boys were learning are useful: carefully deconstructing a text, finding clues hundreds of pages apart, and using those clues to assemble a coherent picture. That sort of puzzle-solving is a skill that more of us could use. Imagine what might have happened a few years ago if more shareholders had read through WorldCom's financial reports and noticed, "Hmm, this line on page 21 doesn't seem to fit with what's implied in the second paragraph of page 76 . . ." Analytical deconstruction of a text is at least as useful as being able to write an imaginative essay about "how you would feel" in a given situation.

Furthermore, the boys were really learning the text. It's impossible to do this mapmaking assignment without reading closely and attentively. I decided to get out my old copy of *Lord of the Flies* to see whether I could make the map myself. I didn't want to read the whole book. I thought I'd just skim it quickly, look for clues, and draw a map. I couldn't do it. The words "north," "south," "east," and "west" never appear in the book. The only way to make the map is to pay careful attention to every detail. I myself have a tendency when I'm reading a novel to skip long descriptions and just go to the next bit of dialogue.

But you can't do that if you want to draw the map. In fact, you have to read the descriptions more carefully than you read the dialogue. So I stayed up until 3 A.M., reading the book straight through. It's a much better book than I remembered from Mrs. Buehler's class—maybe because I was alienated by the assignment. Or maybe I was just too young to appreciate it.

What other strategies work for getting boys excited about reading? Recall the old idea about boys preferring fact to fiction. Some educators have found that assigning articles from the daily newspaper is a good motivator for boys. Edward DeRoche, director of the International Center for Character Education at the University of San Diego, has reviewed about two dozen studies of the effectiveness of newspapers for motivating below-average readers, especially boys. The studies show that "students in such classes score significantly higher in spelling, vocabulary development, and comprehension than comparable students who did not use newspapers." He adds, lyrically, "Something happens to teachers and students when they encounter newspapers together. The four walls of the classroom open to the real world. The class comes alive. Relationships change. Conversations are enriched."[36] DeRoche has found that language arts classes based on newspapers are effective not only at the high school level, but all the way down to the early elementary years.

There are several problems, though, with using the approach of "fiction for the girls, nonfiction for the boys." I'm hearing about middle school reading classes where the girls are reading John Steinbeck and F. Scott Fitzgerald while the boys are reading *Sports Illustrated*. Kids notice that contrast. Boys start to believe that maybe great literature is only for girls.

In fact, there is plenty of great literature that appeals to boys in middle and high school. Few American teachers assign it anymore, though. Boys *do* like fiction, if it's the right kind of fiction: strong male characters doing unpredictable things. Hemingway, Dostoyevsky, and Mark Twain, for starters.

Last summer I met with Darryl, who had just finished seventh grade. "How'd you do in school this year?" I asked.

"Great," Darryl said. "I got straight A's, except for a C in reading."

"How come a C in reading?" I asked.

"It was boring," Darryl said.

"What'd they ask you to read?"

"Well—" Darryl scrunched up his eyes, as though trying to recall a painful repressed memory. "There was *Of Mice and Men*, which is about this retarded guy and all the sad things that happen to him, and then he dies. Then we had to read *Flowers for Algernon*, which is also about a retarded guy, actually, and how he gets smart and then he gets dumb again, and then he dies, too, actually."

Both the books Darryl mentioned are "touchy-feely" books in which weak, disabled male characters are helpless to change their miserable destiny. Most boys don't care for those kinds of stories. Most boys prefer to read about strong male characters who take dramatic action to change their world. There's plenty of great literature that fits the bill. Mark Twain's *Huckleberry Finn* is a good place to start. *For Whom the Bell Tolls* by Hemingway is another good choice. How about *Treasure Island* or *Robinson Crusoe*? Classic boys' literature is "classic" for a good reason.

Critics object that this approach reinforces gender stereotypes. I respond that the most pernicious gender stereotype is the one that says boys don't like to read. Let's break down that stereotype first. Get every child excited about learning. Once kids have discovered for themselves that reading can be fun and exciting, then you can worry about broadening their taste in literature.

Right now I'm seeing many boys who have never had the experience, not even once, of reading a book that really excites them. They've never read a book that punched them in the gut. They've never cried while reading a book. They have no clue how powerful books can be.

The first priority of schools must be education. Social engineering comes second.

When Is an A Not an A?

Remember Melanie, the gifted student who wanted to take physics her senior year? One of the things about Melanie that always impresses me is her willingness to try something new. She is supremely self-confident. In that respect, Melanie is, unfortunately, not your typical girl.

Beth is another girl I know. Beth is every bit as smart as Melanie, but she doesn't have Melanie's self-confidence. Like Melanie, Beth "aced" biology and was a favorite student of Ms. Griffith. But when Ms. Griffith suggested that Beth sign up for physics, Beth hesitated. "I just don't think I'm smart enough for physics," Beth said. "I've never done anything like that, and I don't want to risk getting a B or worse on my transcript." She ended up taking psychology in her senior year instead of physics.

Girls on average outperform boys in school (as measured by report card grades), in most subjects and in all age groups.[37] Because girls do better in school, one might imagine that girls would be more self-confident about their academic abilities and that they would have higher academic self-esteem. But that's not the case. Paradoxically, girls are more likely to be excessively critical in evaluating their own academic performance. Conversely, boys tend to have unrealistically high estimates of their own academic abilities and accomplishments.[38]

Those are some of the paradoxes teachers face: the girl like Beth who gets straight A's but has no real confidence in her own abilities; the boy who's getting B's and C's but thinks he's brilliant. That leads us to a basic difference in teaching style for girls versus boys. You need to encourage girls and build them up. Boys on the other hand more often need a reality check. You have to make boys realize that they're not as brilliant as they think they are and challenge them to do better.

The great mission of education is to enable every child to fulfill their potential, to discover that corner of the field of knowledge they can call their own. Almost every child is a gifted child, I believe. The trick is to discover where your child's talents lie.

Our educational system isn't doing very well in this regard. Girls and boys are being pushed into pink and blue cubbyholes regardless of their individual aptitude. And this pink-and-blue stereotyping is worse now than it was twenty years ago. Twenty years of gender-blind education has not ameliorated gender differences in important educational outcomes; in some cases it has exacerbated them. A smaller proportion of boys now study subjects such as advanced foreign languages, art, and music, and a smaller proportion of girls study advanced math, computer science, and physics.[39]

In the closing chapter, I'll suggest strategies that have been shown to break down gender stereotypes in education, by *embracing* gender differences.

SEX

Contemporary culture encourages precocious sexuality. Too often popular culture and peer groups, rather than parents or other responsible adults, call the cadence in contemporary teenage life.

—Professor Joan Jacobs Brumberg, Cornell University[1]

There was no sense of there needing to be a connection. No boyfriend-girlfriend. Used to be, you know, "Will you still love me tomorrow?" There is no tomorrow. It's all today. "Meet me after study hall at 4, we'll sleep together," and then on to the next partner tomorrow. Slam, bam, thank you ma'am.

—Michelle Burford, journalist, describing her interviews with teenagers[2]

I don't kiss girls on the mouth because if I'm not in a relationship why should I kiss?

—Zachary, age seventeen, talking about "hooking up"[3]

Tina and Jimmy

Tina Jimenez faced a potential triple whammy when she started ninth grade. Ninth grade at a new school isn't easy for anybody. Everybody's trying to figure out who's who, who's cool, where do I fit in. But in addition to the challenge of a new school, Tina also had the additional burden of having just moved to the area, not knowing anybody, and also of belonging to a minority group with almost no representation at her new school. Her family had just moved to the Washington area from Miami, Florida. Both her parents had immigrated to the U.S. in the 1970s from the Dominican Republic.

Being a dark-skinned Hispanic girl at Seneca Valley High—which is overwhelmingly white—might have been a major problem for some girls, but Tina made friends easily. Three weeks into the new school year she was off to a good start. Her soccer teammates were impressed by her fearlessness on the field. She was a skillful player, but she didn't make a big deal about it. The other girls included her in everything they did, adopting her as one of their own.

She and most of the other soccer girls were invited to a party the last Saturday in September at a large house in the older, "nicer" section of Germantown. Tina stayed close to her friend and soccer buddy Jennifer, a tenth-grader. After they had been at the party for half an hour, Tina noticed an older boy staring at her. "Who's that?" she asked Jennifer.

"Who's what?" Jennifer shouted over the music.

"That blond guy over there, wearing the Redskins sweat-shirt," Tina said.

"Oooh. That's Jimmy. Jimmy Mandeville. Senior. Football player. Not so great as a football player. But in other departments he's supposed to be a *monster*," Jennifer winked.

Tina rolled her eyes and shook her head. "I'm *totally* not interested," she said.

Jimmy came over to them, his eyes fixed on Tina. "Hi," he said. His breath smelled of beer—which was not surprising, as he was holding an open Budweiser can in his right hand.

"Hi," both girls said.

Jimmy looked Tina up and down, his glassy eyes lingering on her chest. He was nodding his head in time to the beat of the music. "Wanna hook up?" he asked Tina, point-blank.

Tina's eyes went wide.

"Hey Jennifer!" Another boy appeared out of nowhere and grabbed Jennifer by the arm. "You gotta see this! Come on!" Jennifer gave Tina a sad look as if to say, Sorry to leave you all by yourself. And Jennifer was gone.

Please don't leave me, Jennifer, Tina thought. Her heart sank. Jimmy towered over her. The way he was nodding his head in time with the music began to irritate her. And, she was worried that he might spill some of his beer on her blouse.

"Wanna hook up," he said again, more a statement than a question.

"What do you mean?" she asked, stalling for time. She knew what he meant. But she didn't know how to say "no" without offending him or sounding lame. And as a freshman talking to a popular senior, she didn't have the confidence to just turn her back and walk away.

He snorted in amazement, then burped. "Freshman girl. Come on, I'll show you." He grabbed her by the arm, tossed the half-empty beer can onto the carpet, and pulled her into a small study lit only by a tabletop lamp on a desk. Tina saw another couple already in a corner of the room, fondling each other. Before she could say anything, Jimmy pulled her down to the floor beside the desk.

Jimmy groped at her breasts with one hand while he fumbled with the snap on her pants with his other. Tina's mind was in a whirl. This was crazy. How could this be happening? She wanted to push him off, to scream . . . but what would happen next? The other kids would laugh at her. *Freshman girl. Prude. Dork.*

"Come *on*," Jimmy said. "What's your problem?"

"I—I don't know how . . ." Tina said.

"Seriously? I'll show you," Jimmy said. "Come on!" he snapped, standing up and pulling her to a kneeling position, facing him. He unzipped his fly.

Tina had never given a boy oral sex before. She had heard other girls talk about it, of course, but the idea repulsed her. Why would any girl want to have a boy's you-know-what in her *mouth*? Yuck. Now a total stranger, a boy she had never met, a boy she wasn't even attracted to . . .

Three minutes later it was over.

"Sweet. A little clumsy on your end, but sweet," Jimmy said. "With a little more experience, you could be dynamite, sister. See ya later." Zipping up his fly, he left the room without looking back.

"I couldn't see. Did you spit or swallow?" The question came from a skinny, pimply boy Tina had never seen before, who had apparently been watching from across the room. He giggled.

Tina thought she would vomit.

Hooking Up

Girls and boys face very different challenges when it comes to sex. Most young women enjoy physical intimacy more when it develops in the context of a loving relationship. Few women or girls really understand how different sex is for many men and for most boys. And the type of intimacy most common among teenagers today—hooking up—feeds into the worst kind of male sexuality. "Hooking up"—in case you didn't know—means being physically intimate with the understanding that *no* romantic relationship is implied and none is expected. It's sex without love, sex without the "bother" of a relationship.

"I can't tell you how many girls come in who are bereft about having had sex too soon," says New York psychologist Marsha Levy-Warren. She's seeing more and more teen and preteen girls whose emotional lives are in turmoil after some kind of sexual encounter. "They went to a party . . . they hooked up and did what they assumed everyone was doing. Then, they feel awful." Teachers and counselors are hearing about more and more sexual activity "of a detached, unemotional kind" among preteens and young teens. "I call it body-part sex," says Dr. Levy-Warren. "The kids don't even look at each other. It's mechanical, dehumanizing. The fallout is that later in life they have trouble forming relationships. They're jaded."[4]

"Oral sex is definitely a trend," says Professor Peter Leone of the University of North Carolina at Chapel Hill. "And it's happening in public because teenagers don't see it as a big deal." In some places "oral sex is taken so lightly that it's treated like a racy version of Truth or Dare or Spin the Bottle. . . . At one party, they played something called Make a Rainbow: the girls put on different colored lipsticks and took turns making a rainbow on all the boys' penises [with their lips]." Parties where oral sex predominates are sometimes called "chicken parties," because of the way all the girls' heads are bobbing up and down as they go down on their partner-of-the-moment.[5]

"A girl who did it for her boyfriend on a school bus was upset when she found a line of guys in school the next week wanting her to go down on them," says Tamara Kreinin, president of the Sexuality Information and Education Council. Another girl "went down on a bunch of guys at a party, and then the next week in sex ed, the other kids said, 'Amy was going down on guys at this party—she should teach the class.' The girl wasn't ready for that. I've had lots of kids tell me that they got this sick feeling in their stomachs the next day."[6]

Here's what one sixteen-year-old girl told me: "I was in a hook-up with this guy Zachary. I tried to kiss him and he wouldn't let me. That was weird. I mean, we were doing stuff way beyond kissing, but he didn't want to kiss. I asked him why he didn't want to kiss me and he was like—'I don't kiss girls on the mouth because if I'm not in a relationship why should I kiss.' "

Several boys have told me, in words similar to Zachary's, that they deliberately avoid kissing a girl when they're hooking up. These boys really believe that they're being virtuous—in a weird, twenty-first-century way—by *not* kissing the girl they're hooking up with. These boys believe that kissing a girl on the lips sends the message, "I'm interested in having a romantic relationship with you." They don't want to send that message. By keeping face-to-face interactions *out* of the encounter, by restricting their intimacy to fellatio or a groping "quick feel," these boys believe that they are at least being honest about their intentions—which are purely physical.

Another girl said: "I know it was just a hook-up. But it felt so right, I was sure he would call. I just couldn't believe it when he never called. Then two weeks later, after I hadn't heard from him at all, I saw him at a party and he wanted to hook up again. It made me feel dirty. Like he just wanted to, like, *use* me, use my body. Like I wasn't really even there. Like he was just jerking off, using me instead of some porn magazine."

Choosing Virginity?

The Centers for Disease Control recently reported that the number of high school seniors who say they've had sexual intercourse decreased between 1991 and 2001, from 54 percent in 1991 to 46 percent in 2001.[7] That sounds like good news. Even if it's not a huge change, it's a change in the right direction. Isn't it?

Shortly after the CDC report was released, *Newsweek* magazine ran a cover story entitled "Choosing Virginity." The editors at *Newsweek* interpreted the CDC report to mean that teens have become less sexually active.

The *Newsweek* cover story makes for strange reading. The editors at *Newsweek* were determined to find teens who conformed to the editors' interpretation of the CDC report, teens who would say that they have decided to remain sexually inactive. They had to look pretty hard. In the country town of Longmont, Colorado, they finally found a teenage couple who had mutually agreed not to engage in sexual activity until marriage. Longmont is a small town about forty-five minutes' drive from Denver. "It figures you had to come all the way out here to find a virgin," one local told them.[8]

In fact, the *Newsweek* staff had goofed. They had misunderstood the CDC report. It's true that there has been a slight drop in the rate of *penile-vaginal* intercourse (which was the only sexual activity the CDC report measured). But that's not because teens have become less sexually active. It's because the dominant form of teenage sexuality has changed. It's not penile-vaginal intercourse anymore. It's oral sex.

"Oral sex is the new second base," says Alexandra Hall, a journalist who spent weeks interviewing students at suburban high schools in the Boston area. "Things are very, very different in high school from the way they used to be. Not different from two or three generations ago, but different from just five or ten years ago . . . [There has been a] profound shift in the culture of high-school dating and sex, with no-strings 'hooking-up' replacing dating."[9] "Kids don't date nowadays," agrees physician and bioethicist Leon Kass.[10] "Traditional dating is dead," concurs journalist and author Barbara Dafoe Whitehead.[11]

Monica, a seventeen-year-old high school student, says that oral sex has become the new kissing. "People just assume you do it, because most everybody is."

"No one I know considers oral sex to be sex at all," says Rob, a senior at a private high school. "Oral sex just isn't what [the word] 'sex' means."

"Twenty years ago, teenage sex not only was much less pervasive, it also had a different context. That context was called 'dating,' " says journalist Hall. "These days, something else is much more common. Single boys and girls go in a group to a friend's house (where the parents may or may not be home), drink or smoke pot, then pair off and engage in no-strings 'hook-ups.' A week later, when the same scenario happens again, they hook up with someone else."

Michael Milburn, professor at the University of Massachusetts, agrees that "the days of a boy showing up at a girl's front door and meeting her parents before he takes her on a date are almost obsolete. Dating has been replaced by house parties and a culture of 'hooking up.' "[12]

Don't be fooled by talk of "the new abstinence." The shift from penile-vaginal intercourse to oral sex signifies a shift from personal sex to impersonal sex. That shift is not a cause for celebration.

For many boys, and for some men, sex is an object in itself. The challenge for a teenage boy is to integrate the desires of the soul and spirit with the needs of the body, to weld his sexual drive to his desire for friendship and companionship. For many teenage boys (and for some adult men) that doesn't come easily. Some never reach that level of maturity. But there *are* some things a parent can do to help. First, though, we need to look more closely at basic differences between girls' sexuality and boys'.

Oxytocin, Testosterone, and Rape

What's the relation between love and sex? The neurochemical basis for both love and sex in females involves the hormone oxytocin, the same hormone released when a mother breastfeeds her newborn baby. "Oxytocin's effects on both [romantic] attachment and sexual behavior are estrogen dependent and gender specific," observes neuropsychologist Lisa Diamond, adding that there appear to be "more extensive oxytocin circuits in female than male brains."[13] In males on the other hand the hormone underlying sexual attraction is not oxytocin but testosterone, the same hormone that mediates the aggressive drive.

The first brain-imaging study comparing brain areas activated in women and men during sexual arousal was published in 2002. Doctors found fundamental differences between females and males. The men showed lots of activation at the base of the brain, in the thalamus and especially the hypothalamus, while the women showed proportionately more activity up in the cerebral cortex.[14] Another study, published in 2004 by researchers at Emory University, showed that sexually aroused men show more activity in the base of the brain compared to women, even when the women report *feeling* more sexually aroused.[15]

If you recall our discussion of cortical/subcortical in chapters 2 and 5, you'll recognize the significance of this finding: it suggests that the sexual experience in women is "happening" more up in the cerebral cortex and is therefore more connected with the rest of what's going on in their mind. The sexual experience in men is less connected with the cortex, less connected with the outside world.

I've already mentioned the work of UCLA psychologist Anne Peplau on the difference in how females and males experience sexual desire. Peplau has concluded that "women's sexuality tends to be strongly linked to a close relationship. For women, an important goal of sex is intimacy; the best context for pleasurable sex is a committed relationship. This is less true for men."[16]

You can say that again. For many boys, as for some men, the sexual urge is closely tied to aggression. That's not surprising when you remember that both the sexual urge and the aggressive urge, in males, are mediated by testosterone. In one carefully designed study, a surprisingly high percentage—35 percent—of "normal" college men said that they not only fantasized about rape, they would actually rape a woman if they had the chance and they were sure they wouldn't be caught.[17] In another study of "normal" college men, more than half of the men said they would actually rape a woman if they were assured of not being punished.[18] These men are not Neanderthal cavemen. In fact, researchers have found no association between the liberality of a man's gender-role beliefs and the likelihood that he finds rape sexually appealing. Some men who are strongly in favor of equal rights for women, who approve of women in leadership roles, and so on also say that they would rape a woman if they had the opportunity. Nor is there any association, positive or negative, between a man's intelligence and the likelihood that he will be sexually aroused by depictions of rape.[19] Highly intelligent men are no less likely to fantasize about raping a woman than are men of below-average intelligence.[20] The most common sexual fantasy in sex magazines is rape and/or bondage of a young woman.[21]

If you get mad at your partner, are you more or less likely to have sex *while* you are still angry? For women, being angry is a turnoff. Most women say that if they're mad at their boyfriend or husband, they won't want to have sex with him—at least, not until the argument is settled. They need to kiss and make up first. Not so for men. Many men will have sex with their girlfriend or wife even if they are angry at her.[22]

Even more troubling: for many teenage boys, the idea of inflicting pain on a woman is sexually arousing. Psychologist Neil Malamuth, who has specialized in studying the responses of "normal" college men to rape fantasies, has found that most young men experience greater sexual arousal when the imaginary rapist deliberately hurts the woman he is raping. The greater the victim's pain, the greater the sexual excitement experienced by these young men. For most young men, according to this research, the most arousing fantasy is the rape of a young woman in which the woman experiences both pain and orgasm.[23]

In real life, of course, that never happens. No woman enjoys being raped—although curiously, a substantial number of women answer "Yes" to the question of whether some *other* woman might enjoy being raped.[24] Malamuth found that when women listened to tape-recorded rape fantasies, any sexual arousal the woman listening might have felt was immediately extinguished if the rapist hurt the woman victim.[25] Nevertheless, the myth that some women want to be raped is so pervasive in our culture that it affects women's opinions about how *other* women might respond to being raped.

For young men, sex and violence are so closely tied together that—according to psychiatrist Robert Stoller—"hostility, overt or hidden, is what generates and enhances sexual excitement, and its absence leads to sexual indifference and boredom."[26] (I personally consider Dr. Stoller's statement too extreme and too general. Also: for a minority of teenage boys, about 10 percent, the link between aggression and sexual arousal is not strong at all. We will return to these exceptional boys in chapter 9.)

One thing's for sure. The motivation for sex is fundamentally different for most teenage boys compared with teenage girls. Teenage boys want to have sex to satisfy sexual desire. It's a gut-level, base-of-the-brain impulse, not far removed from the need to have a bowel movement when you feel the urge. Many boys will tell you that the urge feels just that irresistible.

Not so for girls. As psychologist Roy Baumeister recently wrote, "Male desire aims at the sexual activity itself, whereas female desire aims beyond it toward other outcomes and consequences."[27] Professor Joan Jacobs Brumberg, who has written two books about the psychosexual development of teenage girls, agrees. Sexual pleasure is usually not the motivating factor when young teenage girls engage in sex, Brumberg has found. That's especially true for oral sex. Girls today provide far more oral sex for their boyfriends than in previous generations, but Brumberg says that "they do so without pleasure, usually to please their boyfriend or to avoid the possibility of impregnation."[28] Deborah Tolman, a director at the Wellesley College Center for Research on Women, concurs that sex in the twenty-first century remains heavily weighted in favor of boys' needs and desires. With regard to oral sex, Tolman says, "The boys are getting it, the girls no. It's the heterosexual script that entitles boys and disables girls."[29]

When you ask teenage girls and boys why they're having sex, you'll hear very different answers from the girls compared with the boys. Boys usually answer that question with a snort. "Why *wouldn't* I have sex? As long as the girl wants it, too—I mean, as long as she doesn't kick me or slap me or yell 'Fire!'—why shouldn't I?" Boys want to have sex because they feel sexually aroused. Simple, base-of-the-brain motivation.

It's different for girls. In one major study, girls didn't even list sexual arousal as a reason for having sex.[30] Teenage girls have sex for other reasons. Girls may hope that having sex will earn them points in the popularity contest, or they may just want to please the boy they happen to be hooking up with, or they may feel pressured either by the boy or by other girls who *are* having sex. Oprah Winfrey recently devoted a session of her talk show to this topic. She invited several teen girls on to the show to describe why they began having sex so young. One girl, Shana, began having sex at age thirteen. By age sixteen, when she appeared on the show, she had had intercourse with seven different boys.

Oprah Winfrey: When you started having sex, at 13, was it to fit in or was it just because you wanted to have sex?

Shana: It was definitely to fit in, because, I just figured, you know, this is what everyone's doing and I was getting ready to go into high school and I'm like, "this will make me popular."

Oprah: And has it?

Shana: No, it . . . I paid a big price for it. I paid a huge price.

Oprah: What is the huge price you've paid?

Shana: Just socially. Luckily, I didn't get pregnant or anything like that, but emotionally I have scars that are never going to go away. After he leaves, you know, you give him what he wants, then you feel, like, horrible.

Oprah: So if you do that a couple of times, and you know if you do it again, it's going to feel the same, why do you keep doing it?

Shana: I really can't answer that. Honestly, when I get an answer, I'll tell you.[31]

Journalist Michelle Burford appeared on the same show to describe her interviews with young teen girls. Ms. Burford herself was only thirty years old when she spoke with the teenage girls, but she found that a lot had changed since her own student days. Girls she spoke with, some as young as twelve, "were completely cavalier in the stories they were telling me. There was absolutely no sense of shame. There was no sense of there needing to be a connection. No boyfriend-girlfriend. Used to be, you know, 'Will you still love me tomorrow?' There is no tomorrow. It's all today. 'Meet me after study hall at 4, we'll sleep together,' and then on to the next partner tomorrow. Slam, bam, thank you ma'am. It's really shocking."[32]

Gender roles in our society load the dice against girls as well. According to a survey published in 2003, 89 percent of teen girls say they feel pressured by boys to have sex. But in the same survey, more than nine out of ten teenagers (girls *and* boys) agree that a girl can get a bad reputation because she has sex with a boy.[33] The space between prude and slut has narrowed from a broad highway to a tightrope. If a girl refuses to have sex, she's a prude. If she is too willing to have sex, she's branded a "ho" and a slut.

The Male Paradigm

For many teenage boys, sex is an impersonal urge that has its own agenda, not necessarily connected to a relationship with another person. That's not news. Teenage boys have always been that way. For most teenage girls, a satisfying and fulfilling sexual experience is most likely to occur in the context of a loving and mutually caring relationship. That's not news, either. What's changed?

The fundamental change that has occurred over the past thirty years is a change from the female paradigm to the male paradigm. Thirty years ago, a boy usually had at least to give lip service to the notion of being in love if he expected a young woman to be sexually intimate with him. No longer. That's the significance of the hook-up replacing the romantic relationship as the primary sexual mode in teenage culture.

That change has led to a fundamental transformation in the dynamics of sexual activity. In engineering terms, it's a change from linear dynamics to zero-order dynamics. The likelihood of sex is no longer related to the closeness of the relationship. It used to be the case—as recently as ten or fifteen years ago—that the more serious the relationship was between a girl and a boy, the more likely they were to have sex. That correspondence no longer holds. A recent survey by the Kaiser Family Foundation found that teenagers nationwide are now just as likely to engage in sex during a casual "hook-up" as they are in a serious, committed relationship.[34] The major difference in sexual behavior in an ongoing relationship compared with a hook-up, in this study, is *not* in the type of sex the teenagers engage in, but only in whether or not a condom is used. Condoms are used more often in a "hook-up" than in a committed relationship. (A New York school stirred up controversy when teachers proposed passing out fruit-flavored condoms, to make the experience of fellatio more agreeable for the girls.)[35]

What's the result? Barbara Dafoe Whitehead concluded that the effect of today's "sex-drenched teen culture . . . is not to help young people learn how to choose a future life partner" (that's an understatement). At best, it helps them only to "manage their sex lives."[36] But what good is a sex life without any emotional connection?

Dr. Drew Pinsky recently made an important observation about gender differences in hooking up. Both girls and boys are usually partly or totally drunk when they hook up. (Remember the sexual assault Jimmy perpetrated on Tina? He was drunk when he did that.) Dr. Pinsky has found that girls and boys give completely different reasons *why* they get drunk before they hook up. Boys like to get drunk because it slows down their sexual response, allows them to relax, and decreases the likelihood of premature ejaculation. Girls like to get drunk because it numbs the experience for them, making it less embarrassing and less emotionally painful.[37]

Another change: kids are having sex earlier than before. The National Longitudinal Study of Adolescent Health is the largest study ever conducted of teenage behavior in the United States. Over ten thousand teenagers—a representative sample of kids from cities, suburbs, and rural areas, rich and poor, Asian and white and black and Hispanic—were periodically interviewed about everything from cigarette smoking to sex to thoughts of suicide. In 2002 the doctors running the study reported that there has been a "dramatic trend toward early initiation of sex." In 1988, 11 percent of adolescent females fourteen years of age and younger reported having had sexual intercourse; a decade later it was 19 percent. In other words, about one girl in five age fourteen and younger has now had sexual intercourse.[38] A separate study, published in 2003 by the National Campaign to Prevent Teen Pregnancy, independently arrived at the same conclusion: among girls age fourteen or younger, one in five has had sexual intercourse.[39] This study also found that most parents of sexually active daughters are NOT aware that their daughters are having sex. "Parents are overwhelmingly clueless about their kids' sexual experiences and knowledge," agrees journalist Hall. "Most teens [interviewed by Hall] said their parents have no idea what their real sex lives are like."[40]

Clueless

Pediatrician Thomas Young and psychologist Rick Zimmerman wanted to find out just how much parents know about what their kids are really doing. They asked 140 middle school students and their parents about smoking cigarettes, smoking marijuana, drinking alcoholic beverages, and having sexual intercourse.

Question for parents: Does your child smoke cigarettes? 12% of parents said yes.

Question for the kids: Do you smoke cigarettes? 43% of students said yes.

Question for parents: Has your child smoked marijuana? 3% of parents said yes.

Question for the kids: Have you smoked marijuana? 34% of kids said yes.

Question for parents: Does your child drink alcoholic beverages? 5% of parents said yes.

Question for the kids: Do you drink alcoholic beverages?
49% of students said yes.

Question for parents: Has your child had sexual intercourse?
2% of parents said yes.
Question for the kids: Have you had sexual intercourse? 52%
of kids said yes.

The authors titled their report "Clueless: Parental Knowledge of Risk Behaviors of Middle School Students."[41] It's not hard to see why.

Are Boys Human?

Three big changes have occurred since you and I were in middle school and high school:

- Girls and boys are engaging in sexual activities earlier than they used to;
- Girls and boys who are going steady today are no more and no less likely to have sexual intercourse than are girls and boys who are just hooking up;
- Oral sex has become the most common mode of sexual interaction.

Most of the articles and books about these changes in teenage sexual behavior have focused on the harm done to teenage girls. There's no question that teenage girls are the most obvious victims. A girl is more likely to feel used and abused after a typical twenty-first-century sexual encounter. In the most common type of hook-up, oral sex, the girl is far more likely to be servicing the boy than the other way around. And if the hook-up progresses to sexual intercourse, girls bear the risk of an unwanted pregnancy.

The impersonality of twenty-first-century adolescent sex victimizes girls. No argument there. But to focus only on that side of the story misses the harm done to boys. What harm? you may ask. How does impersonal sex harm boys?

I see plenty of harm. By the time a heterosexual young man is in his early twenties, he will rely on his girlfriend or his wife to be his primary emotional caregiver.[42] And that reliance only becomes greater as he moves through adult life. For the great majority of heterosexual adult men, the wife or girlfriend is the man's most important source of emotional support. Straight men who don't have a wife or girlfriend are substantially more likely to become seriously depressed, commit suicide, or die from illness.[43] It's not unreasonable to conclude that a heterosexual man's happiness and maybe even his life expectancy depend on his ability to establish a sound relationship with a woman he loves and who loves him.

Women are different in that respect. Women as a rule have more diverse support systems than men do. Husbands and boyfriends matter to them, sure, but so do their girlfriends, coworkers, and (often) family, especially a sister or mom. One reason for this has to do with the difference between female-female friendship and male-male camaraderie. Remember what we discussed earlier about differences between girls' friendships and boys' friendships. Close friendships between girls are usually intimate and personal. Friendships between boys are usually built around shared activities. David may have a great time playing video games with Juan, but that doesn't mean that David will confide in Juan about how he feels when his parents get divorced.

So here's the irony. Even though many of us think of teenage romance as something that interests girls more than it interests boys, it's the boys, ultimately, who will have greater need for an intimate and durable romantic relationship in their lives.

Playing a Role

Here's what we know:

- Most kids don't date anymore. They hook up instead.
- Kids are just as likely to have sex if they're just hooking up as they are if they're in an ongoing relationship.

As a result, relationships are no longer defined by sexual intimacy. Relationships today are defined by group affiliation. What does that mean?

To use the jargon employed by psychologists who study teenage dating: "Romantic pairs form most often on the basis of rank order rather than personal characteristics." Here's what that means: When fourteen-year-olds form romantic relationships, they do so less on the basis of individual characteristics and more on the basis of how popular the teenager is in the teenager's group. The most popular boy in the group is "going out with" the most popular girl, the second most popular boy goes out with the second most popular girl, and on down the line, with the least popular boy paired with the least popular girl.[44] "Going out with" usually doesn't mean actually going anywhere together. It just means that in the collective consciousness in the group, that girl is linked with that boy. Sexual relationships in this age group, far from involving intimate personal connection, usually are more of an exercise in role-playing.

Journalist Linda Perlstein spent a year living with middle schoolers, much as Dian Fosse lived with the gorillas. Perlstein described what relationships are really like at the middle school she visited. Girls choose who they will "go out with" mostly "because the guy is someone her friends would approve of. It's mostly about the superficial stuff. He's got the right look, he's got the right clothes. . . . The asking out and dumping are done through intermediaries. . . . Jackie and Anton [a girl and boy who are "going out together"] don't go anywhere together. They don't talk much, on the phone or at school. Mainly their relationship means Jackie checks herself in the bathroom every day after lunch and runs around Anton on the playground, except when she carefully ignores him." In this age group, Perlstein observes, *going out together* "doesn't have much meaning. Generally they just realize the roles they are supposed to play and pretend to do so."[45]

The average high school romantic relationship lasts about eleven weeks.[46] In middle school, not even that long. The typical high school romantic relationship—with its two weeks of infatuation, four weeks of relative happiness, and five weeks of gradual disintegration—may be the worst possible preparation for a lasting and loving relationship, for a lifetime commitment to stick together even when times are tough and when both you and your partner are less attractive than you used to be.

We all want our children to grow up to enjoy a loving, mutually supportive and *lasting* relationship. Many parents imagine, reasonably enough, that romantic relationships in adolescence provide good "practice" for more serious relationships in adulthood. You can't run before you walk. Practice makes perfect.

Psychologists who study romantic relationships in adolescence are coming to a different conclusion. Practice makes perfect only if you're practicing the right task. Most adolescents aren't. Psychologists Wyndol Furman and Elizabeth Wehner have studied adolescent romantic relationships for years. For middle school and even most high school students, they report that "adolescents are not very concerned with the fulfillment of attachment or caregiving needs. . . . Instead, their focus is on who they are, how attractive they are . . . and *how it all looks to their peer group.*" Adolescents often develop bad habits in their dating relationships. A boy may get in the habit of regarding his girlfriend as a source of sexual gratification without really connecting with her as a human being. A girl may get in the habit of seeing her romantic partner as a "trophy boyfriend" without any idea of how to integrate him into her life. And both of them may get in the habit of dumping their current partner whenever a better-looking or more popular one becomes available. Over time, Furman and Wehner have found, "these individuals may become more skillful, but more skillful in developing the relationships they have come to expect."[47] By the time they reach adulthood and it's time to build a marriage that will last a lifetime, they've accumulated all sorts of bad habits that they need to break. They might be better off had they never had those teen relationships.

There are other reasons to be skeptical about the value of romantic relationships in early adolescence. According to a large survey published in 2003, kids who become sexually active before fifteen years of age are three times more likely to be regular smokers, four times more likely to have tried marijuana, and six times more likely to drink alcohol once a week or more.[48] Maybe we should regard sexual relationships in the same way we regard alcoholic beverages: as an adult pleasure to be enjoyed by adults only. As with alcoholic beverages, romantic relationships can be wonderful when responsible adults are partaking. But if unprepared teens use them, they can be deadly. Drunk driving kills. So does AIDS. And the boy who gets in the habit of exploiting his girlfriend sexually while ignoring her emotional needs is setting himself up for a lifetime of frustration, loneliness, and failure.

So What Can You Do about It?

I hope I've persuaded you that for most teens, early sexual activity—whether in or out of a romantic relationship—does more harm than good. But so what? Your kid won't ask you for permission to hook up at a party Saturday night. What difference does it make what you think?

It makes a big difference. As much as your teen may mock you and claim to consider your opinions out of date and irrelevant, study after study confirms that teens almost universally regard their parents as being the most important and influential people in their lives.[49] That doesn't mean that you can change your teen's behavior just by telling her or him that you don't think hooking up is a good idea. It does mean that you can have some leverage, if you know what to do and how to do it.

Think about *when* and *how* your teen might engage in sexual activity. Researchers have found that teens typically engage in sex in one of two opportunistic settings. The most common venue for teens to have sex is in their own home or their partner's home, right after school, before parents come home. That leads to rule number one:

- Know *where* your teen is. Make it a habit to call your teen after school. And vary the time you call. If your teen is supposed to be at an after-school activity, verify that she or he actually went to that activity. If you're into high-tech, you can even buy one of the new GPS watches for your teen to wear. You lock the watch on your teen's wrist and then monitor your child's location in real time, online. Some brand names include the Wherify GPS Locator and Lojack for Kids.
- Second rule: Know *who* your child is with. Even when your child is at home, you need to know who she's with. Ask her: Is anyone at home with you? Will anyone be coming over? *Why* are they coming over?
- The third rule has to do with *parties*. You need to know everything about the party: where it is going to be, who your teen is going with, and so on. When your teen announces that she or he is going to a party, ask whose house it will be at. Call ahead and speak to the parents. Verify that the parents will be present and supervising, not just upstairs with the door closed. Announce that you may drop in on the party. (Your teen will be mortified if you actually show up, but the mere possibility that you *might* has some deterrent value.) And don't forget about teen party-hopping: teens often start at one party, then move on to another party later in the evening. Make it an ironclad rule that your teen *must* notify you before going to another party.

If you have a daughter, then there's a fourth rule:

• No more than *three years'* age difference between your daughter and the oldest boy in the group. Girls who go out with substantially older boys are more likely to be pressured into having sex, more likely to get a sexually transmitted disease, and more likely to experience an unwanted pregnancy.[50]

With girls, there's another way to decrease the risk of early sexual activity and teenage pregnancy: encouraging girls-only activities. Girls who participate in activities that are mostly or entirely girls-only—such as a girls-only soccer team, or ballet, or horseback riding—are less likely to be sexually active and much less likely to experience an unwanted pregnancy.[51] Competitive sports have been shown to be especially effective in getting girls to focus on something other than the rating and dating game. The more involved a girl is in competitive sports, the less likely she is to be sexually active and the less likely she is to get pregnant.[52]

That doesn't hold for boys. Boys who play competitive sports are actually somewhat *more* likely to be sexually active than nonathletes. How come? Why does participation ir. sports have opposite effects on girls and boys with regard to sex?

The answer has to do with self-esteem. Athletes, both girls and boys, typically have higher self-esteem than nonathletes.[53] Higher self-esteem increases the likelihood that a boy will have sex, while higher self-esteem *decreases* the likelihood that a teenage girl will have sex. Why the difference? Athletic boys usually rate somewhat higher in the popularity game than nonathletic boys do. So, athletic boys will have more opportunities for sex than boys who are not athletic. More opportunity for sex equals more sex—if you're a boy.

Girls choose to have sex not so much because they want to have sex but for other, more complex reasons. A girl with low self-esteem may be looking for affirmation of her femininity. She may think she's not pretty. She may think she's not popular. A boy who tells her she's beautiful, a boy who listens to her with interest, may be the boy she allows into her bed.

So. Tell your daughter to play sports and everything will be fine? Maybe. Encouraging your teenage daughter to sign up for sports or to continue in a sport she has been playing is not as easy as it sounds. A recent study of teenage American girls found that girls drop out of sports in droves beginning in middle school and continuing into high school.[54] Girls often perceive competitive sports as unfeminine, and girls often become more concerned with femininity as gender becomes more salient. Group membership also becomes more important as kids move through adolescence. In many middle schools and in most high schools, it's become uncool for any but the most talented jock girls to play competitive sports.

Another factor, often overlooked, is that most adolescent girls don't like boys staring at them. Several researchers have found that girls drop out of sports because they don't like the spooky feeling that boys—and even men—are watching their practices and their games just to stare at their bodies. "You can feel them looking at you," says one girl.[55]

So what can you do about that? Make sure that girls-only sports and physical education are available at your daughter's school, for one thing.[56] Psychologist Anna Engel found that girls were much more likely to participate in physical education if P.E. classes were girls-only rather than coed.[57]

More generally, you should encourage your daughter to participate in activities where the focus is on what she *does* rather than on how she *looks*. In cheerleading, poms, ice skating, and ballet, for example, a major focus of the activity is on how you look. Is your uniform clean? Do your socks match? And don't forget to smile! In soccer, field hockey, and basketball, on the other hand, the focus is on what you *do*. Your daughter's soccer coach doesn't (and shouldn't) care whether your daughter's socks match or whether her uniform is spotless. Nor should you.

The two basic rules for guiding your child's behavior are:

First, make clear what's forbidden, and enforce that prohibition.

Second, offer alternatives.

Remember when we talked about violent video games, in chapter 4? I advised: First, prohibit violent antisocial video games such as *Grand Theft Auto*. Second, encourage healthier real-life alternatives, such as playing soccer or football.

In the case of sex, this strategy means: First, make sure your kid understands that you don't approve of sexual activity involving genital contact between young teens. No oral sex. No penile-vaginal intercourse. And you're going to do your best to enforce that prohibition.

Second, offer alternatives. For girls, as I've said, that means sports, ballet, jazz dance, and other all-female activities. We have good data, as you've seen, showing that girls who participate in these activities are less likely to be sexually active.

For guys, it's tougher. There are no alternative activities that are unequivocally proven to decrease boys' proclivity to engage in premature sexual activity. I have a theory about what might work, though: encourage *cross-generational* community activities in which boys and men work together.

A school near my home sponsors a summertime program called Somos Amigos, "We Are Friends." A group of sixteen teenage boys under the leadership of three or four adult men travels to the Dominican Republic for the summer. Their mission: to build three small houses for the local villagers. The boys eat what the villagers eat, mostly beans and rice. No McDonald's, no Burger King, no Pizza Hut. There's no air conditioning. The conditions are brutal: hot and humid all day and all night. The boys are doing work, real work, shoulder-to-shoulder with the adult men: hammering four-by-fours, putting up drywall, installing toilets. Despite the rugged conditions, each year between forty and fifty boys apply for the privilege of spending their summer this way. Those who've participated say it was among the most meaningful experiences of their lives.

Here's what's really interesting, though: the organizers have told me that those boys *subsequently* are more respectful to women. You don't hear about those boys sleeping around with every girl who will let them. That's not scientific proof. But these boys are impressive.

My other hope is that if we can generate enough real change in teen culture—if we can empower enough girls to take charge of their sexual agenda, so that girls will stop providing oral sex on demand—then such a change might offer another way to shift teenage sexuality toward a more person-centered, relationship-oriented basis and away from the impersonal, experience-oriented bias that is skewing teenage sexuality at the present time. We need more girls to say No.

This girlchild was born as usual
and presented with dolls that did pee-pee
and miniature GE stoves and irons
and wee lipsticks the color of cherry candy.
Then in the magic of puberty, a classmate said:
You have a great big nose and fat legs . . .
She was advised to play coy,
exhorted to come on hearty,
exercise, diet, smile, and wheedle . . .
In the casket displayed on satin she lay
with the undertaker's cosmetics painted on . . .
Doesn't she look pretty? everyone said.

—"Barbie Doll," Marge Piercy[1]

Caitlyn

Caitlyn never was a superstar. The youngest of three children, she always seemed content to hang back in the shadows while her two older brothers took the limelight. Alex, the oldest, was smart. Really smart. He earned an A in every class without ever seeming to study and was accepted early to his first-choice school, the University of Pennsylvania.

Aaron, the middle child, was a jock. Soccer in the fall, basketball in the winter, lacrosse in the spring. Aaron was the first sophomore at our high school ever to be named a starter on the high school varsity soccer team. The following year he led his team in scoring. By December of his junior year he had received invitations to visit some NCAA Division I soccer programs, including at Clemson and Virginia Tech.

Jill, their mother, was a full-time mom who attended every one of Aaron's games. Caitlyn seemed happy to tag along and cheer her brother on.

Because Caitlyn had always been withdrawn and shy, parents Jill and Harry were concerned she might have problems when she started middle school. Jill read *Reviving Ophelia* and *Odd Girl Out* and most of the other books parents of girls are supposed to read nowadays. On nights when Jill and her husband went to bed at the same time, Jill would read Harry excerpts from those parenting books. If Harry complained, she would say, "You need to be prepared. She's your daughter, too."

read both [handwritten margin note]

Middle school is supposed to be the toughest time for girls—but Caitlyn sailed through. In eighth grade, she blossomed. Over a period of about ten months, she shed her baby fat and became a slender and attractive teenager.

When she started high school the following year, it seemed as though the phone never stopped ringing. Every weekend she received a barrage of invitations—to go shopping, to go to a party, or just to go to a friend's house to hang out. Nevertheless, her grades actually improved. She became obsessive about homework. By her sophomore year she was spending an average of three hours a night on homework. Her parents, especially Jill, marveled at her stamina, her discipline. "She's our late bloomer," Jill told her husband.

Caitlyn's weekends were filled with homework during the day, then parties or group trips to the movies Friday and Saturday night. Caitlyn begged her parents for more money to buy the latest fashions. Harry objected that Caitlyn's clothes budget was way out of line. "We're spending more on her clothes than we spent on Alex and Aaron *combined*," he said.

"And what she's buying isn't so fabulous, if you don't mind my saying so. We're paying Neiman Marcus prices for Kmart clothes. One hundred dollars for a pair of faded blue jeans?"

"But she's a girl. Girls' clothes cost more. And girls care more about clothes," Jill said. "Boys can wear the same thing over and over again and nobody cares. If a girl wears the same outfit twice in a month, other girls notice." Secretly, though, Jill had to admit that Caitlyn's spending was excessive, and Caitlyn didn't show good judgment about prices. But Jill was so pleased to see her daughter finally coming in to her own, finally taking center stage, she couldn't bring herself to talk to Caitlyn about it. She'll only be a teenager once, Jill thought. Let her have this chance.

talk to teens

The college counselor said that Caitlyn was a shoo-in for the University of Maryland, but Caitlyn wanted to go out of state. As Caitlyn began her senior year, Jill and Harry's biggest concern was whether they would be able to afford tuition for an Ivy League school without cutting back on contributions to their own retirement plans.

In retrospect, all the telltale signs were there. But when the phone rang at 3 A.M. that Sunday morning early in November, Jill had no clue that Caitlyn had been hiding a secret.

Jill thought at first that the phone call must be a wrong number or a crank call. Hello, she mumbled into the phone.

"Hello, my name is Cathy, I'm a nurse at the Shady Grove Hospital Emergency Room. Are you the mother of Caitlyn Morrison?" the nurse asked.

Yes of course, Jill answered.

"Caitlyn's friends brought her here about two hours ago," the nurse said. "Caitlyn is still unconscious. She tried to commit suicide."

"That's impossible," Jill said immediately, instantly wide awake. "How—what makes you say that?"

"We found empty bottles of Xanax and Vicodin in her purse," the nurse said matter-of-factly. "Her tox screen is positive for Xanax and Vicodin. And we found a suicide note."

"A suicide note? How—What does it say?" Jill asked, then before the nurse could answer, she said, "No wait! How is she? How is she?" Please let her be all right, Jill prayed. Suddenly she found it hard to breathe. Tears welled in her eyes. "Will she be okay?"

"Dr. Sorenson just told me that Caitlyn is stable enough to be transferred upstairs to the intensive care unit," the nurse said. "Normally we put teenagers in a special part of the peds ICU, but the peds ICU is completely filled, so she'll be in the regular ICU."

"Oh my God," Jill said, trying to grasp what was happening. Harry was still snoring.

"We've seen two other girls just in the past week, with the same story, exactly the same combination of drugs," the nurse said. "OD'd on Xanax and Vicodin. Those girls came in just like Caitlyn, and I can tell you both of them pulled through okay. So hopefully Caitlyn will pull through this fine, too."

"I'll be right there," Jill said.

Harry slept through the entire phone call. Only when Jill was completely dressed and on her way out of the bedroom did he stir. "What's up?" he mumbled.

You big lump, she wanted to say. Our daughter is in the emergency room! "I'm going to bring Caitlyn home," she said, and she was off.

When Jill arrived at the hospital, Caitlyn was already in the intensive care unit. "I'm sorry, visiting hours don't start until 8 A.M.," the unit clerk told her.

"But I'm her *mother*," Jill said impatiently.

"I understand," the clerk said. "If you'll just have a seat, I'll see whether the nurse can come out and speak with you now."

The nurse, a pleasant middle-aged woman named Rosemary, explained that ICU policy didn't allow visitors in the middle of the night, not even parents. "But don't worry. The moment Caitlyn starts waking up, I'll buzz you in, visiting hours or no," Rosemary said.

"She's still asleep?" Jill asked.

"She's still unconscious," Rosemary said. "But Dr. Feingold

expects her to regain consciousness by morning. If she doesn't, he'll give her some Narcan."

"Who's Dr. Feingold? What's Narcan?" Jill asked.

"Dr. Feingold's the attending physician. He's an intensivist."

"What's an intensivist? And if he can can wake her up by giving her some Narcan, why doesn't he give the Narcan to her *now*?" Jill asked.

"I tell you what, Jill," Rosemary said patiently. "Don't worry about the details of your daughter's medical care. Leave that to us. Caitlyn is going to be just fine, medically speaking. You need to be focusing on other things."

"Like what?" Jill asked plaintively.

"Like what you're going to say to Caitlyn when you see her."

"I'll just tell her I love her. . . ." Jill said, and her voice trailed off. She realized that she still had no idea why her daughter had done this.

"Here's the suicide note they found on her," Rosemary said. "It was in her purse, on the top, where she knew we'd find it." She held out a folded sheet of paper to Jill.

Jill nodded and took the paper without opening it. "Thank you," Jill said.

"Ask the clerk to buzz me if you have any questions," Rosemary said. "I'm working a twelve-hour, so I'll be here when visiting hours start."

Jill waited until Rosemary had gone before she looked at her daughter's note. After the first two paragraphs, she began to cry, so she stumbled to the women's restroom. Mercifully, no one else was there, giving Jill some privacy as she read her daughter's confession:

Dear Mom and Dad,

I'm so sorry to be doing this. I know how much this will hurt you. But there just isn't any other choice for me.

I guess you guys still don't know that I've been doing drugs for a long time now. I started in eighth grade. At first I just used

Dexedrine, to lose weight. And it worked. I really thought I could get away with it. It was so easy to fool you guys, along with everybody else. Everybody just looked at the surface. People saw how thin I got, and everybody thought it was just great. They envied me. They never wondered: How did that fat girl get so thin?

Dexedrine was wonderful—except for the palpitations and the nausea and the headaches. But that seemed like a small price to pay. Then I started having panic attacks. So say hello to Xanax. Even with Xanax, though, I never could get really calm inside. Until I discovered Vicodin.

For a while I thought I could still pull it off. Especially because I knew that other girls were doing it. I felt like I was juggling a dozen balls in the air all at once. Maybe I could just keep juggling forever. I had a routine: Dexedrine in the morning, Dexedrine and Xanax at lunch, Xanax after school, Xanax and Vicodin at bedtime. No problem.

Then the drugs stopped working. Not all at once. Gradually. I tried taking more. I increased the Vicodin to two a day. Then four. Then six. Then ten. The side effects got to be awful. I thought about stopping all the drugs, just going cold turkey. But that would mean going back to being fat and stupid. I could never get the grades I was getting without the boost from the drugs. And I couldn't stand the thought of being fat and ugly and stupid again. Once you've tasted the glory of being everybody's favorite girl, how can you give that up?

The truth is that the real me is an ugly, fat, stupid girl. And I just can't go on pretending, taking drugs and trying to fool people. I hate having to lie to you guys—about what I'm spending all the money on, about how I'm able to stay up all night studying, about how I lost all that weight.

And I don't want to be the person I really am. I don't like that person. She's ugly and stupid and fat.

Please forgive me.

Love always,
Caitlyn

Different Drugs, Different Highs

Girls and boys turn to drugs for different reasons. Girls use stimulant medications such as Dexedrine far more than boys do, for example, as a way to lose weight.[2] Girls use drugs like Xanax and Vicodin to relieve stress, to calm down, and because their friends are doing it.

Boys get involved with drugs for different reasons. Most boys who abuse drugs are looking for a thrill. And, they want the excitement of doing something dangerous. Remember the chapter about risk, about boys' risk-taking behaviors? Boys are more likely to buy illegal drugs from strangers while girls buy most of their drugs from people they know.[3]

What do teenagers themselves say about it? In a nationwide survey of 6,748 adolescents—selected to be geographically and ethnically representative of the entire United States—researchers found consistent gender differences in the reasons teenagers give for using drugs, alcohol, and cigarettes. Girls were sixteen times more likely than boys to say that they smoke in order to keep their weight down, for example. Boys were more than three times as likely as girls to say that they smoke in order to look cool.[4]

Despite the fact that girls and boys use drugs for different reasons and in different contexts, most drug prevention and treatment programs still don't distinguish between girls and boys. A 2003 report from the Center on Addiction and Substance Abuse (CASA) concluded that there's no excuse anymore for failing to recognize fundamental gender differences in drug prevention and drug treatment. "Girls and boys use drugs for different reasons, get drugs from different sources, differ in their ease of obtaining substances and are targeted by the media in different ways . . . Now is the time to replace one-size-fits-all [drug abuse prevention and treatment] with comprehensive approaches tailored to the needs and circumstances of girls and young women," the report concluded.[5] And for young men as well, I might add.

Let's start by looking at some of the reasons why girls and

boys use drugs and alcohol. Then we'll look at what you can do, as a parent, to keep your child from experimenting with drugs and alcohol in the first place or to get them to stop using if they've already started.

Risk Factors

Caitlyn's story illustrates the number-one risk factor for drug use among girls: namely, low self-esteem. Caitlyn thought she was stupid and fat. She compared herself negatively with her brilliant brother Alex and her athletic brother Aaron. There was nothing about herself that she was proud of. Dexedrine helped her lose weight and gave her the energy to stay up late so she could do long hours of homework every night, night after night.

We've already seen how self-esteem works in different ways for girls compared with boys. Girls with high self-esteem are less likely to have sex before age sixteen. Boys with high self-esteem are *more* likely to have sex before age sixteen. The best evidence suggests that a similar phenomenon is at play with regard to drugs and alcohol. Girls with low self-esteem are at much higher risk for using drugs and alcohol.[6] By the same token, depressed girls are more likely to start using drugs and alcohol. With boys, there's no strong relationship either way between self-esteem or depression on the one hand and the risk of using drugs and alcohol on the other.[7] Later in this chapter we'll explore some reasons for the difference.

Caitlyn's story also illustrates how academic stress can perpetuate a girl's use of drugs. Psychologists Suniya Luthar and Bronwyn Becker studied sixth- and seventh-grade girls in an affluent community. They found that for these middle school girls, academic stress was a common pathway to substance abuse.[8] Don't underestimate the stress your twelve-year-old daughter is telling you about. From your perspective as an adult, whether she gets an A or a B in Spanish is not a matter of world-shaking importance. But in her world, it may be.

The best way to protect a girl like Caitlyn from falling into *ways to avoid girl issues*

the drug trap is to find ways to strengthen her self-confidence and self-esteem, and to de-stress her environment. Remember those heartbreaking words at the end of Caitlyn's suicide note: ". . . the real me is an ugly, fat, stupid girl. . . . I don't want to be the person I really am. I don't like that person. She's ugly and stupid and fat." Your job is to change the way Caitlyn evaluates herself, so that she's focusing not on how she *looks* but on who she *is*.

Good parenting requires knowledge, insight, and understanding. It's your job as a parent to know your child—not only to know who she is right now, but also to sense who she could become, where her hidden strengths lie. You have to know your child better than she knows herself. And you have to resist the tendency to push your child in a direction that worked for you or for one of your other children.

In this case, Caitlyn's parents were "programmed," so to speak, by their two older children Alex and Aaron. They had come to think that all kids were either jocks or brains. Caitlyn was neither, so—with all due respect to her parents Jill and Harry—they assumed that Caitlyn didn't have any special talent of her own.

Were they right?

Rosemary, the nurse in the intensive care unit, was right about Caitlyn's medical prognosis. Caitlyn regained consciousness the morning after she was admitted, just as Rosemary had predicted. Jill was at Caitlyn's bedside when she woke up. "I didn't die?" were Caitlyn's first words to her mother. Jill couldn't tell whether Caitlyn was relieved or disappointed.

Two days later, Dr. Feingold cleared her for medical discharge, and Caitlyn was transferred to Potomac Ridge, an inpatient psychiatric facility. After two weeks of group therapy—as well as Wellbutrin and Lexapro (two antidepressant medications)—the doctor said that Caitlyn was ready to go home. "She's so much more relaxed now," Jill told me. "I don't know whether that calmness is just the medications, or whether that's what Caitlyn is really like when she's not taking Dexedrine. I wish she didn't have to take any medication at all."

The psychiatrist, Dr. Himmelfarb, insisted that Caitlyn would have to stay on her medication for at least six months, probably longer. Those were the same six months during which she was supposed to decide which college to go to. She had to take a grade of incomplete in two of her subjects that fall. Caitlyn was worried that her college applications would be in jeopardy because of those incompletes, but I sent letters to the colleges, saying that she'd been hospitalized for three weeks because of an (unspecified) illness. As it turned out, she was accepted at most of the colleges she applied to.

In the meantime, Caitlyn discovered something she enjoyed, something she was really good at. With Dr. Himmelfarb's approval, she started volunteering as an aide at Potomac Ridge. Because she had been an inpatient there herself, and because she was still a teenager, she had a special credibility with the teenage inpatients.

One evening the aides on duty at Potomac Ridge were talking about Malia, a fourteen-year-old girl who had been put in the isolation room again after hitting a nurse's aide. Malia had been at Potomac Ridge for five days. This was her third time in isolation. "That girl's a bad number, a real mean one," said Sophie, one of the aides. "She's the sort who'd just as soon kill you as look at you." Two other aides, Taneesha and Ruthanne, nodded.

"Do you mind if I go in and talk with her?" Caitlyn said.

Sophie, Taneesha, and Ruthanne just stared at her. "You crazy? You want to die?" Sophie finally asked. "That girl will eat you alive and spit out your bones."

Caitlyn shrugged. "Do you mind if I try?" she repeated.

Sophie and Ruthanne watched through the small window of the locked room as Caitlyn sat down on the bed across from Malia. They couldn't hear what Caitlyn was saying, and at first it didn't seem to be having any effect. Malia remained sitting on the floor in a corner, huddled in a tight fetal curl with her head between her knees. But after Caitlyn had been talking for about a minute, Malia looked up. Sophie and Ruthanne were amazed to see an enchanting smile on Malia's face. "You know, that girl is almost pretty when she smiles," Sophie said.

Caitlyn stayed in Malia's room for two hours. When she knocked on the door to be let out, Malia was by her side. "Malia's coming out with me," Caitlyn said, not a question but a statement. "She won't need to be in the locked room anymore."

Sophie looked suspiciously at Malia. Malia nodded. "I won't hit anybody," Malia said. "As long as I can talk with Caitlyn, on the nights when she's here."

Caitlyn went to Potomac Ridge every evening for the next two weeks, spending an hour or more each night with Malia, mostly listening, sometimes talking. Nobody knew what they said to each other, but everybody could see that Malia had changed. She wasn't violent anymore. She didn't shout or scream anymore. And she started sleeping at night.

"What do you girls talk about?" Dr. Osenick, the attending psychiatrist, asked Caitlyn just before Malia was discharged.

"Not much," Caitlyn said. "I tell her about myself a little. I tell her how bad I used to feel, how I used to hate my body, hate my life."

"You know," Dr. Osenick said, "if you ever become a professional therapist, one of the first things you'll learn is that you shouldn't tell your client too much about yourself. The focus of therapy should be on the patient, not on the therapist."

"Then I guess I won't ever be a professional therapist," Caitlyn said mildly.

Caitlyn was accepted to Cornell. She went to visit the campus in late April. She still hadn't decided which college she would go to, but Cornell was the only Ivy League school to which she had applied. She stayed overnight in one of the dorms.

"How'd you like it?" her mother asked her.

"It was scary," Caitlyn said. "All the kids seem so grown up. And some of the girls there are really skinny. And it's out in the middle of nowhere. I mean, Ithaca is like a gazillion miles from anywhere."

When Caitlyn said "some of the girls there are really skinny," a chill went through Jill's heart. Caitlyn had gained thirty pounds in the months since her suicide attempt. She was up to 140 pounds (at five-feet-four-inches tall). Jill thought Caitlyn looked beautiful, but she was worried. On the other hand: What parent wouldn't want their child to go to an Ivy League college?

In May, Caitlyn decided to decline the offer from Cornell and to go to Towson instead. "I need to stay close to home," she said. "And I want to keep volunteering at Potomac Ridge at least a few days a month. I'm going to be a therapist someday."

I think it's clear in retrospect that Caitlyn's talents lay in her ability to care about people. It's easy to be critical after the fact, but maybe Caitlyn wouldn't have started using drugs if her parents had tried harder, earlier, to find Caitlyn's areas of strength instead of just taking her along to watch Aaron play soccer and lacrosse. When Caitlyn was younger, she loved to be around animals. Suppose the parents had signed Caitlyn up to volunteer at the zoo, or at an animal shelter in our town where no animal is ever euthanized. Empathic children like Caitlyn love to care for animals. If her mother had driven Caitlyn to volunteer at the zoo, even if it meant missing some of Aaron's games, Caitlyn would have gotten the message that her interests mattered just as much as Aaron's triumphs on the field.

I mentioned a moment ago how the stress of high academic expectations can lead girls to start using drugs. What can you do about that? You have to show your daughter that there are other ways to relax besides taking Xanax or getting drunk or smoking a joint. Join her for a long walk in the park, or introduce her to prayer or meditation—but only if *you're* proficient and comfortable with those methods, of course. Share with her your own ways of coping. You can build a bond, and hopefully decrease the risk that she will turn to drugs when she needs to relax. One mom I know likes to bake a cake when she's feeling stressed, and she's taught her two daughters to do the same. Maybe that's not the lowest-calorie way to relax, but it's a lot safer than illegal drugs. "Comfort cooking," she calls it.[9]

None of this works for boys, though. Boys are different.

Ethan

Mike and Uta adopted Ethan when Ethan was almost two years old. Like many African-American children given up for adoption, Ethan had been in a series of foster care placements from birth until the time Mike and Uta adopted him.*

Mike was a research physicist at the National Institute of Standards and Technology. Mike had always been a geek. He'd met his wife, Uta, while doing a three-year postdoctoral fellowship at the Max Planck Institute in Germany. Mike and Uta shared a love of the novels of Thomas Mann, the music of Gustav Mahler, and Mosel wine. They used to refer to themselves as the 3M club: Mann, Mahler, and Mosel. Mike in particular was a great believer in the power of a good upbringing. He was confident that he would be able to raise his young son to share his tastes and his hobbies.

Wrong. Uta and Mike soon were getting a crash course in infantile masculinity. Ethan loved to smash things, throw food, collide into furniture head-on at full speed. Within a few weeks of Ethan's arrival in the home, Uta had packed everything breakable away in boxes, labeling the boxes carefully and then stacking them in the basement. Ethan found his way into the basement, tore open one of the boxes, and stomped on the china Uta had so carefully packed away. After that, they started

---

*Actually, Ethan's birth mother was Irish-American while Ethan's birth father was a light-skinned African-American. Ethan was as much Irish as he was African. But in North America, if you have *any* African ancestry, our society labels you as African-American, period.

calling Ethan "the little criminal," and they treated him like one, too. They barricaded those parts of the house that were off-limits to Ethan, and they kept him on a leash—literally—at the mall. Uta and Mike had originally planned to adopt two or three children, but after Ethan arrived, they decided one was enough.

I first met Ethan when he was fifteen years old, five-feet-ten-inches tall, 180 pounds, and in ninth grade. He was already a star in basketball and football. We even heard a rumor that one of the big high schools down-county was already trying to steal him away to play for their teams.

Ethan's grades had been mediocre all through middle school: C's and D's across the board, except for an A in physical education. But when grades came out for the first marking period of ninth grade, they were worse: he had failed English and Spanish, with D's in his other subjects. He still had his A in physical education, though. His father, Mike, decided that it was time to make a change.

"He can finish the football season," Mike said to me. "There are only two games left in the football season. But no basketball. Sports are taking up too much of his time. There's just no way he should be spending two or three hours a day on sports when he's failing English and Spanish. Don't you agree?"

I paused. "Honestly, I'm not sure I do," I said. "I'm not convinced that taking Ethan out of sports will improve his academic performance. In fact, it might backfire."

"Doctor, with all due respect," Mike said, "that makes no sense. The more time he spends on sports, the less time he has for school."

Mike and Uta pulled Ethan out of sports. "We want what is best for you," Uta told Ethan. "We want for you to be able to go to college."

"I don't want to go to college," Ethan said.

"Sometimes you have to do things you don't like, in order to get the things you want later," Mike chimed in.

"But what I want is to play basketball right *now*," Ethan complained. "How is taking me off the basketball team going to help me play basketball?"

Uta and Mike looked at each other, the same despairing glance they had exchanged so many times over the years. Why can't Ethan understand? was what the glance said.

When he started high school, Ethan had hung out with the jocks. But you can't hang with the jocks if you're not on the team—or it's hard, at any rate, especially if you're a freshman. One month into basketball season, Ethan was drifting. He was supposed to come straight home every day after school and work on his homework, but he wasn't. Instead, he was hanging out in the high school parking lot, catching rides to Rockville and the District of Columbia with the older boys, coming home late at night.

The first week of December, Uta smelled the sweet, pungent odor of marijuana on Ethan's clothes. She spoke with Mike that evening. They decided to confront Ethan. To their surprise, he didn't deny using pot.

"Yeah, I smoke pot. So?" he said.

"But you never smoked pot before," Mike said.

"That's because no ATHLETE's gonna smoke pot, because pot messes with your re-ACTION time," Ethan said, raising his voice. "Your re-ACTION time is what it's all about, see. But you made me quit basketball. So why the HELL shouldn't I smoke some pot?"

"Please don't swear, Ethan," Mike said.

"Right. No god-DAMN swearing allowed in THIS house," Ethan said. "No NOTHIN allowed in this house."

"Ethan, we're just concerned for you, because pot damages your brain. You said it yourself. Pot slows your reaction time," Uta said.

"I don't need this shit," Ethan said, and walked out the door.

They didn't see him again for three days.

After Ethan had been missing for two days, they notified the police. "We need to report that our son is missing," Mike told the officer at the police station.

[handwritten margin note: lost friends]

The officer listened to Mike's story. Then the officer said, "He's not missing. He's a runaway."

"What's the difference?" Mike asked.

"Missing means you don't know what happened to the person. Maybe they were abducted. You don't have any idea. Runaway means a juvenile under eighteen deliberately left home. Your son is a runaway."

"Runaway" seemed like the right word to describe the cascade of events over the next six months. Ethan began stealing money from his parents routinely, brazenly, once even taking money out of Uta's purse while Uta watched him do it. Uta and Mike bought a safe. They began locking their valuables in the safe at all times, even when they were at home.

Ethan flunked ninth grade. Mike and Uta consulted with a psychiatrist who specializes in adolescent drug addiction. The psychiatrist recommended that Mike and Uta allow Ethan to play football. "According to school rules, Ethan will be allowed on the team only if he can maintain his GPA above flunking. Right now, Ethan's got no motivation to succeed," the psychiatrist told them. "At least being on the team will give him some motivation. And we'll get him in a random drug testing program. If he tests positive, he's off the team."

At six feet, two hundred pounds, Ethan towered over the other JV football players the following fall. But the coach kept him on JV just the same. "He needs to learn some discipline," the coach said. Sure enough, Ethan brought his grades up—to a C average. But rejoining the team didn't eliminate Ethan's drug habit. He wasn't stealing anymore, but he was still using drugs. Uta could smell pot on his clothes, and she found traces of pot or drug paraphernalia—mostly cigarette wrapping papers—in his clothes.

"Where is he getting the money?" Uta asked Mike one night as they lay in bed together. "And how is he able to pass the drug tests?"

"I don't want to know," Mike said, and turned on his side away from his wife. "I'm going to sleep."

This Is Your Brain on Drugs

Remember what we talked about in the chapter on risk? Danger doesn't reliably deter boys. It may even spur some boys on. Educating boys about "the dangers of drugs" can be counterproductive. You may stimulate the behavior you're trying to discourage.

Did you ever see that old commercial where the man shows an intact egg and says, "This is your brain"? Then he cracks the egg, puts it in a frying pan, it sizzles, and he says, "This is your brain on drugs"? That sort of commercial works reasonably well with girls. Girls watch the commercial and think, Hmm, I don't want my brain to end up like an egg frying in a pan.

Not so with boys—especially not with the sensation-seeking, risk-taking boys who are at greatest risk. Those boys see the frying egg, hear the narrator say, This is your brain on drugs, and think: "Way cool! Where can I get some of that stuff?" I know a teenage boy who's wallpapered his room with the "This is your brain on drugs" poster and other posters like it, warning of the dangers of drugs. This boy uses drugs and he wants everybody to know it.

As a society, what we are doing right now is *not* working. The United States government recently announced that its five-year, $900 million ad campaign intended to discourage drug use among teens was a total failure. Teenagers who saw the government commercials were *more* likely to use drugs than teenagers who never saw the commercials.[10]

Mike and Uta meant well when they warned their son about the dangers of drugs. Mike after all had always been one of those 10 percent of boys who are highly risk-averse (we'll come back to those boys in chapter 9). And Uta, like most women, thought that telling her son about the dangers of drug use would decrease the likelihood that he would use drugs. After all, any sensible person would avoid using a substance that damages the brain, right?

Right. But most fifteen-year-old boys are not sensible people. They are fifteen-year-old boys.

[handwritten margin note top: playing sports deters girls because it raises self-esteem]

What could Mike and Uta have done differently? Of course, I think they should have followed my advice in the first place as far as leaving Ethan on the team. Would that have prevented Ethan from using drugs? Maybe. Maybe not. Participation in competitive sports *has* been proven to be an effective strategy for decreasing the risk of drug use among teenage *girls*. But it's not been shown to make a big difference for boys.

Epidemiologist Deborah Aaron and her colleagues at the University of Pittsburgh studied how playing sports affected the likelihood of drug and alcohol use among adolescents. They found that boys who played sports were slightly *more* likely to drink alcohol, whereas playing sports had a *protective* effect for the girls. Playing sports decreased the likelihood that a girl would smoke cigarettes, for example.[11] Those findings were confirmed and expanded by the 2003 report from the Center on Addiction and Substance Abuse that I mentioned earlier in this chapter. According to that report, teenage girls who participate in three or more extracurricular activities during the school year are half as likely to smoke as those who don't participate in any activities. The active girls are also less likely to drink alcohol and much less likely to use marijuana.[12] Participating in sports and other extracurricular activities just doesn't have those kinds of benefits for boys.

Why the difference? It goes back, I think, to issues of self-esteem. Participation in extracurricular activities, and especially in competitive sports, raises girls' self-esteem. Low self-esteem is a major risk factor for drug and alcohol use among *girls*, so raising self-esteem lowers the risk of drug and alcohol use among *girls*.

But boys are different. Boys don't drink or use drugs to assuage low self-esteem. Boys drink and use drugs because they're sensation-seeking or because they want to look cool. Playing sports doesn't decrease their interest in sensation-seeking or wanting to look cool. It may be the case that boys who are the greatest risk-takers are also the most likely to participate in competitive sports, in which case participation in sports may be a

[handwritten margin note right: uses examples and it illustrates self-esteem is relative]

[handwritten note bottom: Boys do drugs for risk taking so sports don't help]

marker for boys who are at higher risk for drug and alcohol use—without being the *cause* of that increased risk.

Look in the Mirror

We've laid out some of the basic differences between girls and boys in terms of why they use drugs and alcohol as well as a few of the risk factors and protective factors that increase or decrease the likelihood of their using drugs and alcohol. Now let's talk about concrete action you can take to decrease the likelihood that *your* daughter or son will use drugs or alcohol.

Look in the mirror. If you have a drinking problem, don't waste your time talking to your daughter or son about drugs or alcohol. Your word has no credibility.

If you smoke cigarettes, you're stepping up to bat with two and a half strikes against you. "You smoke twenty cigarettes a day. I smoke two joints a week. What gives you the right to tell me that what I'm doing is wrong?" That's what one teenage boy told his mother after she warned him about the dangers of smoking pot. Mom tried to answer that marijuana is more dangerous than tobacco. Her son responded with facts and figures purporting to show that tobacco is more dangerous than pot. Mom thought that her son was inventing most of the facts and figures, and maybe he was. But you don't want to get bogged down comparing the relative risks of marijuana and cigarettes.

If you've used drugs in the past, don't mention it unless you have no choice. Don't try saying, "I used pot when I was your age, so that's how I know how bad it is." Your teen has many good responses ready for that one, including:

- "Maybe it was bad for you. Maybe it wouldn't be so bad for me. You're not me."
- "Why shouldn't I be allowed to try something you did yourself?"
- "You turned out okay, didn't you? So it couldn't be that bad."

If your teen confronts you and demands to know whether you used pot, tell the truth. But don't boast or brag. Acknowledge your mistake, but don't try to use your prior experience for any advantage when you talk with your child.

Just the Facts, Please

When you talk with your kids about drugs, stick to the facts. But keep in mind that the relevant facts are different depending on whether you're talking to a daughter or a son.

For your daughter, make sure she understands the harm of using drugs. If you're not sure of the facts yourself, start with a balanced, unbiased, noncommercial source of information. I recommend the National Library of Medicine, a division of the National Institutes of Health. Go to their "layperson's" website, www.medlineplus.gov, type in the name of the drug that you want to learn about, and you'll get reliable, accurate information.

Remember that girls get most of their drugs from friends, and that the transaction usually takes place in a private home.[13] Know where your daughter is. Know who her friends are. Talk to her friends' parents. Ask her to check in with you frequently throughout the day. Consider purchasing one of those personal GPS trackers I mentioned in the last chapter. Keep tabs on her. Make sure she knows that you will be checking up on her. And verify her statements, openly, with her cooperation. If she says that she's at Melissa's house, ask her to call you back using Melissa's home phone rather than the cell phone. Look at your caller ID: Does the number match Melissa's home phone number? Make sure your daughter understands what you're doing and why. That knowledge will actually empower your daughter to refuse unsafe requests. If her friends invite her to go downtown to somebody else's home, she can tell them: "No, I can't, because my mom makes me call her from everybody's house and she'll see from her caller ID that I'm not where I told her I'd be." For thirteen- and fourteen- and fifteen-year-old girls, that technique really does work. "I wish *my* mom cared that much about me" is what one girl said after another girl I know explained her mom's requirements.

What about boys? My experience is that the approach I just outlined for girls is ineffective for boys. First of all, the trick of asking your teen to call you from the home of a friend is a nonstarter with boys. Boys who "check in" with their parents will be ridiculed by other boys, as your son will quickly learn. Second, remember that boys are more likely to purchase drugs from a stranger, outdoors, in a park or on the street. So keeping track of which particular house your son is visiting is less relevant.

Regarding drug education: the evidence of the past thirty years suggests that educating boys about the dangers of drugs is a waste of time. On the contrary: emphasizing the harmful, mind-blowing, damaging effects of drugs can boomerang. That approach will pique the interest of thrill-seeking boys. Remember that these are the same boys who go snowboarding down a steep mountain without taking a lesson first.

So what works with boys? My recommendation is: clear and consistent discipline. Tell your fourteen-year-old son, "If I catch you drinking or smoking or using any kind of drugs, we'll take the PlayStation and lock it away for the three months that you're grounded." Teenage boys prize mobility and independence. Tell your fifteen-year-old son: "If I catch you using drugs, you won't be driving until you're seventeen, not sixteen." Tell your sixteen-year-old son: "If I catch you drinking or using drugs, you lose the car keys for six months. *Minimum* of six months." These measures may seem extreme, but they can also be lifesaving. And I haven't found anything else that works—for boys.

What's for Supper?

We've been focusing on what I call "negative discipline." Punishment for bad behavior. What about *positive* discipline? What positive interventions have been shown to decrease the risk of drug and alcohol use?

positive discipline

Answer: eating supper together. According to the Center for Addiction and Substance Abuse, "The more often teens have dinner with their parents, the less likely they are to smoke, drink or use drugs."[14] The protective effect of teens having dinner with their parents is greater for girls than for boys, but it's significant for both sexes.[15]

Why are kids who eat supper with their parents less likely to use drugs? Several reasons come to mind. First, parents who insist on eating supper together with their kids are more likely to be parents who know what their kids are doing. Kids whose parents are involved in their lives will be kids who are less likely to use drugs and alcohol, compared with kids whose parents don't bother to make the effort.

Second, if it's an ironclad rule that your kids have to be home for supper, then there's less opportunity for them to be somewhere else. If your son isn't home when you get home, and he doesn't arrive home until ten or eleven or midnight, then you really don't have a clue what he's been up to, do you?

I know you're busy. Everybody's busy. But please, try your best to make dinner at home a family affair. And here's one rule you should never break: when all family members *are* at home at supper time, all family members should eat together. I see more and more families for whom eating separately is an accepted way of life. Dad brings a pizza home, but neither of his kids answer when he announces that he's home, so he eats alone in the kitchen. Twelve-year-old Dean darts into the kitchen a minute later, grabs three slices of pizza, and goes back to his room, closing the door behind him. Fifteen-year-old Diana sneers at the pizza, takes a cup of yogurt out of the refrigerator and grabs a spoon, all the while talking on her cell phone. Mom arrives home half an hour later. It's too late to make a proper supper, and besides, everybody's already eaten, so she just tosses something in the microwave for herself.

Your kids won't starve if they have to wait a few minutes for supper. Maybe another reason kids do better in families that eat supper together is because with everybody's busy schedules, eating supper together ~~requires~~ you to stay in touch with one another during the day. It gives you a reason to call your child (aside from custodial checking-up). "I'm running late," you tell your son on the phone at 4:30 P.M. "You're good at making spaghetti with meatballs, so you're the cook tonight." (Your son groans.) "Check in the kitchen to make sure you have everything you need," you tell him. "I'll call you back in fifteen minutes."

The Day Everything Changes

Most parents I've known don't think their kids are doing drugs. Other kids, maybe. But not their kid. Then comes the day when they find out. Mom discovers drug paraphernalia in her son's pants pocket. Or Dad finds an incriminating e-mail message on his daughter's computer.

What do you do now?

Remember the principles we talked about earlier:

1) establish the prohibition;
2) offer alternatives.

Whether you have a daughter or a son, you need to make clear that drug use is prohibited. But the right alternative depends on whether we're talking about a girl or a boy. If your daughter is smoking in order to relax, you need to help her find other ways to loosen up. If your daughter is using Dexedrine to lose weight, you need to offer her safer ways to lose weight. Join an exercise club with your daughter. Or better yet, help her to accept herself as she is, and shift the focus away from how she looks.

If you have a son who's a risk-taker, a son who's using drugs because he's looking for a thrill, you need to help him explore safer, healthier ways to get that risk-taking tingle. Snowboarding, skiing, mountain biking, motocross, mountain climbing.

Wait a second, you're thinking. You've just discovered your

son is using drugs. I'm telling you to buy your son a snowboard or a mountain bike. Am I saying that you should reward your son for using drugs? What about punishment?

We'll talk more about discipline in the next chapter. I'm *not* saying that you can't discipline your son, or your daughter. But it's not enough just to take away your daughter's cell phone or your son's driving privileges. You have to offer alternatives. Positive alternatives that ease your daughter's hurt or satisfy your son's desire for excitement.

The other objection I hear from parents of sons in this situation is that the alternatives I'm suggesting are risky. Your son could break his leg snowboarding. He could crack his skull mountain biking.

That's all true. But those risks are healthy risks. When your son allows a drug dealer to stick a needle in his arm, your son has entered a much darker world.

punishment not enough must offer alternatives

DISCIPLINE

*I was so concerned about being a friend that I sometimes forgot to
be a parent.*

—Mother of seven children[1]

Kristen

I first met Kristen when she was eleven and a half years old.
Diane, her mother, brought her in for a routine checkup.
"What's your favorite thing to do at home, Kristen?" I asked.

"Smoke cigarettes," she responded immediately.

I glanced at her mom. Mom looked embarrassed but didn't
say anything. "What else?" I asked.

"Listen to music. Watch TV. I don't know. Talk to my friends.
What does anybody do?" She yawned.

"Are you tired?" I asked. Kristen didn't answer. "What time
did you get to sleep last night?" I asked.

"Three," she said.

"Three A.M. this morning?" I asked.

She nodded.

"What were you doing between midnight and 3 A.M.?"

"Talking with my friends," she said.

"On the phone?" I asked.

"Some on the phone. Mostly online."

"Instant messaging?"

She nodded.

"Do you often stay up till 3 A.M.?" I asked.

"Yeah," she said, exasperated. "Everybody does."

"I don't want you to be online at three in the morning," Diane interjected.

"I don't see the problem," Kristen said.

"I know you don't," Diane said. "But I just don't think it's safe, or smart, for an eleven-year-old girl to be online at 3 A.M."

"How would you know," Kristen said. "See?" she said to me. "That's what I mean. My parents are so boring. They haven't got a clue. Not a clue."

I spoke to her mother later. "How do you discipline Kristen?" I asked.

"What do you mean?" Diane asked.

"Well, smoking for instance. Kristen's only eleven. Do you punish her for smoking?"

"You mean, like spanking her?" Diane asked.

"No of course not," I said. "I mean, like taking away her privileges, telephone privileges, things like that."

Diane shook her head. "It'd be hopeless to try," she said. "My husband, David, smokes. Whenever I say anything to Kristen about smoking, she just says, 'Dad smokes, so why can't I?' She says we're hypocrites. She gets mad. And when she gets mad, she throws things. She threw her dinner plate across the kitchen last week. The plate broke, but what scared me was she just barely missed hitting David. Two inches the other way and she could have really hurt him."

"Did you punish her?" I asked.

"What do you mean?"

"After she threw the dinner plate, did you punish her?" I asked.

"Well . . ." Diane paused. She seemed to realize that some sort of punishment was called for. Or maybe she understood merely that *I* expected her to have punished Kristen, and she was trying to think up the "right" answer. "After it happened, I was mainly just trying to calm her down. I didn't want her to throw anything else."

"It sounds as though you were afraid of her," I said.

"I was," Diane said, nodding.

This story does not have a happy ending. Later that year, Kristen was suspended from school after she threatened a teacher. The following year she was arrested for possession of cocaine. She was stealing money from her parents to buy the drugs. One year later, after her second arrest, her parents sent her to a nearby drug treatment facility. That didn't work. So one week after her fifteenth birthday, Kristen's mother drove her three hundred miles to another drug treatment facility, which looks suspiciously like a prison. As I write this, Kristen is still there. Her mom tells me that the counselors at the facility are disappointed by Kristen's lack of progress.

What could Kristen's parents have done differently to avoid this outcome? We'll come back to that at the end of this chapter. It's not an easy question.

The Oozing of Parental Authority

If you're like most people, you've never heard of sociologist Norbert Elias. His name is not well known, neither in his native Germany nor in his adopted home, England. But those who do know his work regard him as one of the great social critics of the twentieth century. In 1989, one year before his death at the age of ninety-three, he published an important essay on the fundamental ways in which our society changed between 1939 and 1989.[2]

Perhaps the most significant change in our society in those fifty years, according to Dr. Elias, was the *transfer of authority from parent to child.* Think about the way parents used to choose a high school for a teenage son, for example. If, in the summer of 1940, a mother and father told their son that they would be enrolling him in a Catholic boys' high school that September, you could bet that he would indeed be going to a Catholic boys' high school that September. The son might complain, he might sulk, but nobody seriously expected the parents to change their mind just because he didn't like their decision.

No more. Today most parents would *consult* with their son about which school he would attend in the fall. The parents might suggest, or cajole, or even beg. But the final decision would in most cases be up to the boy.

The result of this loss of parental authority is, to use the phrase coined by Dr. Elias, *status uncertainty* (*Statusunsicherheit*— which can also be translated "status *insecurity*"). Parents no longer know what authority they have over their children. Their recollections of their own childhood provide at best an unreliable guide. Another consequence of this relocation of power from parent to child is an "informalization" of relations between the generations. I know many children who address their friends' parents by their first names, for example.

The informality of today's family relations puts parents at a disadvantage. On one hand, it may be somewhat easier for parents today to be *friends* with their children. But it's harder for parents today to be *parents*. A friendship is a reciprocal relationship between social peers. The parent-child relationship is not a reciprocal relationship between peers, nor should it be. You tell your child what she can watch on TV, for example. She doesn't have the authority to tell you what *you* can watch, nor should she.

If you shouldn't be your child's best friend, and you don't have the authority to be a real parent, then where are you? You're in limbo. Dr. Elias observed that such a profound change "inevitably causes a pervasive feeling of uncertainty . . . The conventional code governing behavior [between parents and children], which was adapted to a more strictly hierarchical order, no longer corresponds to the relationships as they actually are."[3] Parents are adrift at sea without a compass.

Even for younger children, I'm finding that parents seldom feel that they have the authority to *tell* their child what to do. Instead, the best parents can do is *suggest*. Recently I was talking with the mother of Sally, an obese eight-year-old girl. "I'm really worried about this coming summer," Mom told me. "Sally goes to my husband's parents' place at the beach for at least a few weeks each summer, and my mother-in-law spoils her terribly. They go to the boardwalk and buy funnel cakes, taffy, ice cream, all that junk food. Sally doesn't eat anything healthy for a month, and when she comes back she's angry when I serve vegetables."

"How about signing her up for a sleep-away summer camp?" I suggested. "There's a good one about two hours west of here, near Deep Creek Lake. The girls swim and hike and camp outdoors overnight. There's no junk food and no vending machines. The camp is run by three women. . . ." I trailed off as I saw Mom shaking her head.

"I already asked Sally about going to a summer camp, and she threw a tantrum," Mom said. "She's really looking forward to a vacation at the beach."

"But Sally's never been to summer camp. She might love it," I said.

"I know," Mom said. "But what can I do? I can't force her."

Of course, Mom *can* "force" her eight-year-old daughter to go to summer camp. But this mom, like most parents today, doesn't feel that she has the authority to compel her child to do anything against her will.

Like many adults, most children prefer the certainty of the pleasure they know to the uncertainty of something they've never experienced. If you *ask* them whether they'd like to do something they've never done before—like going to summer camp—they'll probably say no. I remember one snowy weekend when I was a child. My two brothers and I had nothing planned except watching football on TV. My mom suggested that all of us go skiing—which none of us had ever done before. All three of us protested, none louder than my oldest brother Steve. We weren't in the mood to go out into the ice and snow, and we didn't want to miss the football game on TV. But Mom insisted. This was back in 1968, when most parents still had the authority to assert their will in such matters. We all went skiing, and we all loved it, especially my brother Steve. He became an ardent skier, and he remains one today. But today many parents would back away from the same suggestion if all three sons loudly protested against it.

When I talk to parents about the transfer of authority from parent to child over the past sixty years, some parents respond that this is a change for the better. Giving children more authority makes them more responsible, these parents believe.

I don't agree. The best evidence suggests that taking authority away from parents and giving it to young children results in:

- *More fat kids.* Most young children prefer chicken nuggets and french fries over broccoli and brussels sprouts. Most kids prefer a dish of ice cream over an apple or an orange. Most kids would rather drink Coke or Pepsi or Sprite than a glass of milk. Fifty years ago, french fries, ice cream, and soft drinks were special treats to which kids had only occasional access. In the era of His Majesty the Child, kids eat and drink this stuff every day. No wonder more kids are fat. According to the Centers for Disease Control, boys today are four times more likely to be overweight than boys were thirty years ago; girls today are three times more likely to be overweight than girls were thirty years ago.[4] The Surgeon General, Dr. Richard Carmona, was recently quoted as saying that "Generation Y is turning into Generation XL."[5]

A Duke University study of 991 children published in 2003 reported that obese children are much more likely to be disobedient than normal-weight kids are. The authors of this study couldn't say which way the arrow of causality pointed. They speculated that maybe obesity somehow causes oppositional and defiant behavior through some mysterious mechanism involving serotonin or other neurotransmitters.[6] I think that the arrow of causality more likely points the other way. I suspect that kids who are disobedient—kids who insist on having their own way and who are allowed to eat whatever they want, whenever they want—are more likely to become fat.

- *More teenage sex.* Most parents in most cultures throughout most of human history have sought to restrict their children's sexual freedom. In many cultures girls and boys did not mingle until they were of marriageable age. In North America before 1950, parents generally tried to keep their children (especially their daughters) out of sexual relationships prior to marriage. In just thirty years—between 1960 and 1990—a radical change occurred. The sexually active teen, previously the exception, became the norm. Many factors contributed to this change, among them the introduction of reliable oral contraception. But the loss of parental authority was a major contributor. The United States has probably gone further in this direction than any other developed country. That may be one reason why American girls between the ages of eleven and fifteen are *five times* more likely to get pregnant than same-age girls in other countries.[7]

In recent years, some people have argued that increased sexual activity among teenagers isn't a bad thing. Practice makes perfect, these people believe. Sexually experienced teenagers are more likely to have fulfilling sex lives as adults, these people claim.[8] The evidence suggests otherwise. As we discussed in chapter 6, most studies indicate that early sexual intercourse increases the risk of adverse outcomes such as depression and unwanted pregnancy.

- *More teenage criminals.* Teenagers who no longer respect their parents' authority are less likely to respect society's authority. Between 1965 and 1990 the rate of teenage criminal activity increased by more than 300 percent (measured as number of arrests per one thousand teenagers).[9] Before 1965, a teenage criminal was a rarity, usually a boy working at the behest of an adult—often his father or another relative "in the business." Today the teenage criminal is a common cliché on television and in the movies. He or she is more likely to be a gang member, less likely to be working for the family.

The transfer of authority from parent to child has major implications for discipline. If parents today cannot compel their child to go to sleep-away summer camp, how are they going to *discipline* their child?

In the shifting quicksand that is American culture today, the first step, I believe, has to be to take nothing for granted. Don't assume. Be explicit. For example, if you're married, make sure your child understands that *both* parents must "sign off" on major purchases or commitments. If your child says, "But Dad said I could stay home from school to get ready for the party!" remind her that all major decisions need to be approved by both Mom *and* Dad.

Keep family matters in the family. Make sure your child knows that special requests should not be made in public and never in front of neighbors or friends. Suppose your daughter asks you whether she can go to Sheila's party, with Sheila standing right next to her, while you and your daughter both know that your daughter is grounded for the next three days. If you enforce the grounding, you embarrass your daughter in front of her friend. If your daughter's friend Sheila says, "Oh please, just this once?"—now you're in the awkward situation of having to explain your disciplinary decisions to your daughter's *friend*. But if you give way, you've undermined your own authority. Insist that all discipline decisions be discussed only within the family, with no outsiders listening.

Positive Discipline

One pediatrician told me that it's silly for me to write a separate chapter on discipline. "You can't separate discipline from the rest of parenting. If parents have a warm and loving relationship with their child, then the child understands what's expected and *wants* to please the parents," she said. "If that relationship isn't there, then talking about discipline in isolation from everything else is a waste of time." There's a lot of truth to that. Discipline is only one aspect of parenting. If you don't have a well-rounded relationship with your child—if the only time you interact with your child is to discipline her—then no discipline strategy will be effective.

But this pediatrician agreed with me about the importance of parents asserting their authority. The key is to assert your authority not only to discipline your child, but also to introduce your child to new things to do, new hobbies, new adventures. One of your responsibilities as a parent is to broaden your child's horizons. For example, you might insist on a summer camping vacation for the whole family. (It's remarkable how many strong families go on summer camping vacations *as a family*.)

I like to use the phrase *positive discipline* to refer to using your authority in positive ways, either to broaden your child's horizons or to reward good behavior. Let's suppose you are considering a family vacation. You and your spouse are thinking about taking a trip to Mexico, but your three kids vote for Disney World. Two of your kids have never been to Mexico, and the oldest was last there when she was four years old. In this situation, your kids don't get a vote. A well-run family is not a democracy. Asking your child whether she'd like to go to Mexico if she's never been there is like asking her whether she'd like curried chicken when she's never had it before. Her answer isn't based on experience. *Tell* her: "We're going to Mexico, and you're coming along." Don't promise her that she'll love it, because she might not. Your job is not to maximize your child's pleasure, but to broaden her horizons. Those two objectives do not always coincide.

A word of caution. This sort of putting-your-foot-down coercion works reasonably well for most girls under twelve and boys under fourteen. Older kids may be so annoyed at being compelled to go somewhere or do something against their will, they will manage to have a bad time no matter what you do. That's particularly true if you've previously been the typical twenty-first-century parent, which is to say, you usually defer to your child's whims.

Here's the general rule for positive discipline, for girls twelve-and-under, and boys fourteen-and-under: *Don't ask. Tell.* Let's suppose you and your five-year-old are at the local park. Your child is having a great time in the sandbox with some other kids. You look at your watch and realize you'll need to leave soon. *Don't* say: "Honey, it's later than I thought, we need to go soon, okay?" *Do* say: "Hey sweetheart. We're leaving in five minutes. Time to start packing up."

Don't ask. *Tell.* You're not making a request. You're giving an order. Child psychologist Dana Chidekel points out that adding "Okay?" to the end of your sentence leads your child to perceive your statement as a question, a question to which your child has the right to answer "No."[10] If your child says "No" and continues to play in the sandbox, you're at a disadvantage. If you now put your foot down and insist on leaving, your child will feel deceived. You were only pretending to ask a question, which wasn't a question at all. You would have been better off being firm in the first place.

Chidekel says that many parents today are afraid their children won't like them if they are firm or "strict." Some parents even resort to bribing their children, often without fully realizing what they're doing. In the example just given, such a parent might say, "Let's go get a Happy Meal at McDonald's" as a way of prying the child away from the sandbox. Don't use the promise of food as a bribe. If you find yourself bribing your child to do something, stop.

Dr. Chidekel also discourages parents from explaining their commands. *Don't* say: "If you don't turn off the TV, you won't get your homework done." Dr. Chidekel points out that this statement doesn't actually tell a child to do anything. It's just information, which most children feel free to disregard. *Do* say: "Turn off the TV and do your homework. Now."

Don't bail out your child. Let's suppose you reminded your

twelve-year-old son two days earlier that he should stop playing video games and work on his report for school. He ignored you. Now his report is due the next morning and he hasn't finished it. The teacher has said that late reports won't be accepted. If your son doesn't turn something in, he could get a bad grade in the course. He asks you for help.

I've heard from too many parents who've found themselves in this situation. You'd be surprised how many will stay up all night and write the report themselves. Usually parents download something from the Internet and try to customize it to the assignment.

These parents know they're doing the wrong thing. But they rationalize it. "Just this once," they say. Fat chance. By bailing your child out of this difficult situation, you're guaranteeing that it will happen again. Hard as it is for many of today's parents, here's what you have to say: "When you see your teacher tomorrow, ask her if she'll give you an extension." Your son may insist that the teacher won't give an extension, and maybe she won't. But your son will learn a valuable lesson by going through the painful process of requesting it.

One area of increasing difficulty and concern for parents to-day involves the use of personal computers. I've seen many middle-class parents purchase a computer just for their child's use at home. Understandably enough, they install the computer in the child's bedroom. A few months later they realize their mistake, but it's too late.

Installing a computer in the bedroom of a child or teenager is asking for trouble. You can't possibly police the sites your child is visiting.* You can't see what your child is doing on the computer. One couple I know purchased software that allows them to keep a record of all their daughter's instant messaging. They

---

*If you think Web safety programs protect your child from pornographic or violent sites, you haven't spent much time on the Web. The purveyors of these sites have figured out many ways to defeat those programs, such as inserting hyphens into words that the safety programs look for (s-e-x), misspelling words (sexx), or replacing letters with other characters (g!rls).

brought me in a long printout of their daughter's instant messaging, including all sorts of incriminating statements about buying and using drugs. "What do we do now?" they asked. The instant messaging transcripts seemed to prove that their daughter was using drugs, something their daughter vehemently denied when they asked her about drug use. The parents don't want to show their daughter the evidence—the transcripts—because they don't want to tell their daughter that they've been surreptitiously monitoring her instant messaging. That's a tough situation. If you're going to use such software, tell your child *in advance* that you are doing so.

If you must buy your child her own computer, put the computer in the family room—or the basement, rec room, study or work area, even the breakfast nook—some sort of "public" area where your child knows you can look over her shoulder at any moment. Just the knowledge that you *can* look over her shoulder without warning will make it easier for her to follow your rules.

"But shouldn't I respect my child's privacy?" some parents ask. Of course you should. You should always knock on the door before entering your teenager's bedroom, for instance. But you also need to know what your child is doing online. The only way to reconcile the necessity of privacy with the need to monitor your child's Internet use is to have the computer in a shared family space, such as the family room or the basement. And of course, if the computer is for the use of more than one child or the whole family, then it needs to be in a shared space.

Your child may object to this arrangement. She may point out that there's plenty of room in her bedroom. Why crowd the family room with a computer when she's got space in her bedroom? It's a reasonable question. Don't hem and haw in your response. Be straight with her. Tell her that you need to be able to see what she's doing online, and you don't want to invade her privacy in the bedroom. And remind her that you have the right to monitor her e-mails and her instant messaging.

For somewhat similar reasons, there should be no television set in your child's bedroom. Your child's bedroom should be for sleeping or reading or studying. Putting a TV set in the room creates a distraction. I hear about so many kids who stay up late watching TV or playing video games, and then they're too sleepy for school the next morning. They trudge off to the bus like zombies, barely half awake. Their parents get tired of yelling at them every night: "Turn off the TV! It's past your bedtime!" The simplest solution is not to have a TV in the bedroom in the first place.

Some parents respond that they (the parents) want to watch a news program or a professional sports game while their daughter wants to watch *Gilmore Girls*. That's why they need a TV set for their child. All right. I won't quarrel with having two television sets in the home (although I know of many families who do fine with just one). But the second TV should be in a "public" family space such as the basement or the kitchen, not in a child's bedroom.

And finally, one more rule: Keep your own secrets secret. As I said in the last chapter, your children do not need to hear about how you used marijuana in high school and that's how you know how dangerous smoking pot can be. Sharing such stories—regardless of their educational value—erodes your authority and blurs the distinction between who's the parent and who's the child.

Some single parents are especially vulnerable to the temptation to use their children, especially their teenage children, as willy-nilly confidants. That's a mistake, says Paul Kropp, author of *I'll Be the Parent, You Be the Child*. As adults, we each have our own emotional needs: to confess our wrongdoings perhaps, or to get advice, or maybe just to share a juicy piece of gossip. But you're an adult. Find another adult to satisfy your needs. "Parents who are looking for confession, psychotherapy or a best friend should approach the appropriate people in an adult way," Kropp says. "Kneel, pay the fee or buy the beer. Leave your kids alone."[11]

Look in the Mirror, Again

Amy Denison was fifteen years old when her dad caught her creeping back home at 6 A.M. on a Sunday morning.

The night before, she had changed into her pajamas, gone to kiss her father good night, and innocently asked him, "Are you staying up all night long? It's late!"

"You're right," her father, Sam, said. "I'm going to bed."

Amy went back to her bedroom and closed the door. It was just about 11 P.M., Saturday night. She took off her pajamas and put on her new outfit: short black skirt, black pantyhose, white silk blouse. A quick check of her e-mail showed a new message, the one she was waiting for. She punched in a number on her cell phone. "It's me," she whispered into the phone. "I'm ready. My dad's just gone to bed. Pick me up at the corner in five minutes."

Amy's parents had allowed her to have a lock installed on her door six months earlier. "I need some privacy," she had said, and it was true that her younger brother liked to barge into her room unannounced. Now she turned the key in the lock, from the inside. If her parents happened to check the door, they'd find it locked, and they wouldn't knock because they would assume she was sleeping. She opened the window, swung her stockinged legs up and over, and stepped out onto the dewy grass in her tennis shoes (she was carrying her high heels). As silent as a cat.

At the corner, her boyfriend—nineteen years old—picked her up and drove her to the apartment in Germantown where students from the community college were having a party. For a fifteen-year-old girl, this was the epitome of cool: to party with the college kids. And they accepted her completely. She had a great time. All the young men wanted to meet the hot new girl. She was the dancing queen.

Amy's father would never have known anything about it if the family's dog hadn't whined to go out at 6 A.M. the following morning: precisely when Amy happened to be tiptoeing across the backyard to her still-open window.

Sam rubbed his eyes as he opened the back door to let the dog out. Someone was walking across the backyard—and it looked like Amy, but Amy was in bed asleep, right?

"Amy? Is that you?" he called out.

Two days later Sam was in my office. "I don't understand what happened next," he said. "She didn't apologize. She didn't explain. I got so angry I felt that I could explode. I felt this burning in my chest. Like my insides were on fire. But instead of yelling at her, I just started to cry. I felt so stupid. A grown man crying. 'How could you do this to me?' I said. I could smell the beer on her. She claimed she hadn't drunk anything, that one of the boys poured a can over her hair. 'What am I supposed to tell your mother?' was all I could say to her." Sam's wife, Lynn, was away on a business trip.

"Did you punish her?" I asked.

"I thought about it," Sam said. "I wasn't sure what to do."

What should I tell this man, I wondered. Perhaps I should suggest that he take away Amy's cell phone, or remove the lock from her bedroom door so he could look in on Amy without waking her up. Maybe he could move her bedroom upstairs (visions of Rapunzel flickered in my head).

But a second look at Sam made me hesitate. Something wasn't right. "You don't look so hot," I said. "How are you feeling?"

"To be honest? I feel like crap," Sam answered. "My stomach's in knots, I still have this pressure in my chest, all my muscles ache. I feel like I could throw up."

"You know what?" I said. "Let's start by doing some tests on *you*." I didn't suggest anything regarding Amy. Not that day, anyhow.

Two days later I was looking at Sam's blood test results. His chemistry profile showed a pattern of abnormalities suggesting damage to the liver caused by chronic alcohol abuse. I picked up the phone to call Sam.

In retrospect, Amy's behavior made perfect sense. Mom's behavior made sense, too. Mom was coping with her husband's alcoholism by taking every opportunity to do business out of town. Lynn knew that you can't make someone stop drinking if they don't want to stop. She didn't see the point in hanging around and fighting with Sam every day about his drinking. But she didn't want a divorce, either. So the life of a traveling businesswoman—with plenty of money in salary and commissions—seemed to be the best bargain she could make.

This example shows, incidentally, how far astray counselors and pediatricians can go when they focus only on the child without first really knowing the family. You might spend months working with Amy in this situation before she'd share her concerns about her father's drinking, and even then you wouldn't *know* he was alcoholic; you'd only have her allegations.

I'm happy to report that Sam decided to quit drinking the day I called to tell him about his liver damage. Better late than never. He hasn't had a drink since, and that was almost three years ago. His wife, Lynn, requested and received a "sideways promotion" with her company, so she could spend more time at home. And Sam removed the lock from Amy's door.

The first step in disciplining your child is to discipline yourself. I'm not talking about analyzing every imperfection. For the sake of your children, you can't allow yourself to be paralyzed by your awareness of your own shortcomings.

But: if you have a major, glaring problem in your life—alcoholism and drug addiction being the most obvious examples—then there's no way you can effectively discipline your child. "Do as I say, not as I do" just won't wash. You can't discipline your child if you can't discipline yourself.

The Punishment Must Fit the Crime— and the Gender, and the Age

We've talked about "positive discipline": encouraging your child to do the right thing by modeling good behavior, by rewarding good behavior, and by gently discouraging bad behavior. What happens when your child does something that requires sterner measures? What do you do when your daughter lies to you about her report card? What do you do when your son intentionally destroys your daughter's favorite toy? What do you do if you catch your daughter sneaking home from a party she wasn't supposed to be at? In those circumstances, you have to resort to *punishment.*

Claire Hughes, Kirby Deater-Deckard, and Alexandra Cutting recently published what may be one of the most important studies ever done of sex differences with regard to punishment.[12] First, they analyzed parents' disciplinary styles—from strict and authoritative at one end of the scale all the way to gentle and permissive at the other—using a combination of interviews with the parents, ratings of disciplinary styles by independent observers, and coding of behavior derived from actual videotapes made in the homes of the 125 families studied. Then they looked to see whether there was any correlation between the parents' disciplinary style and the child's social skills, after controlling for the effects of socioeconomic status, IQ, and parents' occupations.

The results were completely different depending on whether the child was a girl or a boy. Boys responded well to strict and authoritarian discipline, which included an occasional spanking. The stricter the parents' disciplinary style, the better the boy's social-cognitive skills (of course, none of these families used *abusive* punishment). Remarkably, a "warm and fuzzy" parenting approach appeared to *retard* boys' acquisition of social-cognitive skills. For girls, the results were just the opposite. The "warm and fuzzy" approach promoted social skills whereas strict discipline had a slight negative effect on girls' social development.

You might imagine that parents of boys were generally stricter than parents of girls. In fact, the researchers found a significant tendency in the opposite direction: parents tended to be stricter with girls than they were with boys. Many parents today have been so misled by parenting misinformation—particularly (in my judgment) by the push to enhance the "emotional literacy" of boys—that they're doing exactly the wrong thing: they're being strict with their daughters and gentle and permissive with their sons.

Everybody agrees that the punishment should be appropriate to whatever the child has done wrong. Everybody knows that the right punishment for a three-year-old is different from the right punishment for a fourteen-year-old. What many parents don't realize, however, is that the right punishment depends on the child's *gender* as much as it does on the child's age.

Induction

Ask traditional authorities on parenting to name the number one disciplinary method they recommend for children ages three to sixteen, and they'll give you some variation on a technique known as *induction*. "Induction" means helping your child to imagine herself in the position of the person being harmed. "How would you feel if someone did that to you?" is the prototypical inductive question. But induction is not the best method for all children.

Child psychologists Christina Sinisi and Mark Barnett asked children of different ages which kind of discipline they thought works best—not just to punish a single occurrence of the behavior, but to discourage the same behavior in the future even when parents are not around and not aware of the misbehavior. According to the children themselves, induction works best for girls while power assertion works best for boys.[13] ("Power assertion" means physical restraint, corporal punishment, or the threat of same.) The children also said that their mothers were more likely to use induction, regardless of the child's offense, while their fathers were more likely to use power assertion. The children approved of induction as a disciplinary technique when a girl was the transgressor, but were more likely to favor power assertion when the boy was the transgressor.

What does this study tell us? Children themselves recognize that different disciplinary techniques work differently, depending on whether the child is a girl or a boy. Children themselves believe that induction works better for girls and power assertion works better for boys. But what I find equally interesting is the children's recognition that parents lack this fundamental insight. Instead, the children observe (correctly) that Mommies tend to use induction for both daughters and sons while Daddies tend to use power assertion for both daughters and sons. In other words, parents use the technique that feels right to *them*, regardless of whether it's the right choice for their child.

Child psychologist Nicole Horton and her associates at Auburn recently reported on gender differences in the way children respond to induction. They found that girls were sympathetic to parent-oriented induction. For example, suppose your child gets in trouble at school for bullying another child. You might say to your child: "Just think how embarrassed and ashamed I felt, when the teacher told me that my child is the class bully." In technical jargon, your comment is an example of "parent-oriented induction." Dr. Horton found that parent-oriented induction works well for girls. Girls respond to that kind of comment. Girls consider it fair for the parent to make such comments. Girls can imagine themselves in their parent's position, feeling ashamed.

Boys respond differently. For boys, parent-oriented induction is a waste of time. "If you feel bad, that's *your* problem," I once heard a boy tell his mother. *Victim*-oriented induction is a more effective technique for boys. For example, in the case of the parent who's just been told that their son is a bully, the parent might say to the son, "How would you like it if a bigger boy came along and slapped *you* around?" That kind of approach works modestly well in fifth- and sixth-grade boys, Dr. Horton found. For younger boys, inductive techniques may not work. After all, induction begins with some variation on the sentence "How would you feel if . . ." And as we saw in chapter 5, any sentence that begins "How would you feel if . . ." is a nonstarter with young boys. In any case, *parent*-oriented induction scores a big zero with boys at all ages.[14]

Discipline Begins in the Nursery

Most of the discipline strategies we've considered so far involve verbal communication. What about the infant? How do you discipline a child who doesn't understand language?

Maggie was a first-time mom. I had just finished examining her baby Justin for his four-month checkup. "You've got a beautiful baby boy," I told her. "Justin looks great. But *you're* looking exhausted, if you don't mind my saying so." One virtue of family practice is that I know Maggie as well as I know her baby. Maggie wasn't looking right. "What's up?"

"I just don't feel that I have any *time*," Maggie said. "I don't know how mothers manage with more than one child. I spend half my day breastfeeding. I finish breastfeeding, and it seems I barely have time to get dressed before Justin wants to breastfeed again."

"I don't understand," I said. "Breastfeeding shouldn't take more than fifteen minutes, twenty minutes max. Remember we discussed this in the hospital?"

"I remember that's what you told me," Maggie said. "But Justin just won't stand for that. If I try to stop after twenty minutes, he cries and cries until I let him latch on again."

Justin just won't stand for that. Justin is four months old. "Whoa," I said. "Wait a minute, Mom. You're doing one breast per feeding, right?"*

Maggie nodded.

"All right. So you breastfeed for fifteen, maybe twenty min-

---

*When the breast is full, the first milk to come out is thin and watery. That's the appetizer. Then comes the regular breast milk, the entrée. Finally, when the breast is nearly empty, comes the high-fat hindmilk. That's dessert. The hindmilk satisfies baby and puts baby to sleep. But, if Mom switches breasts during a feeding, baby and Mom have to start all over with the second breast. The result is that baby consumes more and is less satisfied. One breast per feeding, that's the rule.

utes, and then you're done," I said. "You gently pull Justin off the breast. What happens next?"

"He smacks his lips, but then, after a moment, he starts to cry. He's not satisfied," said Maggie, looking as though she were about to cry herself. "So I let him latch on again."

I shook my head. "Look. A four-month-old baby has three main occupations. Eat, sleep, and poop. Eating is a lot more fun than sleeping or pooping. If you leave it up to your baby, he'll be at your breast all day long. He's not really eating. He can't be, because the breast is empty, right?"

Maggie nodded.

"So he just enjoys being close to you and being latched on," I said.

"What's wrong with that?" Maggie asked.

"Nothing, except that you have other things to do in your life besides breastfeed," I said. "You're not a milk cow. You're Mom. You're the boss. He's the baby. When the twenty minutes are up, stop. Gently pull Justin off the breast, burp him, and put him in the crib."

"But he'll cry."

"Of course he'll cry, because he'd rather be latched on to you than lying in his crib. But after three minutes, he'll fall asleep. Guaranteed."

"Guaranteed?" Maggie asked, doubtful.

"Well, maybe after five minutes. Ten tops."

When I saw Justin for his six-month checkup, he still looked great, and Maggie looked better as well. "I took your advice," she said. "About the breastfeeding. It was hard at first, because I hate to hear my baby cry. But after three days, the crying stopped. Like magic. It was as though he suddenly understood that when we're done, we're done. It doesn't seem to bother him anymore. He's more interested in playing with his toys now."

In your child's first year, you must communicate one basic fact to your baby: you are the parent. You are the boss. If you can't be firm about breastfeeding with your four-month-old, you're laying the groundwork for endless arguments about bedtime with your eight-year-old and quarrels about curfews and "home by midnight" rules with your fifteen-year-old. But if your baby understands that your rules don't change—and babies are amazingly good at figuring out this sort of thing—then that comprehension forms a solid foundation for discipline throughout childhood and adolescence.

The same rules apply for meals. At six months of age, it's time to start offering solid foods. Bananas, apples, peas, and carrots. Mashed peas and carrots may not appeal to you, but they are a good choice for your baby. How you feed your child is one of the most basic discipline issues for children ages six months to two years.

Babies double their birth weight between birth and four months of age. They triple their birth weight by one year of age. The average baby weighs about seven pounds at birth; the average twelve-month-old weighs about twenty-two pounds. Never again in your child's life will she need to increase her lean body tissue at such a rate: never again will she have to triple her weight in one year. Which means: never again will she eat the way she did during that first year.

Parents who don't understand this often are concerned when their one-year-old simply stops eating. "She hasn't eaten *anything* in three days except for a grape and a cracker. And she only ate half the cracker!" one concerned mom wailed. "She must be sick."

"She looks fine to me," I told Mom.

"But she's not eating."

I reminded this mom that her child, like all healthy one-year-olds, will not starve herself. "When she's hungry, she'll eat. Don't bribe her to eat with cheese and chicken nuggets. When she's hungry, she'll be happy to eat the fruit and vegetables you offer her." I see toddlers who seem to be living on potato chips, french fries, and candy. Their parents have lost authority over what their kids are eating, to the detriment of the children—both nutritionally and with regard to discipline.

Lay down the rules and stick to them. You know the rules. If you didn't eat your supper, you don't get any snacks later. No filling up with chippies at four in the afternoon, because then you won't have any appetite for vegetables at dinner. Stick by these rules with your one-year-old and your two-year-old, and life will be easier later on.

Nuts and Bolts

At each age, there are certain disciplinary techniques that work best for each sex. Let's go through some of those techniques for girls and boys, starting with toddlers and moving up.

Girls ages two through four. Verbal correction means that you gently but firmly correct your child. "We don't slap" is the right thing to say when your daughter tries to slap her playmate. If that doesn't work, you move on to inductive techniques. In this age group, stick with victim-oriented induction. Help your daughter think about how she would feel if she were the victim of the misbehavior. "How would you feel if someone slapped *you*?" For girls in this age group, you may need to pose the inductive question several times in different ways. "Has anyone ever slapped you? How did that feel? Would you like it if they slapped you again?"

If verbal correction and induction have not been effective, then it's time for a time-out. Remember that in order for a time-out to be effective, it must follow the bad behavior *immediately.* Let's imagine that your four-year-old daughter is misbehaving in a restaurant. Let's suppose that she doesn't like her meal and dumps it all over the floor. It won't do any good to put her in time-out when you get back home one hour later. You must *immediately* remove her from the restaurant, take her to the car, put her in the child seat and close the door, with you standing outside. Stay there for four minutes. (The general rule for time-outs is: one minute for each year of age. Four-year-olds get four-minute time-outs.) Then open the door and ask her to apologize to you for her misbehavior. If anyone else in the restaurant was on the receiving end of her bad behavior, she should return to the restaurant and apologize to them as well.

Many parents don't really understand the concept of time-out. One mom was telling me how her three-year-old son had gotten into the "bad habit" of slapping other children. I asked her how she responded when he slapped another child. She told me she uses time-outs.

Tell me what the time-out is like, I asked. What do you do?

"When he slaps another child," she explained, "I hold him in my arms for three minutes, and I massage his arms and legs, and I whisper to him, 'We don't do that. We don't slap.' " I reminded Mom that her son may actually *enjoy* this contact with his mother, and that in any case what Mom is doing doesn't qualify as a time-out. The essential ingredient of time-out is *isolation*: separation from parents and from other children. Put your child in a room, alone, and close the door.

One two-year-old I knew threw a full-blown tantrum when his parents put him in his room and closed the door. His parents wanted to punish him, so he was going to punish *them* by reducing his room to a shambles. So, Mom and Dad started using a car seat *indoors* for their two-year-old's time-outs. That puts the child in a safe, secure place. You set the timer for two minutes, and you know that when you return in two minutes, both the child and the bedroom will be reasonably intact. (If you're going to use that method, be sure that the car seat you use for this purpose looks, feels, and *smells* different from the car seat in your car: otherwise, your child may misunderstand a routine trip in the car and think that she or he is being punished.)

Boys ages two through five. One big gender difference in this age group is that induction *doesn't* work well for boys this age. The moral understanding of the typical four-year-old girl is well beyond that of the typical four-year-old boy. Inductive reasoning works reasonably well with most girls in that age group. "How would you feel if someone slapped *you*?" Once you get a girl that age to imagine being on the receiving end of a slap, then she'll be less likely to slap in the future. The same technique doesn't work well on the typical four-year-old boy. You say, "How would you feel if someone slapped *you*?" and the boy—if he's confident that he can say what he thinks instead of what you want to hear—might answer, "I'd slap him back! Then I'd punch him! Then I'd kick him! Then I'd *sit* on him! Then I'd *choke* him!" Psychologist Martin Hoffman and others have observed that boys this young often just don't understand inductive disciplinary techniques.[15] As I just mentioned, the question "How would you *feel* if . . ." doesn't work well for boys. They reinterpret that question as "What would you *do* if . . ." and they may give an answer very different from the one you had in mind.

With a four-year-old boy, start with simple verbal correction as you would with a girl. "We don't slap." If that doesn't work, go directly to an enforced time-out. If your son's bad behavior persists, you can lengthen the time-out—or, if you're comfortable with spanking, then a spanking is appropriate. Remember: spanking means two swats on the behind, and that's all. Never spank a boy in anger. Never spank a girl, period.[16]

Girls four through eight, boys five through ten. In this age group, you have all the techniques available that you used for younger children, plus a new one: withdrawal of privileges. Children have an inalienable right to food, clothing, shelter, and medical care. Everything else is a privilege. Toys, video games, using the phone, watching TV, shopping, having friends over . . . those are all privileges that need to be earned.

Most parents understand how to use withdrawal of privileges. If your seven-year-old daughter has just taken her brother's favorite toy and thrown it into a pond, it doesn't make sense to let her go to a friend's birthday party later the same day. Going to a birthday party is a privilege, not a right. Likewise, if your six-year-old son has—for the third time—kicked another child at school, it's reasonable to say "No Game Boy for the next three days."

Sticking to it can be tough. It's easy to say "No Game Boy for three days," but two days later, after your son has been a little angel for two whole days, it feels heartless to insist on another day of deprivation. Likewise, when the mother of your daughter's friend calls to ask whether your daughter is coming over, it's hard to say "No, she's not coming, because she is grounded." Many parents err in imposing too harsh a withdrawal of privileges; then they err again by reversing their own decision a day or two later. Once pronounced, your judgment for a child in this age group must be *final*. Even if you secretly recognize that perhaps your judgment was too harsh, you should NOT change or reverse it. Doing so opens the floodgates to a deluge of *negotiation*.

Negotiating disciplinary matters with a child in this age group (girls four through eight, boys five through ten) is almost never appropriate. Negotiation sends the message that nothing you say is final, that everything can be bargained for. Once you open the door to negotiation, it's hard to close that door. What's for dinner, when is it time for bed, how many hours of TV can be watched on a school night . . . all becomes open to negotiation. Negotiation undermines the fundamental idea that the rules of good behavior are fixed. Negotiation subverts the process of *moral internalization*, the process by which your children internalize your sense of right and wrong and affirm it as their own. Remember that what's right for you as an adult may not be right for your child. As an adult, you expect the right to negotiate, so you may unthinkingly extend the same right to your child. Don't.

Girls nine through fourteen. Time-out no longer works in this age group. And your other disciplinary techniques—verbal correction, induction, and withdrawal of privileges—don't work as well as they used to, either. This is the age of *Reviving Ophelia* and *Queen Bees & Wannabes*. Cliques and peer pressure reach their peak importance for girls in this age group.

For girls in the nine-to-fourteen age group—more so than for girls in any other age group, and more so than for boys at any age—behavior that you perceive as aberrant may be normative for your daughter's peer group. If you find out that your twelve-year-old daughter is smoking even though you have strictly forbidden her to smoke, you need to know more about her social group. Are all of the girls in her clique smoking? If they are, then *none* of the disciplinary techniques we discussed will be effective. You'll succeed only in driving a wedge between you and your daughter. Your daughter will be convinced that you just don't understand . . . and she'll be right.

What can you do if your daughter's behavior is motivated by the bad behavior of the other girls in her clique? The best solution, and maybe the only one that really works, is to remove her from the clique. It's the best solution, but it's also the most difficult. You can't ask your daughter not to affiliate with other girls. So you can't just ban her from the group she's in. You have to find an alternative group she can join. As we discussed earlier, that might mean signing her up for a dance class, or riding lessons, or some other activity with other girls her age. Changing schools is an extreme measure, but if it's the last resort you may have to think about it.

Verbal correction, induction, and withdrawal of privileges all remain in your discipline repertoire for girls in this age group. But you've got to know your daughter and her situation. Is she the "queen bee"? Are you asking her to do something that jeopardizes her status in the clique? Be creative. Let's suppose that your twelve-year-old daughter wants to go to a rock concert with three other girls, let's call them Ashley and Amanda and Laura. The concert is at the football stadium. The girls plan to take public transportation. Four twelve-year-old girls with no adult escort, at a huge stadium, after dark. Not a good idea. But, if you just tell your daughter that she's not allowed to go, you may compromise her standing in the eyes of her friends. That erodes your political capital, making it harder for you to exert your authority the next time something comes up.

Instead, call the parents of the other girls. See whether you can agree on a solution. Then all of you can present a united front to your daughters. You can say, "I talked with Ashley's mom, and with Amanda's dad, and also with Laura's parents. Ms. Fielding and Mr. Jefferson both volunteered to escort you girls to the concert. All of us parents agreed on these two options: the four of you can go to the concert with Ms. Fielding and Mr. Jefferson, or you can stay at home." In this age group you can't discipline in isolation from other parents. You may need to be calling those other parents almost as often as your daughter is calling their daughters.

Boys ten through fifteen. With older boys you need to make two changes in your disciplinary strategies. First, whatever your beliefs about corporal punishment for younger boys, corporal punishment is no longer an option for boys in this age group. To begin with, it's not particularly effective for boys this age. A simple swat on the behind just doesn't hurt a thirteen-year-old boy that much, and more severe corporal punishment is not acceptable. And, it's not wise to try to spank someone who may be stronger than you are and who can run faster than you can. More fundamentally, corporal punishment sends a very different message to a thirteen-year-old than it does to a seven-year-old, a message that can easily backfire. Two spanks on the rear end tell a seven-year-old boy that he did something very wrong and he better not do it again. Spanking a thirteen-year-old boy sends a different message, essentially saying, "You're just a little boy, you need to be treated like a little boy, so I'm going to spank you to remind you that you're still just a little boy." A thirteen-year-old boy wants you to see him as more than a little boy. Spanking him may motivate him to prove to you how grown-up he is. He may think, on some subconscious level, that if he comes home smoking a cigarette—or (God forbid) if he impregnates a girl—*then* you'll see how wrong you were to think of him as a little kid.

The second change in your disciplinary armory for boys in this age group is that you *can* begin to use induction—but with a twist. Instead of asking "How would you *feel* if . . . ," ask "What would you *do* if . . ." Let's suppose that your fourteen-year-old son deliberately threw his sister's favorite magazine out in the garbage. *Don't* say: "What you did made your sister and me feel sad." Boys this age seldom connect with discussions of other people's feelings. *Do* say: "What would you do if your sister took your favorite PlayStation game and destroyed the disk?" That question can lead your son to recognize the appropriateness of the punishment, which in this case would probably involve a withdrawal of privileges.

Girls fourteen through eighteen, boys fifteen through eighteen. If you've been a pushover parent for the first fourteen years of your child's life, now comes the really fun part. You will reap the whirlwind. Even for parents who have been consistent and firm since Day One, this age group presents new challenges. Our culture today—as manifested in TV commercials, popular movies, and teen magazines—encourages teenagers to consider themselves as autonomous players in society. Obeying parents is the height of uncool. That means it's more difficult than ever for you to assert your authority with kids in this age group. It also becomes harder to work with other parents, because there is no societal consensus about what kids in this age group should and should not be permitted to do. To continue with the example above, most parents would agree that four twelve-year-old girls shouldn't be out by themselves at a rock concert after midnight. But many parents would see nothing wrong with four sixteen-year-old girls being out by themselves after midnight.

Assert your authority. You are the parent. You are not your fifteen-year-old's best friend. At times your kid may feel that you are not her friend at all. That's fine. If your fifteen-year-old daughter proposes taking a weekend trip to a rock concert fifty miles away with three twenty-year-old college students whom you've never met, the answer is No.

Pick your battles. If your daughter wants to get her nose or belly button pierced, think twice before you object. This particular battle may not be the right battle to fight. You've got to save what influence you have. Issues involving your teenager's safety take priority over issues of dress, piercing, tattoos, music, and so on. And, letting her have her way with regard to piercing and other fashion expressions gives you more credibility when you *do* put your foot down.

Isn't Spanking a Form of Child Abuse?

In our discussion of appropriate discipline for boys ages two through ten, I included spanking as one method of discipline, to be considered when inductive techniques and time-outs either are not appropriate or just aren't working. I don't encourage spanking, but I don't necessarily oppose it in families where both parents consider it appropriate. For some boys, especially, parents tell me that spanking was an essential "tool" to have available. They may have spanked their son only twice in his entire life, but those two spankings made a huge difference (or so they tell me).

Some people go ballistic at this point. Even some experts regard spanking as a form of child abuse. Others claim that children who are spanked are more likely to be maladjusted as teenagers or adults. Spank your son and he'll grow up to be a criminal. Alice Miller attracted attention for her book *For Your Own Good*, in which she seriously claimed that Adolf Hitler became the evil monster he was because his father spanked him.[17]

Such far-fetched claims aren't supported by the available data.[18] About ten years ago, Christine Johnson and Ronald Simons published an ambitious study of corporal punishment.[19] At the beginning of the study, they determined which families used corporal punishment. But they also ascertained the *level of parental involvement* in the child's life. Then they came back three years later to see how the kids were doing. These researchers found that the key determinant of good behavior was the degree of parental involvement in the child's life (as measured at the beginning of the study). The kids of highly involved parents turned out fine. The kids of parents who were uninvolved had problems. In this particular study, parents who used harsh corporal punishment were more likely to be uninvolved.

If the only time a father spends with his son is when he's spanking him, then that boy is not going to do well. But the boy's bad outcome doesn't appear to be a result of the spanking. It's a result of the father's lack of involvement.

I tell parents to keep the "seven-to-one" rule in mind. Think of the time you spend with your child and divide it into "fun time" and "discipline time." Fun time includes all the fun things you do with your child: playing games, shopping (for girls), wrestling (for boys), going on a ride at the amusement park, seeing a movie together, and so on. The ratio of fun time to discipline time should be way above 1:1. I tell parents to shoot for a 7:1 ratio. If you're spending more time disciplining your child than you're spending enjoying life with your child, then you need to spend more time having fun with your child.

Regarding the idea that children who are spanked are more likely to be criminals as adults: if you test this idea across cultures and across eras, it doesn't hold up. As Harvard psychologist Jerome Kagan has observed, the standard of child-raising in Puritan New England included very harsh punishments for children. Nevertheless, these children usually grew up to be model citizens who believed in the value of corporal punishment and applied it to their own children. The level of crime in Puritan New England was extremely low, Kagan observes, and rose over time as parents moved away from using corporal punishment.[20]

One sometimes hears the claim that "it's a slippery slope from spanking to child abuse." Once again, though, available research doesn't support this claim. Parents who love their young son and spank him only occasionally when he does something really outrageous are at no more risk of becoming child abusers than are parents who never spank. There is certainly no evidence that actual child abuse is less prevalent in countries like Austria, Denmark, Sweden, and Cyprus, where parents are forbidden by law from spanking their children, than it is in South Africa and Barbados, where spanking is common and even administered regularly in public schools, with full approval of the parents. Sweden, for example, passed a law in 1979 making it illegal for parents to spank their children. But a Swedish government study conducted in 1995 showed a fourfold *increase* in child abuse in the years following passage of the law.[21] Of course, that doesn't mean that the law somehow caused an increase in child abuse. But it certainly provides no support for the theory that outlawing spanking will decrease child abuse.

Psychologist Diana Baumrind has pointed out that there is a fundamental and qualitative distinction between parents who love their child and occasionally spank him when he does something outrageous versus abusive parents who frequently beat their child in anger.[22] And there is no evidence that the one type of parent is likely to turn into the other.

Spare the Rod, Sedate the Child?

Forty years ago, American kids who misbehaved were likely to be punished. Today parents are much less likely to exert any kind of strict and consistent discipline. So what happens to modern kids who misbehave—to the seven-year-old boy who bites his mother, for example, and who would have been spanked in the "olden days"? There's growing evidence that these kids are instead being put on calming behavior-modifying drugs such as Ritalin, Adderall, Concerta, and Metadate.

According to the United States Drug Enforcement Administration, the amount of methylphenidate (marketed under the names Ritalin, Metadate, and Concerta) prescribed in the United States increased by over 500 percent between 1991 and 1999, while the amount of amphetamines (primarily Adderall) prescribed during the same interval increased by over 2000 percent.[23] In other words, American doctors wrote *twenty times* more prescriptions for amphetamines for children in 1999 than they did in 1991. The Colorado State School Board has approved a resolution officially advising teachers statewide not to recommend or suggest psychotropic medications for any student.[24]

The board concluded that "psychiatric prescription drugs have been utilized for what are essentially problems of discipline."[25] According to a nationwide survey conducted in 2004, American families now spend more on drugs to control children's behavior than on any other class of medication—more than on the previous leaders, antibiotics and asthma medications.[26]

Ritalin, Adderall, and Concerta aren't the only medications being dispensed to children much more readily than ever before. As we discussed earlier, antidepressants such as Prozac are also being prescribed for young children at a rate more than three times higher than was the case ten years ago. Dr. Julie Zito has studied doctors' prescribing of these medications for children. She recently noted that the increase in the prescribing of antidepressants seems to have followed the increase in the prescribing of stimulant behavior-modifying medications such as Adderall, Concerta, and Ritalin. She asked, "What's the chicken and what's the egg? Is the depression following the use of the stimulant?"[27] Among American kids age ten through fourteen, roughly one kid in seven is now on a medication to control behavior.[28]

Who benefits when children are drugged in this way? I suppose that parents and the teachers may benefit, perhaps, in some sense, in the short term, since the kid is easier to control. The drug companies certainly benefit, as well. But does the child benefit? "Other than zonking you, we don't know that behavioral management by drug control is the [best] way [for a child] to learn to behave properly," said Dr. Zito. "If we are using drugs to control behavior, that doesn't change the underlying problem" of a child who hasn't internalized society's rules for how to behave.[29]

The chickens are coming home to roost. The four-year-old boy who is not disciplined firmly for persistent misbehavior is likely to become the eight-year-old boy whose parents—frustrated and overwhelmed by their child's acting up at home and at school—take him to the doctor with a desperate question: "What's wrong with my child? And what can we do to make it better?" The result of that visit is often a prescription for psychiatric medication. In a bizarre turn of events, it's become politically incorrect to spank your child, but it's okay to drug him.

Something fundamental has changed. There has been a transformation in the way we think about children. Throughout most of the history of Western civilization, parents have assumed that children are naturally inclined to misbehavior. This assumption is manifest in the Calvinist doctrine of total depravity, in the Catholic doctrine of Original Sin, and in the Jewish belief in the *yetzer hara*, the evil impulse. The role of parents—it was thought—was to guide kids along the straight and narrow. Without strict parenting, children were innately inclined to misbehave. Or such was the common belief.

Today the dominant ethos reflects a 1960s-era flower-child belief in the innate goodness of children. Children are born good, according to this worldview. If kids behave badly, it must be because of

- bad parenting
- poor nutrition
- lack of prenatal care for Mom when she was pregnant
- environmental toxins
- attention deficit disorder
- video games (or violent television shows, or movies, or music)

Take your pick.

Even the language used by parents and professionals to describe the disobedient child has changed. Fifty years ago a teenage boy who stole from other kids was a thief. Today he's a boy exhibiting "adolescent conduct disorder with maladaptive social functioning." The change in language results from a change in the way people think about juvenile misbehavior. Fifty years ago, bad behavior was considered a *disciplinary* problem. If you misbehaved, you needed to be punished. Today bad behavior is more often considered a *psychiatric* problem. Kids who misbehave are referred to a specialist for a diagnosis—and for treatment, often with medication.

And psychiatrists have plenty of diagnoses at their disposal. The most recent edition of the *Diagnostic and Statistical Manual of the American Psychiatric Association*, known to practitioners as *DSM-IV*, lists half a dozen "diagnoses" that could be applied to plain old disobedience. Consider the official description of "Oppositional Defiant Disorder," *DSM-IV* 313.81:

> The essential feature of Oppositional Defiant Disorder is a recurrent pattern of negativistic, defiant, disobedient and hostile behavior toward authority figures that persists for at least 6 months and is characterized by the frequent occurrence of at least four of the following behaviors: losing temper (Criterion A1), arguing with adults (Criterion A2), actively defying or refusing to comply with the requests or rules of adults (Criterion A3), deliberately doing things that will annoy other people (Criterion A4), blaming others for his or her own mistakes or misbehavior (Criterion A5), being touchy or easily annoyed by others (Criterion A6), being angry or resentful (Criterion A7), or being spiteful or vindictive (Criterion A8).

What is the difference between these two sentences?

- A parent says: "More often than not, it seems, Tommy is disobedient and disrespectful toward me and other adults."
- A child psychologist says: "Tommy meets *DSM-IV* criteria for Oppositional Defiant Disorder, code 313.81."

Both sentences could be describing the same boy. But there's a big difference between the two sentences. If you, the parent, acknowledge that Tommy is disobedient, then the natural next step is to ask what disciplinary strategy might help Tommy to be more obedient. On the other hand, if a paid professional tells you that Tommy meets formal criteria for a psychiatric disorder, then the natural next question is: Would medication be helpful? Parents who might balk at drugging their child as a method of discipline will be much more comfortable doing so as a method of treatment, especially when the diagnosis has been certified by the appropriate specialist. I call this process "the medicalization of misbehavior."

A recent news story described how preschool day-care centers today are doing something that was unheard-of just fifteen or twenty years ago: they are expelling three- and four-year-olds. Some of these kids are totally out of control. In one case, a three-year-old called his teacher an obscene name. Apparently he uses that language at home without punishment, so why not use it at the day care? At another day-care center, a boy was throwing rocks at other children and kicking adults without any sign of remorse. He was enjoying himself. A third boy met a visitor with the threat "I'm going to kill you." The visitor did not think the four-year-old boy was kidding. It turns out that boy's parents live in fear of their four-year-old child. They still spoon-feed him—he refuses to eat any other way—and they enforce no bedtime. Another child refuses to eat anything except pancakes and doughnuts.

What do today's experts suggest for these children? One expert recommends "a sensory routine that includes stroking his skin as many as ten times a day, and softly pressing on his finger and arm joints every two hours . . . Accommodate [his] need for extra sensation. [Let him] go to a splash sink or a sandbox whenever he wants."[30] One mother who is doing her best to follow these expert recommendations admits to wondering, "Can I really keep doing this? Can I keep everyone safe? What happens when he's twelve?" When she shared these concerns with her child's psychologist, the psychologist recommended that Mom be treated for an anxiety disorder. More drugs.

Before you pooh-pooh strict discipline, allow me to ask you this question. What do *you* propose instead for Tommy, an incorrigibly disobedient four-year-old boy who mocks his parents and spits at his teacher? If you haven't worked with a boy like

Tommy, if you haven't struggled with such a boy and agonized late at night about the best way to help him, then you should pause before you deny his parents the right to discipline him. The only alternative may be a bottle of pills.

Kristen, Interrupted

The last we heard from Kristen she was fifteen years old, on her way to a drug rehab center, and the prognosis was not good. In retrospect, could Kristen's parents have done anything differently? The problems with Kristen began very early. Kristen's mom admitted to me that she felt very uncertain about disciplining Kristen even when she was a baby. Kristen was their first child. Both parents were inexperienced. "We let her get away with a lot of things. We were stricter with Lisa [their second child]." If two-year-old Kristen didn't want to eat her vegetables, her parents gave her chicken nuggets and french fries instead. Kristen never had to eat anything she didn't want to eat. She never had to go anywhere she didn't want to go, or do anything she didn't want to do. Although Mom is still a devout church-goer, she gave up taking Kristen to church when she was eight years old after she threw a tantrum during a church service. "Kristen's temper was sort of cute when she was five," her mom told me. It was a lot less cute when she was eleven. By that time it would have been hard for the parents to institute real discipline, after eleven years of accommodating Kristen's every whim.

But it's easy to say, "You should have done things differently when your child was younger." The real question is: What should you do *now*?

Here's what Kristen's parents might have done at age eleven. First, sit down with Kristen and explain that there are going to be some new rules enforced from now on. Kids need to know what the rules are. Be detailed and specific. In that age group, you'd want to specify, for starters:

- Bedtime: when is it, and what does it entail (no instant messaging after 10 P.M., for instance);
- Household responsibilities: taking out the garbage, keeping your bedroom clean;
- Acceptable mealtime behavior: Kristen's parents had actually begun making special trays for her so that she could watch TV in her bedroom, as they were afraid of another outburst at the dinner table;
- TV and computer privileges: remove the TV and computer from Kristen's room and put them in the family room;

And so forth.

Kristen's behavior during her visit with me was totally unacceptable. She showed disrespect for her mother in front of a stranger (me) by saying that her mother "hasn't got a clue" and that her parents are "boring." Kristen is entitled to her opinions, but no child is entitled to show disrespect for her parents in front of a stranger. Kristen boasted of her disobedience: smoking and staying up till 3 A.M. Appropriate punishment at that time would have included grounding for at least two weeks, including "computer grounding": a suspension of all computer and Internet privileges including instant messaging and e-mail.

Kristen had clearly fallen in with a bad group, a group in which disrespect for parents was considered cool. I've already said how you sometimes have to take your daughter out of one group and try to help her find another group to join. That's what Kristen's parents needed to do. They could have blocked phone calls from the homes and cell phones of the girls in the bad group. They could have enrolled Kristen in an all-summer-long sleep-away camp. They could have tried to get her involved in organized sports or at least in some organized activity where she could make friends with girls who weren't so negative about family. (I know another situation in which the parents were struggling with a daughter who "hated" them and herself. Enrolling that girl in an Irish dancing class literally turned the girl's life around.) They might even have transferred her to another school, if absolutely necessary.

Nobody said this would be easy. There's no one-size-fits-all solution. Parenting is an art, not a science. But you can't duck this responsibility. If *you* don't discipline your child, nobody will.

9

LESBIAN, GAY, BISEXUAL, TRANSGENDER, SISSY, AND TOMBOY

Daniel

You know how TV reporters always interview the neighbors after some guy does something terrible? "We never would have expected this from him," the neighbors always say. "He was always such a friendly guy, such a *normal* guy."

I felt as though I were trapped in one of those interviews, listening to Wendy and Paul describing their son Daniel, who was just starting eleventh grade. "Daniel was a perfectly normal little boy," Wendy was telling me. "I mean he was all boy. He loved his trucks and his trains. He played football, T-ball, soccer, everything little boys love, you know? There wasn't anything sissy about him."

"Right now he's playing on the varsity football team. He plays linebacker on defense, tight end on offense," Paul added. "Coach told me last week he's got a shot at playing college ball if he kicks his game up a notch."

"And then we found *this*," Wendy said, handing me a sheaf of pages.

Daniel's parents had printed out about a dozen pages of Daniel's e-mails and instant messaging. I read them carefully:

... If you jerk off over a picture of a guy, does that mean you're gay? I try jerking off over pictures of chicks, but I keep imagining it's a guy. I look at the girl's neck and I pretend it's a guy's neck. I know it sounds really sick, but I keep wishing it were a guy in the picture instead of a chick. I can't help it.

I flipped to the next page:

If I really am gay, I'll kill myself. I'll drive my car off the Bay Bridge. I think it could be really cool, actually. I could rent a convertible and just soar through the air, right off the bridge and into the sky. I'll get high right before I do it. One super rush and then you die. No problem.

I'm just worried I *won't* die. I might just get brain damaged or paralyzed or something. I'll end up like Christopher Reeve—only without his money—just hooked up to tubes and things. If I'm gonna kill myself I have to make sure I do it right the first time cause I might not get a second chance. You got any ideas?

Daniel's correspondent had typed back:

Shoot yourself in the head while the car is in the air. Just to make sure you die.

That's helpful, I thought. "Who is Daniel sending these messages to?" I asked.

"We don't know. 'Skibum678@hotmail.com'—hotmail addresses can't be traced. We don't know who 'Skibum678' is," Paul said.

"Does Daniel know that you're reading his e-mail, that you've seen these messages?"

Wendy and Paul both shook their heads.

"What led you to search his e-mail messages in the first place?" I asked.

"I was cleaning his room, and I found this stash of pornography under his bed," Wendy said. "*Hustler* was bad enough, but there were also all these porn magazines for gay men. I showed them to Paul, and—"

"Wendy asked me whether boys normally go through a phase where they look at gay porn. I said *Hell no!* I've never seen anything like this stuff. I didn't even know this kind of stuff existed," Paul said.

"We have some questions for you," Wendy said, glancing at the list she had prepared. "Our first question is: Do you think Daniel really is gay, or is it just a phase? Our second question is, if Daniel is gay, what should we do about it? Our third question is, how did this happen? What did we do, or not do, that might have led to his becoming gay?" Wendy was reading, but she was close to tears. "Will he outgrow it? We went online to research this, but there were so many different Web sites, we didn't know which ones we could trust, you know? So we thought we'd start by asking you."

"There's no way he's gay," Paul said before I could respond. "I mean, look at the girls he's taken out! He's dated some really good-looking girls. What about that girl he took out last month, I think her name was Ingrid something. She was gorgeous."

"Ingrid Rasmussen. She's a lovely girl. Nordic blond, you know?" Wendy added, trying to be helpful.

"Why would a boy who's gay go out on a date with a pretty girl?" Paul asked.

"Plenty of reasons," I said. "Here's one: most gay boys Daniel's age aren't a hundred percent sure yet that they're really gay. They're still wondering whether they might be bisexual, or even straight. They may think that if they can find just the right girl, a girl who can get them sexually aroused, then they'll be straight and everything will be fine."

"Daniel and Ingrid only went out that one time," Wendy said. "I asked Danny how it went, and he said 'Fine.' I asked him whether he would ask her out again, and he just shrugged his shoulders and said, 'Maybe, maybe not.' "

"Even if a boy knows he's gay, he may still ask a girl out on dates, because he doesn't want *other* people to know," I continued. "He may even be physically intimate with a girl, even have sex with a girl, to quell any rumors about his sexual orientation."

"How can a gay guy have sex with a girl?" Paul asked.

"Easy," I said. "The guy just imagines that he's having sex with another guy."

"That's sick," Paul said.

"It's the same way heterosexual men in prison have sex with other men," I said. "They imagine they're having sex with a woman. Sexual arousal is more about what's going on in your head than what's going on between your thighs."

Paul and Wendy took a moment to ponder this.

"Very few teenage boys are ready to 'come out' as gay," I continued. "Most gay boys are terrified by the possibility that their sexual orientation will become public knowledge. At the same time, they're desperate for someone to talk to, someone they can trust. And, like all teenage boys, they're experiencing strong sexual feelings. They're looking for an outlet."

"Maybe he's just bisexual, not a hundred percent gay," Wendy said hopefully.

"Men who are truly bisexual are rare," I said. "Many men who call themselves bisexual are actually gay men who are reluctant to acknowledge their sexual orientation, even to themselves. There's less social stigma attached to being bi than being gay."

"What about my other question? Will he outgrow it? Could it be just a phase?" Wendy asked.

"Here's one way to think about homosexuality," I said. "Biologically, the difference between a gay man and a straight man is something like the difference between a left-handed person and a right-handed person. Being left-handed isn't just a phase. A left-handed person won't someday magically turn into a right-handed person."

"Some people are in-between," Wendy said hopefully. "Some people are ambidextrous."

"Some people *are* in-between," I agreed. "But the biological differences are analogous. In both cases there's a biological basis. Some children are destined at birth to be left-handed, and some boys are destined at birth to grow up to be gay."

"So you're saying it's not our fault," Wendy said. "It's not something we did wrong raising him. I suppose that's a relief. But what do we do now? What about that e-mail? He's thinking about suicide! Are we supposed to ignore that?"

"Of course not," I said. "I suggest you contact one of the local support groups for gay teenagers. Talk with one of their counselors first. They can give you some guidance about how to proceed, and they can advise you about how to put Daniel in touch with their people."

"I can't believe you seriously want to send our son to some gay clinic," Paul muttered. "He might catch AIDS or something."

I ignored Paul's remark. "Let me give you those phone numbers. Or if you're shy about making the phone call, I'll call myself, right now, while we're all here together."

The Passion of Simon LeVay

In 1991, neuroscientist Simon LeVay announced that the brains of gay men are different from the brains of straight men.[1] Scientists have long known that certain areas at the base of the brain—the interstitial nuclei of the anterior hypothalamus, or INAH—are dramatically different in women compared with men. One of these nuclei, INAH-3, is about twice as large in men as it is in women. LeVay reported that in gay men this nucleus is small, about the same size as it is in straight women.

LeVay's announcement caused an immediate media sensation, and not only because he was the first to claim that human sexual orientation could be associated with a specific neuroanatomical variation. LeVay himself was part of the story. LeVay's partner of twenty years, an emergency room physician, had died in 1990 after an agonizing four-year struggle with AIDS. While caring for his dying partner, LeVay decided to switch careers. He would abandon his research on the brain's visual system—his field of study for two decades—and instead try to do something for the gay rights movement. He would start by finding a neuroanatomical basis for homosexuality in men.

LeVay's findings received wide coverage in the media. No similar coverage was provided for the subsequent, less sensational reports that documented that LeVay had made a mistake. More recent work using more accurate methods has failed to demonstrate any differences in the brain between gay men and straight men. Specifically with regard to LeVay's findings: the brains of gay men are indistinguishable from the brains of straight men, and the brains of both gay men and straight men differ in the same way from the brains of women.[2] LeVay himself abandoned brain research after his paper was published, instead choosing to devote himself to political advocacy on behalf of the gay and lesbian movement.[3]

This is not to say that male homosexuality doesn't have a biological basis. Male homosexuality certainly derives at least in part from genetic factors. That fact has now been proven beyond a reasonable doubt.[4] Recall the analogy that I used with Daniel's parents: no one doubts that there is a biological basis to left-handedness. No one questions that left-handedness is "real." No one seriously asserts that left-handed people choose to be left-handed because those people were raised a certain way, or because left-handers are trying to strike back at their parents. However, no one has yet discovered a consistent brain marker of left-handedness. You can't look at any particular person's brain and say whether that person is left- or right-handed. The absence of an identified neuroanatomical substrate for a certain characteristic doesn't mean that the characteristic is not genetically programmed. It just means that the neuroanatomical substrate is subtle. The differences between the brains of straight men and gay men—whatever those differences may be—are likely to be on orders of magnitude more subtle than the differences between women and men, or between girls and boys. Anatomic differences in the brain based on *gender* are easily demonstrated. Anatomic differences in the brain based on *sexual orientation* are—with current technology—too small to be reliably detected.

Hearing the Difference

There's a popular notion that gay men are somehow "in between" straight men and straight women. According to this notion, most gay men are effeminate, with interests and hobbies more similar to those of straight women than those of straight men. If this stereotype applied at the neural level, we might expect to see that homosexual men have acoustic thresholds somewhere between the sensitive thresholds of straight women and the less-sensitive thresholds of straight men.

In chapter 2 we established that girls hear better than boys. Dennis McFadden and Edward Pasanen at the University of Texas at Austin studied the hearing of gay men, using the same technology Professor Cassidy used with newborn babies to demonstrate gender differences in hearing sensitivities. But McFadden and Pasanen did not find any evidence that gay men had better hearing than straight men. All the men—regardless of their sexual orientation—had less sensitive hearing than any of the women had.[5] In fact, the gay men actually had *less* sensitive hearing than the straight men!

Dennis McFadden has written recently about the apparent "hypermasculinization" of the hearing system in gay men.[6] McFadden's team has repeatedly found that women have significantly better hearing than straight men, and straight men have somewhat better hearing than gay men. Far from being intermediate between straight men and straight women, gay men appear to be somewhat *more* "masculine" than straight men—at least as far as the auditory system is concerned. Hearing isn't the only realm where gay men appear to be "hypermasculine" compared with straight men. On certain skeletal anatomic measures, gay men appear to be hypermasculine compared with straight men.[7] And on the most salient "anatomic measure"—whose penis is bigger?—gay men are hypermasculine. That's right: gay men have bigger penises, on average, than straight men do.[8]

Ears and penises aren't the only areas where gay men appear to be "more masculine" than straight men. Sexual behavior itself is another area where some researchers have used the term "hypermasculine" to describe gay men. In chapter 6 we talked about how most girls, and most women, are looking first and foremost for a *relationship*. Most boys, and many men, are interested first and foremost in *sex*. Many teenage boys and young men—both gay and straight—purchase pornography and hire prostitutes (male or female as the case may be). Buying pornography and hiring prostitutes are activities that are about as far removed as possible from having a mutual, ongoing relationship. You can't have a relationship with a picture in a magazine. Girls and women (whether lesbian or straight) very seldom hire prostitutes or purchase pornography. Girls and women, whether lesbian or straight, are more likely to be looking for a meaningful relationship rather than a one-night stand.

William Masters and Virginia Johnson, in their exhaustive study of homosexuality, found that many gay men are "hypermasculine" in the sense that they often engage in sex for its own sake rather than in the context of a relationship.[9] Masters and Johnson interviewed hundreds of gay men over many years. Many gay men told them about having dozens or even hundreds of sex partners, sometimes more than one partner in a single evening. Many gay men described having anonymous sex with men they didn't even know. Lesbian women, by contrast, almost never have sex with women they don't know.

Curiously, some Native American tribes regard the gay man as hypermasculine. "The most masculine men [in these tribes] have sex with other men. Men who have sex with women are perceived as less masculine."[10]

I don't want to push this idea of the "hypermasculine" gay man too far. But I do want to raise some doubts about the popular stereotype of the gay man as being some sort of effeminate creature midway between the straight man and the straight woman.

Queer Eye for the Straight Guy

In the summer of 2003, Bravo launched *Queer Eye for the Straight Guy*, a weekly TV show that *Entertainment Weekly* declared the summer's breakout hit.[11] Each week the "Fab Five"—a squad of five gay men—swoop in on an unfashionable straight man and make him over into a suave, debonair hunk. The makeover takes about three days. The straight man is initially clueless in matters of taste. The gay men buy him new clothes, redecorate his apartment, teach him how to shave, and so on. It's a funny show. But how accurate is the show's message—that gay men are naturally more competent—more "feminine"—than straight men in matters of fashion and personal appearance?

Louis Bayard, a gay man and a self-described slob, wrote an op-ed piece for the *Washington Post* in which he described how the show has become "a major problem for some of us in the gay community . . . [The] show is placing enormous pressure on me and on the great silent majority of gay men who really aren't that fab." Bayard then proceeded to give a detailed account of just what a slob he is. Spider webs and insect carcasses are everywhere in his apartment. The cat litter hasn't been changed "at any time in the last decade." He burns bacon to a shriveled black crisp that sets off the fire alarm . . . and then he eats it. He wears a red T-shirt with blue-and-white plaid shorts. He hasn't shined his shoes in years. And so forth. "Slovenliness knows no sexuality," he says.[12]

Are gay men really that different from straight men? More to the point, are gay boys different from straight boys? Are gay boys less likely to enjoy sports, less likely to be aggressive, more likely to understand inductive discipline, and so on, than straight boys are?

Different researchers have offered different answers to this question. Lisa Serbin reviewed studies comparing "real boys" with gender-atypical boys: boys who like to sew and play hopscotch and who are quite comfortable articulating their feelings. She found no evidence that "sissies" were more likely to become homosexual than the "real boys" were.[13] But other authors have vigorously disputed her conclusion. A large study conducted in San Francisco, comparing about 1,000 gay men and lesbian women with about 500 heterosexual men and women, found that gay men were more likely to report gender-atypical behavior and preferences than straight men were. For example, gay men were more likely to say that they hadn't liked sports when they were boys, and that they had enjoyed hopscotch or playing house.[14]

There are all sorts of problems with those retrospective studies. How do we know that gay men in San Francisco who volunteer for a study of homosexuality are characteristic of all gay men? Many gay men keep their sexual orientation secret, even as adults. Such men aren't likely to volunteer for a study comparing gay men with straight men. The subset of gay men who live in San Francisco and volunteer for studies of homosexuality may not be representative of gay men as a whole.

But even in the San Francisco study, less than half of the men said that they had enjoyed sex-typical activities such as playing house or hopscotch. So, more than half of the men were gender-typical in that regard. I suspect that a significant fraction of gay men are indeed anomalous males, males who in some respect show characteristics usually associated with females. Later in this chapter we'll consider anomalous boys (and girls). But the great majority of the gay men I've known over my fifteen years of clinical practice are as gender-typical as straight men are. They'd rather watch football than ice skating, and they hate talking about their feelings. Gender-anomalous behavior is one parameter. Sexual orientation is another. While there may be some correlation between gender-anomalous behavior and homosexuality, I suspect that the correlation is low. Many gay men are indistinguishable from straight men in all the dimensions we've discussed in previous chapters: they like playing competitive sports, they don't listen very well, they're more interested in having sex than in talking about relationships, and so forth. Some gay men are gender-atypical. But the fact that a man happens to be gay doesn't necessarily mean that he is gender-anomalous in other aspects of his life. Conversely, an effeminate boy won't necessarily grow up to be a gay man.

Maybe the term "gay" or homosexual just is not precise enough. Some experts have suggested that some men who are classified as gay—and who may consider themselves gay—are actually *trans*sexual rather than *homo*sexual.[15] There's a big difference between those categories, when you look at the brain.

Take a Walk on the Wild Side

I've already mentioned how, in the early 1990s, there was a flurry of media noise following Simon LeVay's claim that gay men have brains similar to those of straight women, and that more thorough investigations subsequently showed that those initial reports were wrong. There are no obvious differences between the brains of gay men and straight men.

What about transsexuals? A transsexual is a person who is born into one sex but feels herself or himself to be a member of the opposite sex. A transsexual boy feels that he is really a girl trapped in the body of a boy.

Dick Swaab, Frank Kruijver, and their associates at the Netherlands Institute for Brain Research studied the brains of transsexuals. They wanted to see whether men who felt that they were "really" women had brains that appeared in any respect to be like women's brains. In some of the most important areas of the brain, the areas that translate sexual feelings into endocrine responses, Swaab and his team found that the brain of a transsexual man resembles the brain of a woman, even if the man has not yet received any treatments with feminizing hormones.[16]

You have to make distinctions. Gay is one thing, transsexual is something else. Gay men are comfortable with their masculine identity. Think about Sir Ian McKellan, the great British actor who played Gandalf in the *Lord of the Rings* movies. He's very comfortable with his masculinity—and he has said so, repeatedly, as an outspoken advocate for gay rights. He's a gay man. He's not transgender or transsexual. Sir Ian doesn't have any interest in dressing in women's clothes, and he certainly doesn't want to *be* a woman.[17]

Transgender men—men who dress and act as females—are different. They are not comfortable with a masculine identity. They feel themselves to be women. They're interested in stereotypically feminine interests such as clothing and interior decorating—as much or more so, on average, as "real" women are.[18]

The experiences of transsexuals can (I believe) offer genuine insight into the subjective experience of womanhood and manhood. As a young boy, James Boylan always felt as though he were a girl trapped in the body of a boy. Finally, at the age of forty, he underwent sex-change surgery. His penis and testicles were surgically removed, he began receiving estrogen, and he changed his name from James to Jennifer. Now, at forty-five years of age, Boylan has written about the experience. "The first thing I lost when I started taking estrogen was the sense of invulnerability and confidence I had always had as a man. As a guy, much of the turbulence of life just bounced off me, like a pebble hitting a windshield. As a woman, though, things tend to get under my skin. My sorrows and joys tend to lie very close to the surface now. . . ."[19]

Scientists have only just begun studying transgender identity in a serious way. We still don't have any objective way of distinguishing the true transsexual—the man who feels that he is a woman and therefore wants to dress as a woman and act as a woman—from mere trans*vestite* behavior—a man who dresses in women's clothes because wearing women's clothes is sexually arousing for him. Nor does anyone really know yet whether the Netherlands study is accurate, or just another false alarm like

Simon LeVay's 1991 study. Does a transsexual man really have the brain of a woman in the body of a man? Does a transsexual woman really have the brain of a man in the body of a woman? Perhaps in another ten years we'll know more.

Lesbian: Born or Made?

Twenty years ago many experts believed that female homosexuality derived from experience, whereas male homosexuality was thought to be hardwired and innate. Boys, it was thought, were born homosexual or heterosexual. Girls' sexual orientation was more malleable, they believed. If a fifteen-year-old girl was brutally gang-raped by four men, the odds were much higher that she would ultimately develop a lesbian sexual orientation. Or so it was thought. Researchers provided vivid, sometimes horrifying stories of girls who suffered all sorts of sexual maltreatment, stories that corroborated their hypothesis.[20]

More recent research, however, suggests that female homosexuality is genetically programmed, at least in part. Debra Peters and Peggy Cantrell interviewed lesbian and heterosexual women, with special attention paid to sexual experiences in childhood and adolescence. Peters and Cantrell didn't find any difference between lesbian and straight women in terms of childhood or adolescent sexual experience. They concluded that female sexual orientation *cannot* be explained in terms of early sexual trauma or negative heterosexual experiences.[21]

As we've discussed, women and men experience sexuality very differently, regardless of whether they are gay or straight. Professor Lisa Diamond has recently questioned whether the categories "gay" or "straight" even have the same meanings for women compared with men. Professor Diamond spent five years talking with women who were in a sexual relationship with another woman. In many cases, a woman became sexually involved with another woman not so much because she was consciously seeking a lesbian sexual relationship, but simply because she loved the woman so much that sexual intimacy seemed a natural next step.[22] Many of these women reject the labels of "lesbian" or "straight" or "bisexual." They insist that they relate to each person as an individual. If they love that person in a romantic way, if they want to be close to them and hold them and kiss them, then sexual intimacy may just come naturally.

What's the connection between sex and love? We touched on this topic in chapter 6, but Professor Diamond has explored how this question relates to the issue of gay versus straight. Most people, and even most psychologists, have assumed that romantic love usually arises in the context of sexual desire. In fact, for most of the twentieth century, psychologists believed that romantic love was little more than a sublimation of the urge to have sex. But Diamond and many other psychologists, in the past fifteen years especially, have questioned that assumption. Recent work suggests that romantic love derives from different biobehavioral sources than sexual desire—especially in women. Psychologists have noticed that romantic love and long-term romantic relationships share many characteristics with the relationship between a parent and child.[23] Maybe it's no accident that lovers sometimes address each other as "baby." Maybe love and affection come from a different part of the brain than sexual desire does. Maybe romantic relationships derive from the *same* part of the brain that parent-child love comes from. This notion is central to the new idea in psychology known as *attachment theory.*

If attachment theory is correct, then we may have to rethink our assumptions about same-sex relationships. "Infants do not become selectively attached to other-gender versus same-gender caregivers," Diamond points out.[24] Parent-child attachment isn't programmed for one sex or the other. Mothers don't naturally bond better with sons, and fathers don't naturally bond better with daughters. But if parent-child attachment isn't weighted in favor of the opposite sex, and if the neural basis of parent-child attachment forms at least part of the basis for romantic attachments in adulthood, then it might be possible even for a "straight" woman to experience romantic feelings for another woman without *necessarily* wanting to be sexually intimate with her.

Diamond suggests that those kinds of relationships happen all the time, especially among women. Two women may form a passionate friendship, may want to spend lots of time together, may even cuddle together and snuggle together. But they might not want to have sex with each other. They might even find the notion of lesbian sex "disgusting." Still, their relationship with each other might be more intimate and more emotionally fulfilling than the *sexual* relationships they have with their boyfriends or husbands. How meaningful is it then to classify those women as gay or straight? "What does sexual orientation orient?" Diamond asks. She suggests that maybe our rigid categories of gay versus straight get a little blurred when talking about women. Few straight men in our culture have close, physically intimate relationships with other men—although Diamond informs us that men in locales such as Melanesia, Guatemala, and Samoa often do.

So what about lesbian women? If at least some lesbian relationships arise not from sexual urges but from close friendships, how do we account for the evidence of a genetic component for homosexuality in women? What are the genes coding for? Perhaps what's genetically coded—in women—is the *possibility*, the willingness to engage in lesbian sexual activity, if the right woman comes along. The implication of Diamond's work is that many women who consider themselves heterosexual might actually be bisexual, if the right woman came into their lives. And for that matter, some women who consider themselves lesbian might also be bisexual, if the right *man* came along.

Now we're ready to talk about anomalous children: boys whose behavior and interests are more typical of girls, and girls whose behavior and interests are more typical of boys.

Martin

Sally first realized she was pregnant while sitting in the office of her divorce lawyer. She'd been married for four years, and she was at the end of her rope. Even though she worked longer hours than Mark and brought home more money, Mark still expected her to be the housekeeper, picking up his clothes, cleaning house, cooking all the meals. He even had the nerve to complain when supper was late, when he'd been home all afternoon watching TV while she worked her tail off at the bank. She'd suggested marriage counseling; Mark refused. He didn't have the slightest clue how badly the marriage was broken and apparently had no interest in fixing it.

A friend at work gave her the name of a good divorce lawyer. At the first visit, the lawyer was going through a checklist of questions.

"Any children?" the lawyer asked.

"No," Sally answered.

"Any possibility that you might be pregnant at this time?"

Sally was about to answer "No, of course not," but then she paused. When did she have her last period? For that matter, when was the last time she and Mark. . . . Then she remembered that Saturday night about a month ago, when she had thought that just *maybe* this marriage could still be saved. That moment in the attorney's office was the first time she realized that her period was late. "I don't think so," Sally answered at last.

"You don't *think* so?" the attorney repeated quizzically.

Eight months later, she gave birth to Martin. In the meantime, Mark had moved to Los Angeles and Sally was contemplating life as a single mother.

Many mothers imagine that their children are above average, but Sally was *sure* that her son Martin was precocious. And she was right. By one year of age, Martin had a vocabulary of about twenty words, including "zebra." By age two he was talking in full sentences. By age four he was sounding out words in preschool. When he started kindergarten, the teacher immediately put him in the accelerated reading group. Martin was the only boy in that group of six children.

From the beginning, Martin loved school. He always sat in the front row, raised his hand to answer every question, was always polite. His teachers adored him. "If all boys were like Martin, life would be a joy," said Mrs. Messner, his first-grade teacher, wistfully. "I just wish he would go outside at recess."

"Martin doesn't go outside at recess?" Sally asked.

"Lately, no," Mrs. Messner said. "He begged me. He said, 'Mrs. Messner, why should I waste time going outside and just standing around? Why can't I just stay inside and read?' He just doesn't like recess. All the other boys are running around like wild animals, and Martin stays close by me or one of the other teachers."

"I was like that, too," Sally said. "I never liked recess."

By the end of third grade, Martin was reading at the sixth-grade level. He started writing poetry, taking great care in the arrangement of words on the page. His favorite font on the computer was *Palace Script*. His handwriting flowered into an elaborate cursive, and he began making little circles for the dots over "i" and "j."

Sally's friends warned her that Martin was becoming a bookworm. She should sign him up for some sports, they said.

That sounded like a good idea. "What would you like to play?" she asked her son. "Soccer? Basketball? Football?"

"I don't like any of those," he said. Pause. "But I do like bowling with Karen and Samantha," he added at last.

"Bowling's not a sport," Sally said.

"Yes it is," Martin said. "They have tournaments on TV."

Finally Martin agreed to take some tennis lessons, but his heart wasn't in it. "My schedule is too busy," nine-year-old Martin announced to Sally one day, a few weeks after the tennis lessons began. "I need more time to practice piano. The tennis lessons are a waste of time and money." Martin could be very firm, especially when negotiating with his mother.

"All right," Sally said. No more tennis lessons.

At least he has friends, Sally thought. She and Martin agreed on eight children to invite over for his tenth birthday party: seven girls and one boy, as it happened. Martin wanted the party to have a *Lord of the Rings* theme. Martin claimed that all of his friends liked the *Lord of the Rings*. Sally asked her son which character he liked the most.

"Frodo, of course," Martin said.

"Really? Why 'of course'?" Sally asked. "Why not Gandalf? Or Legolas? Or Aragorn?"

"Aragorn is a very unrealistic character," Martin said dismissively. "Frodo is much more believable."

"But Aragorn at least is a human being," Sally answered, determined to win one of these debates for once. "Frodo is a four-foot-tall 'hobbit' with hairy feet. How can you say Frodo is more realistic than Aragorn?"

"Because Aragorn is so strong, so talented at everything. It's just not believable. He's always fighting off somebody evil—orcs or Urûk-hai or Nazgûl, whatever—and he always wins against ridiculously long odds," her son said. "It's just not plausible. Frodo is weak. He's small. He doesn't fight anybody—except Gollum at the very end, and Gollum is even smaller and weaker than Frodo is, and anyhow Frodo basically lost that fight, anyway. Gollum bit the Ring off his hand."

Sally wanted to compliment her not-quite-ten-year-old son on using the word "plausible" correctly in a sentence, but she paused as she considered the implications of what Martin had just said. Being strong and talented was unrealistic, according to Martin. Winning against long odds was unrealistic. Being *weak* was realistic. She needed to sort this out.

The court had granted sole physical custody of Martin to Sally. Nevertheless, Sally made a point of inviting her ex-husband to spend time with Martin, especially over the summer months. Mark had mellowed and matured in the years since the divorce. He'd had two children by his second wife, and he seemed to be a good father to them. (Sally suppressed the urge to ask Mark's wife, Jennifer, whether he had gotten any better at helping around the house.) Mark called from California one evening to ask Sally whether Martin could join him and his six-year-old son Jared on a fishing trip. "My company is chartering a forty-foot-boat. About a dozen people are going. We'll sail to Catalina Island, do some fishing out there, then that night we'll be at sea on the open ocean. There's nothing like it, Sally. The stars are so bright, it's like they're just ten feet over your head."

"It sounds like fun," Sally said sincerely.

But Martin refused. "There's nothing more stupid than fishing," he said authoritatively. "You sit on a boat waiting for some poor fish to chomp down on your hook, then you viciously yank on the hook, which is stuck in the fish's mouth, and then you drag the fish up on the boat and cut out its guts. What fun. I don't *think* so. No thank you."

"But Martin—" Sally began.

"Besides, I'm supposed to be at my music camp then," Martin said. "You're not asking me to give up my music camp, are you?"

Sally and Mark continued to talk after Martin got off the phone. "Martin doesn't want to do *any* regular guy things," Mark said. "He says fishing is stupid, even though he's never tried it. He wouldn't go to a football game with me, even when I had those tickets for a Redskins game when I visited you guys last November. He doesn't want to play soccer. Jeez, he wouldn't even play video games with me when we went to the video arcade."

"So what difference does any of that make?" Sally said defensively. "He's getting straight A's. He has friends. He's happy."

"But what does he do for fun?" Mark asked.

"He plays piano. He writes poetry. He reads."

"You call that fun?" Mark asked incredulously.

"For Martin, those things *are* fun. Martin is very intellectual. That's just who he is. Besides, where is it written that every boy has to like football? Or video games? Or fishing?"

"So what's this music camp he's going to?" Mark asked.

"It's a very good music camp. Martin really wants to work on piano over the summer."

"What kind of piano music does he play?" Mark asked.

"Lots of different kinds," Sally said.

"Oh yeah? Can he play jazz? Fats Waller?"

"No, of course not," Sally said. "He only plays classical. Beethoven. Clementi. Debussy. You should hear him play 'Clair de Lune.' "

"Jeez, give me a break," Mark said.

The other boys didn't really start picking on Martin until middle school. That's when Sally began getting phone calls from the guidance counselor. Somebody had stuffed tampons into Martin's locker with a note attached saying, "You need these." Then a week later somebody spray-painted the word "fag" on his locker. The following month two boys bumped into Martin in the hallway, pretending it was an accident, and knocked him over. Sally was horrified by the bruise on Martin's cheek where his face had hit the floor.

"Doesn't it bother you that the other boys pick on you?" she asked her son.

"Not really," he said with a shrug. "They don't understand me. All they understand is video games and sports. They're afraid of what they don't understand, and they respond the only way they know how. With violence. I just need to be careful, stay away from them, that's all."

"But why don't any of your friends stand up for you?" Mom asked.

"I don't have any friends," Martin said matter-of-factly.

"How can you say that? What about Karen? What about Samantha?" Mom asked.

"They're not my friends anymore. Ever since the boys starting picking on me. Karen and Samantha are friends with those boys now. Especially Karen. She's always hanging out with them. When she saw how the boys hate me, she started avoiding me."

"That must hurt. You must feel terrible," Mom said.

"No, I don't. It doesn't bother me. Besides, I do have friends."

"Really?" Mom said eagerly. "Who?"

"I'd say my best friends right now are Isaac Asimov and Robert Heinlein," Martin said calmly.

Mom had to pause for a moment, searching her memory to recognize the names. "But Isaac Asimov and Robert Heinlein . . . are dead," she said. A chill ran down her spine. "They're dead science fiction writers."

"Right," Martin said. "Isaac Asimov wrote the *Foundation* trilogy. It's about a mutant who's more powerful than all the normal people. He looks small and weak, but he's actually stronger than anybody because of his special powers. Robert Heinlein wrote *Stranger in a Strange Land*."

"But both those authors died long ago," Mom repeated.

"So what?" Martin said. "They're still my best friends. I have tons in common with them."

The Anomalous Male

There is plenty of variation *within* the sexes. Beyoncé Knowles, Sally Ride, Serena Williams, Justice Ruth Bader Ginsburg, and Anna Nicole Smith don't seem to have much in common. Nor for that matter do Bill Clinton, Pee Wee Herman, Tiger Woods, Sylvester Stallone, and Michael Jackson. But how significant are the differences? How do those differences affect what we've discussed earlier in this book?

The answers to those questions are different for girls and boys. One way to begin to understand those differences, I think, is to consider a study published by scientists at NASA who were studying astronauts on the space shuttle (this study was published shortly before the loss of the *Columbia*). One of the less-well-known facts about spaceflight is that women who fly in the space shuttle are typically very dizzy after they return to earth. Their blood pressure tends to drop for several days after the flight. If they stand up too suddenly, they get dizzy. The same phenomenon has been reported in male astronauts, but much less often. Wendy

Waters and Janice Meck at the Johnson Space Flight Center in Houston wanted to study this phenomenon. So they tested female and male astronauts right after the astronauts returned from a mission on the space shuttle—thirty-five astronauts in all.[25]

Their findings confirmed what many previous reports had suggested. Every female astronaut they tested was extremely prone to dizziness after the flight. Few of the men were. The stress of spaceflight had very different effects on most of the men compared with all of the women. If you recall our earlier discussion of sex differences in the biobehavioral response to stress, then this finding shouldn't come as a surprise.

The extraordinary finding in this study concerned those few men who *were* dizzy after spaceflight, men who showed the female-typical *drop* in blood pressure in response to stress. These men were less often pilots by training, more often mission specialists: biologists, physicists, or computer geeks with no background in aviation, men who were on board just to run a particular experiment. Among the "real" astronauts, the men who *fly* the shuttle, the anomalous female-typical pattern was rare. But one in four male mission specialists showed the female-typical pattern.

None of the females showed the male-typical pattern. Very few of the "tough guys" showed the female-typical pattern. But among the geeks, one out of four men showed the female-typical pattern. What's going on?

There's growing evidence that a small subset of boys (and men) have female-typical physiology. Different researchers have used different terms for these boys, and different criteria to define them, so it's hard to consolidate the findings across the different studies. But there's reason to believe that these boys have a lot in common.

Harvard professor Jerome Kagan has spent many years studying these boys, whom I'll call "anomalous males."* Kagan began

---

*Kagan calls these boys "highly reactive," but that term can be confusing because in some circumstances these boys are shy, passive, and withdrawn while other boys are outgoing and assertive.

by analyzing baby boys who were only a few weeks old. He would simply touch the babies gently and see how they responded. Most baby boys don't mind being touched, but a few react intensely. When touched, those boys begin crying and thrashing their arms and legs. Kagan followed these boys for years, from infancy through childhood and into adolescence (he's been doing this work for forty years now!). He found, first of all, that about half of these boys never outgrow their dislike of novelty. As teenagers, these boys shy away from strangers and new adventures, just as they did when they were babies.

Even more striking, Kagan found that these boys have other characteristics in common. Specifically, these "anomalous males" are:

- More likely to have allergies, asthma, or eczema than other boys;[26]
- More likely to have a regular resting heart rate[27] whereas most boys have heart rates with lots of beat-to-beat variability: the heart speeds up when they breathe in and slows down when they breathe out;
- More likely to have a narrow face, a facial width-to-height ratio less than 0.55;[28]
- Unwilling to engage in rough-and-tumble play.[29]

Sociologist Patricia Cayo Sexton also described such boys. She found other characteristics in addition to those identified by Kagan. According to Sexton, these boys also typically:

- are precocious, particularly with respect to language skills;
- are often loners with few close friends;
- may enjoy sports, but typically prefer noncontact sports such as tennis, track, bowling, and golf.[30]

The anomalous male then appears to represent a distinct physiological type and a real challenge to parents—who often don't see that there's a problem. On the contrary, many parents, especially mothers, react the way Sally and Mrs. Messner did. Martin was quiet, well behaved, and never got into trouble. What's not to like?

Many parents don't recognize that their anomalous son is heading for a special kind of trouble . . . until middle school begins. When the tidal wave of puberty hits, the neatly arranged life that seemed so stable and peaceful in elementary school is washed away. For many of these boys, their closest friends during the elementary school years were girls. When puberty arrives, the girls leave. Hanging out with the right kids becomes intensely important in middle school, and the anomalous male is not a cool guy to hang with. So: the girls are gone.

Sexton found that these boys become intensely anxious about sex around this time. Some begin using pornography. Others become suicidally depressed. The "geek" becomes a loner, withdrawn and resentful, finding solace in his books and his fantasies. "I am a rock, I am an island" are the words of the disturbing Paul Simon song that so accurately portrays such a boy:

> *I have my books and my poetry to protect me.*
> *I am shielded in my armor.*
> *Hiding in my room, safe within my womb,*
> *I touch no one and no one touches me.*[31]

Let's follow the anomalous boy into high school. His grades are good but his life is empty. I've seen plenty of these boys in my fifteen years of clinical practice. All too often they've developed a smug facade that hides the hurt they feel inside. After all, they have the approval of the adult world. Why should they care if other kids make fun of them or spray-paint nasty epithets on their locker? As Sexton observed, these boys are "reluctant to acknowledge the connection between school honors and feminization, or to inquire into whether their success can be attributed more to acceptance of female norms than to brilliance or superior intellectual endowments . . . Few feel victimized; they feel more like heroes and victors."[32] By the time such a boy is in high school, I don't know whether anybody could change him or broaden his horizons. He may grow up to be a mission specialist on the space shuttle, but he'll never be the pilot.

However, Jerome Kagan has presented evidence that parents who intervene early—ideally, before the child is three years old—can pull their anomalous son out of the tendency to withdrawal and feminization. Kagan has suggested that *parenting style* is a critical factor in determining whether a boy outgrows his fearful, withdrawn tendencies or whether he remains stuck in that mode. Protective parents who are "sensitive" to their child's preferences have the *worst* outcomes. Baby boys who are fearful and withdrawn become more so if their parents shield them from minor stresses and injuries. Such a parent, Kagan found, "made it more, rather than less, difficult for the child to control an initial urge to retreat from strangers and unfamiliar events. The equally accepting mothers who made age-appropriate demands [for their boys to mix and mingle] helped their highly reactive infants tame their timidity. . . . Mothers who protect their [timid] infants from frustration and anxiety in the hope of effecting a benevolent outcome seem to exacerbate the infant's uncertainty and produce the opposite effect."[33]

If a boy is fearful and timid and "highly reactive" in early infancy but his parents believe in firm discipline, the odds are good that by two years of age the boy will have outgrown those tendencies. In fact, in Kagan's study, every single boy who did outgrow timid tendencies in infancy had a parent who believed in the importance of discipline. Conversely, in Kagan's study, if the parent of a timid child believed in being "sensitive to a child's needs" and did not place a high value on obedience, *in every case* the timid baby boy grew up to be a timid, fearful child.[34]

So what can you do if your son is an anomalous male and he's five, six, seven, eight years old? Number one: adopt and maintain a firm disciplinary style (reread the last chapter if you're fuzzy on what this means). Number two: encourage competitive sports. Your son will tell you he doesn't like football or soccer or basketball. But he's probably never played these sports. Tell him he needs to give them a chance. Your spouse may tell you that your son isn't talented athletically. Maybe he isn't. Makes no difference. As Sexton observes, "Athletics, like other subjects, has become over-specialized and too much the property of the expert and the star. If anything, the physically unfit need coaching and a chance to play more than does the star."[35]

Next, you have to take an honest look in the mirror. If your son is an anomalous male, there's a good chance that you have been overly protective, too careful to shield him from the scrapes and bumps of everyday life. (Again, see Wendy Mogel's book *The Blessing of a Skinned Knee*.) Sexton also has shown that these boys are more likely either to have no father in the house or a father who is himself an anomalous male. She is blunt in her assessment and blunt in her prescription: these boys' problems come "from overprotective parents and can best be remedied through association with a normal adult male." Sexton then asserts that a "normal adult male" is "a rare figure in most schools."[36] If that's true at your school, then you might try signing your son up for the Boy Scouts or for an all-boys summer camp with lots of camping and hiking and sports. Avoid computer science camps, arts camps, music camps, and the like.

Also, if you belong to a synagogue or church or mosque, check with them to see what kinds of all-male retreats they offer. All the major religions still remember what most North Americans today have forgotten: namely, that gender differences are real, and that genuine spiritual transformation is more likely to occur—in both sexes—in a single-gender setting.

Amy

Amy was the firstborn of two daughters. Her parents, Barbara and Howard, didn't realize what a tomboy Amy was until their second child, Zoe, was born. "Amy and Zoe were like night and day," Barbara told me one day in the office. Barbara had asked for an appointment to talk with me, but she wouldn't tell the receptionist what she wanted to discuss. I told the receptionist to allow forty-five minutes for the visit. I had a pretty good idea what Barbara wanted to see me about. "When Amy was six months old, if a stranger came into the room, Amy would crawl across the floor and tug on the stranger's shoelace," Barbara continued. "Zoe was so different. When Zoe was six months old, if a stranger came into the room, Zoe would just start crying and crying until I picked her up. Then she'd just bury her face in my chest."

"And as they grew older?" I asked.

"Amy was your classic tomboy," Barbara said. "She was always playing with the boys, building forts, throwing snowballs, climbing trees. She loved building forts."

"And Zoe?" I asked.

"Zoe was into girly things. Dolls and dress-up and baking cakes. My husband and I were big believers in going against gender stereotypes, you know—"

"Sure," I said. "I know exactly what you mean."

"So when Zoe was three years old, we bought her a set of toy earthmoving equipment: a little dump truck, a backhoe, a front-end loader. Amy loved that sort of stuff, so we bought three brand-new toys like that for Zoe."

"Did she like them?" I asked.

"She loved them," Mom said. "But she didn't use them the way they're meant to be used. First she put all three vehicles in a little circle, facing each other, and then she put little ribbons on the dump truck. 'That's not quite how the dump truck is supposed to work, sweetie,' I remember telling her. 'But it's the dump truck's *birthday*,' Zoe explained to me, very patiently. 'And here are its two *best friends*,' she said, pointing to the backhoe and the front-end loader. Later that afternoon I came into her room and she very loudly told me 'Shush! They're sleeping!' She had carefully laid all three toys—the dump truck, the backhoe, and the front-end loader—in her bed, and drawn the covers up over them so you could just see the headlights of each of them."

"That's cute," I said. "What about Amy?"

"Right. Well, you know," Mom said, "Amy was talented in sports. Competitive sports. We signed her up for MSI [the local soccer league]. She was really brave, even when she was just six or seven years old. She was never afraid of the ball. Most of the other girls were, but not Amy. She didn't mind getting bumped or bruised. And you know, she's built more *solidly* than Zoe. She has a stockier build. Zoe is more delicate."

"Maybe that's a result of the differences in their interests," I suggested. "Maybe if Amy played with dolls while Zoe ran around on the soccer field, then maybe Zoe would be the stocky one."

"Maybe," Barbara said doubtfully.

"Well, let's move along," I said, glancing at my watch. "What can I do for you today?"

Barbara sighed. "I cleaned up Amy's room while she was at school yesterday," she said. "And I found *these*. Hidden in one of her dresser drawers, actually in one of her kneesocks." Mom handed me a package of Seasonale, the birth control pill I had prescribed for Amy five months earlier. "According to the label, you are the prescribing physician," Mom said. "Did you prescribe these pills for my daughter?"

"Yes, I did," I said.

"Did Amy tell you that she had my permission, or her father's permission, to take birth control pills?" Mom asked.

"No, she didn't," I answered. "In fact, Amy made it very clear that you and your husband didn't know anything about it."

"So how could you do this?" Mom said, not angry so much as bewildered. "Isn't it against the law for a doctor to give an underage girl birth control pills without her parents' consent?"

"Not in Maryland it isn't," I said. "Maryland courts have consistently ruled that in matters pertaining to contraception, the doctor-patient relationship between the doctor and the teenage girl is privileged. It's ironic," I continued before Mom could interrupt, "because the result is that under Maryland law, I can give your daughter birth control pills without your knowledge, but the school nurse can't give her a Tylenol without your consent. The law is not very consistent. It doesn't make a whole lot of sense. But that's the law."

Mom sighed again. "I'm not really angry with you, Dr. Sax," she said. "It's just that I don't want Amy to be sleeping around. My God, she's only sixteen. When I was sixteen, I was barely allowed to go out on dates, and I had to be home by 10 P.M. I don't want her to be doing this."

"I agree with you. Completely," I said. "But Amy isn't asking your permission, or mine. She's already decided that she's going to be sexually active. And given that decision, I actually think it's very responsible of her to have made arrangements to take the pill."

"But you're encouraging her!" Barbara said.

"Mrs. Shaw," I said, very slowly, "please hear me out. There are few things worse for a teenage girl than an unwanted pregnancy. When a sixteen-year-old girl becomes pregnant, there are only three options. None of them are good options. Abortion is not a good option. The second option—carrying the child to term and then giving it up for adoption—is wrenching. And the third option—for you and your daughter to try to *raise* the child while Amy is finishing high school—"

"And don't forget I work, forty-plus hours a week!" Barbara said. "Plus doing the laundry. And the cooking. And cleaning—"

"That's my point," I said. "Our top priority here has to be to prevent an unwanted pregnancy. I agree that the best thing would be for Amy not to be sexually active. But Amy has taken that option off the table."

"So what should I do?" Mom said. "I found the pills. Are you telling me to put them back where I found them and pretend nothing has happened?"

"No," I said. "You should sit down with Amy, this evening, just the two of you—your husband's away on a business trip, right?" Barbara nodded. "Tell Amy that you found these birth control pills in her room. Tell her how disappointed you are that she is sexually active. Remind her of the risks—"

"I can never win any debate with that child," Mom said hopelessly. "She can talk circles around me."

"But at least she'll know how you feel," I said.

"What good does that do," Mom said, more a statement than a question.

After she had left, I thought back to that day five months earlier, when Amy had marched into the exam room and demanded that I prescribe birth control pills for her. "And I don't want my mom or dad to know I was here," she said. "I'll pay your bill myself. In cash. I have money."

"The money's not the issue," I said. "Don't you think it's unwise to try to keep a secret like this from your parents?"

"I'm just trying to protect them," Amy said. "What they don't know won't hurt them. I'm just trying to spare them some mental anguish and distress."

"You're trying to spare them mental anguish and distress," I repeated.

"Well, to be honest, I'm trying to spare myself the bother of a big argument," she said, and she flashed me a winning smile. Amy might not be slender or particularly graceful, but she could be charming, even captivating, when she wanted to be.

Amy has her act together more than most teenagers. She knows what she wants—in school, from her friends, and from the boys in her life. She makes whatever arrangements are necessary to secure her objectives. She's an Honor Roll student, captain of the girls' soccer team, she has a variety of hobbies—including, curiously enough, cross-stitch and macramé—and she is popular with the athletic crowd at her school, both girls and boys. But she's not your typical girl.

Differences

Over the past thirty years a handful of scholars have compared anomalous boys like Martin with anomalous girls like

Amy. Once again the most important contribution has been made by sociologist Patricia Cayo Sexton, who found that while the anomalous boys

> ... were noncompetitive, non-athletic and fearful, the [anomalous] girls were fearless, independent, and competitive. Girls who were bold and daring from ages ten to fourteen became the most intellectual women as adults. . . . Among girls, strangely, high intelligence was associated with both greater masculinity and greater femininity. Bright girls were more likely than other girls to be dominant and striving and at the same time have more feminine qualities.[37]

Boys with many feminine characteristics tend to be less popular and at higher risk for social maladjustment, especially in middle school and high school. By contrast, the anomalous girl appears *more* likely to be more popular and well adjusted than her peers. The girl who is the captain of the lacrosse team is more likely to be a top student than the girl who plays no sports. On the other hand, the *boy* who's at the top of the class academically is *less* likely to be a good athlete. The tomboy—the girl who prefers some male-typical activities—should be encouraged to pursue those gender-atypical activities. Girls who show some male-typical characteristics—such as a willingness to confront others openly—generally do *better* than average socially. On the other hand, boys who show female-typical characteristics such as a reluctance to engage in rough-and-tumble play are more likely to have more problems socially.

Anomalous girls have an advantage in school and in life; their social horizons are likely to be broader than those of other girls. Anomalous boys have an advantage in school but they pay a steep price for that advantage, and their social horizons are likely to be narrower than those of other boys.

10

BEYOND PINK AND BLUE

Adults need to get serious on the question of gender. . . . Adults stuck in the '70s have declined to take on the responsibility of helping our children develop a powerful pro-social meaning for masculinity and femininity. . . . The result of our society's indifference to the deep meaning of sexuality is social chaos—the kind of social chaos that can occur only when adults abandon adult responsibilities and leave children to create social meanings on their own, guided by Madonna and Madison Avenue.

—Maggie Gallagher, 2003[1]

A Gender-Blind Society?

We live in what is—or at first glance appears to be—a gender-blind society. Girls and boys are taught to have similar expectations regarding their adult careers. Gone, thank goodness, are the days when all girls were expected to become homemakers. American girls and boys today are offered the same subjects in the same grade at the same schools and have opportunities to play most of the same sports: soccer, basketball, lacrosse, tennis, golf, track and field, and so on.

For the past thirty years, any suggestion that there are innate differences between girls and boys in how they learn or think or interact with one another has been viewed in many quarters as chauvinistic backsliding. The education establishment has indoctrinated teachers and parents in the dogma that girls and boys should be taught the same subjects in the same way at the same time. Any differences in how girls and boys learn are socially constructed, not biologically based. Or so we were told.

Parental authority oozed away over those same three decades. As we discussed in chapter 8, parents seldom *tell* their children what to do anymore. Instead, parents *consult* with their children, they *make suggestions*, they *inform* their children about the choices available. Thirty years ago parents were more often than not the chief decision makers in their children's lives, with no apologies made. Today parents routinely *ask* their six-year-olds what sports they want to play, even what foods they would like to eat. And many parents regard it as an item of good parenting to dutifully fulfill the whims expressed by their six-year-old.

To sum up the transformation in North American (and Western European and Australian) society since roughly 1970:

- Society has blurred any distinction between female and male in terms of social roles;
- The educational establishment has erased any gender distinctions in the curriculum;
- Children have assumed more authority for the important decisions in their lives.

What has been the end result of these changes? If the 1970s theorists were correct in their assumption that girls and boys are cut from the same cloth, then we should expect to find that we now live in an era of unprecedented gender equality, an era in which girls and boys both are free to fulfill their individual potential without regard to gender stereotypes.

That's not what has happened. On one hand, the range of opportunities available to young women today has expanded dramatically in comparison with previous generations. Every person who favors individual liberty must welcome that change. Women have entered all the professions in unprecedented numbers. In the 1960s, women earned less than 5 percent of the law degrees granted by the nation's law schools; today that number is close to 50 percent.[2] Similar gains have been reported in medical schools[3] and in many graduate school programs.[4]

But the news is not all good. Psychologist Jean Twenge carefully examined the records of children from the 1950s to the present. She found that children today are significantly more anxious and depressed than children were in the 1950s and 1960s. In fact, the *average* child today is more anxious than the typical child referred to a *psychiatrist* in the 1950s.[5] To put it another way: the average child today would have been considered a "mental case" fifty years ago.

Twenge suggests two main causes for the increased anxiety of today's children. The first is the unraveling of the social fabric over the past fifty years. Children in the 1950s were more likely to be embedded in an extended family, living in close proximity to grandparents, cousins, aunts, and uncles with whom they would frequently interact. Children today are less likely to have that kind of extended family in the neighborhood and far more likely to be raised by a single parent.

The second cause identified by Twenge is an increased sense of instability and threat in the personal lives of children. Children feel less sure that the parents they are living with today will be living with them two or three years down the road. And, children today feel more vulnerable to physical violence— even if their statistical risk of being a victim of physical violence is no greater than it was in the 1950s.

I would like to suggest a third cause in addition to those two. I think many children today feel less rooted in their gender than children did in the 1950s. The neglect of gender in the raising and educating of children has resulted in a loss of direction for the growing child and especially the adolescent. The adolescent today is like an explorer without a compass in a trackless wilderness, unsure of the path or the destination.

I'm suggesting that one reason girls and boys are more anxious today than fifty years ago is because they're less sure of their gender, they're less sure of what it means to be a girl or a boy, what it means to become a woman or a man. A study published in 2004 provides substantial support for that idea. Researchers in Florida found that the more comfortable a child was with his or her gender, the better that child's psychological well-being. Gender-comfortable kids were more self-confident and less anxious than kids who were gender-atypical.[6] These researchers also pointed out that their findings contradict the general teaching of the past three decades. From the early 1970s through the late 1990s, psychologists thought that children who "conformed to gender norms" were likely to be kids who were bound up in gender straitjackets. Most psychologists expected that those kids would be less happy, less fulfilled, than other kids. But those psychologists were wrong. *Feminine girls and masculine boys are as a rule happier, and are likely to feel more fulfilled, than masculine girls and feminine boys.*

This doesn't mean that you should force a tomboy daughter to play with Barbies if she prefers to play with trucks. But it does suggest that if you have a son who's "all boy," there's nothing to be gained by taking away his trucks and insisting that he play with a doll. My point is that each child's gender is a big part of who she or he is. Human nature is gendered to the core. Work *with* your child's nature, work *with* your child's innate gender-based propensities, rather than trying to reshape them according to the dictates of late-twentieth-century political correctness.

Let me give you an example of how things might be done differently. I was in Toronto recently, giving a talk about sex differences in how children learn. After my presentation, I had the opportunity to get feedback from some of the more than four hundred educators in the audience. One teacher told me how a local man, a retired electrician, had volunteered to come to his school to help the high school boys with their robotics class (this was an all-boys school—all-boys schools are very popular in the Toronto area). The boys absolutely worshiped this old man. They were fascinated to hear his stories about working with high-voltage power lines. They hung on his every word about the technical details of soldering copper wire to a metal post. "There was more going on here than just the transfer of information," the teacher told me. "A *tribe* was being formed."

That teacher's on to something. The foundation of every durable human community has always been the molding of the younger generation by the older: and this interaction is facilitated in *single-sex* contexts. In almost every culture, in almost every era of recorded human history, opportunities for single-sex interactions between generations have been plentiful. In North America until recently, girls participated in sewing circles with their mother's friends, or girls got together with women to bake before a big social event, or attended all-female Bible study together or Girl Scout troop meetings.[7] There are fewer opportunities for such activities today. Likewise for boys: whether you're talking about hunting together or working a farm or going to sporting events, North American society until recently was characterized by a collective male sensibility to which almost every male could connect. An older white man and a young black man fifty years ago might have had very little in common, but they could have conversed about Jackie Robinson and Branch Rickey with passion informed by conviction. More likely than not, they would also be able to draw on shared experiences changing oil filters and tinkering with recalcitrant carburetors. Opportunities abounded for boys to learn from older men in the community: whether in the church or synagogue, or in the Boy Scouts, or in the wood shop at school. I still remember how my brother Steve learned to make an inlaid wooden coffee table from his woodworking instructor, Mr. Waddell, and how proud Steve was when that table was finished.

My brother's woodworking class—which was all-boys back when Steve took the class, thirty-five years ago—no longer exists at our local public high school. In its place the school now offers a computer drawing and design class. Coed, of course.

I don't want to go back to the bad old days of woodworking for boys and home economics for girls. But we need to recognize that our society lost something in the process of dismantling opportunities for boys to learn from adult men in an all-male setting. We lost something when we eliminated many opportunities for girls to learn from women in an all-girls setting.

Socialization is the name psychologists give to the process whereby children learn the customs and mores of their society. In almost every culture of which we have any record, the process of socialization has been primarily a function of _single-gender_ communities. More than just mothers with their daughters and fathers with sons, the women of the whole community pass the traditions and mores of the culture down to the girls while the men teach the boys.[8] This job is too big for just the parents: the whole community takes part. That's what is meant by the old African proverb "It takes a village to raise a child."

Our society wasn't such an anomaly one hundred years ago or even thirty years ago. Back then parents had lots of help with the socialization process. The typical child took part in many single-sex activities: adult women with girls, the men with the boys. Most of those activities now are either gone or they've become coed. You can have a perfectly reasonable coed robotics class, but you won't build a _tribe_. Those kids will learn how to solder copper wire to metal posts, but a genuine connection between the generations is less likely to be established.

It's tough being a parent today. Tougher than in previous eras, I think. Parents today carry more of the burden of socializing their children. Parents have fewer people to whom they can look for help. It's less likely that a grandparent or a cousin or uncle will be available to help out because it's more likely that the family lives far away from other relatives. _socialya~a_

The neglect of gender in education and child-rearing has done real harm. The failure to recognize and respect sex differences has led to the pathologizing of normal female and male attributes. Restless boys are drugged with Ritalin and Concerta so that they will sit still and be quiet in classes taught by soft-spoken women who bore them. Shy teenage girls are medicated with Paxil with the approval of their anxious, misinformed parents. Don't tell me that this doesn't happen. I see these kids every day.

Ironically, some of the harm has come from the inappropriate *intensification* of gender roles as well as from the *sexualization* of childhood at an earlier age than ever before. Once again I think of the old Latin proverb: "Try to drive out nature with a pitchfork; she will always return." If you refuse to affirm a child's gender identity explicitly, children will find other ways to announce their gender identity—ways that may lead them down the wrong road. Seven-year-old girls today wear short shorts to school, sporting phrases like "Hot Stuff" across their derriere. Fourth-grade boys, referring to oral sex, casually ask girls whether they spit or swallow.[9] Sixth-graders gather at parties where the preferred mode of interaction is "grinding": the boy grinds his pelvis into the girl's butt, announcing his masculine role without ever seeing the girl's face. "Kids don't dance face to face anymore," Linda Perlstein observed during the year she spent with middle schoolers. "Girls [are] not sure if they want these guys they don't know grinding against their behinds, but what can they do?"[10]

Boys are hungry for an answer to the question: What does it mean to be a man? But the formal structures of our society—schools in particular—no longer offer any answers to that question. So the market steps into the vacuum. Not long ago I saw an ad in a video game magazine trumpeting that a particular video game is "real man stuff." The ad depicts a fantasy female—long legs, tiny waist, large breasts—astride a motorcycle. The ad is telling teenage boys that being a man means playing a video game with a two-dimensional Barbie doll in a virtual world, a world where girls never talk back, never have an agenda of their own.

You and I know that real manhood has nothing to do with playing video games. You and I know that being a man means using your strength in the service of others. That's the secret to

the popularity of Somos Amigos, the program I discussed earlier in which sixteen teenage boys led by four adult men spend their summer building houses for peasants in the highlands of the Dominican Republic. The boys love it because it's real. It's not a video game. These teenage boys really are putting their strength and their sweat to work in the service of others. *That's* "real man stuff."

Girls are searching, too. Joan Jacobs Brumberg has studied how the psychosexual development of girls has changed over the generations. The most fundamental change Brumberg documents is that girls in generations past worried about their *character.* Today most girls' first concern is with their *appearance.* Whereas the typical fifteen- and sixteen-year-old girl in generations past made solemn resolutions to be a better person, the fifteen- and sixteen-year-old of today makes solemn resolutions to lose weight, tone her tummy, and find a hairstyle that suits her face.[11] The relentless message of our culture—in TV shows and commercials, in movies, in magazines—is that *being a woman means looking sexy.* No wonder so many girls are so concerned about their appearance. We have no structure in place to teach girls that becoming a real woman is not about how you look on the outside, but about who you are inside.

Paradoxically, the ostensibly gender-neutral child-raising and educating of the past twenty years has had the effect of pushing girls and boys into pink and blue cubbyholes. Boys have withdrawn en masse from subjects such as art, dance, and foreign languages. Girls' participation in physics and computer science peaked twenty years ago and has been declining ever since.[12] Art, music, dance, drama, and foreign languages have become largely the provinces of girls and feminized boys (as discussed in the previous chapter). How can we break down those gender stereotypes?

I suggest that the solution is first of all to recognize the differences in how girls and boys develop, and second to embrace gender-separate educational and sports opportunities for both. Recall the quotes at the beginning of the chapter on school. Professors Myra and David Sadker claimed that our schools shortchange girls. Christina Hoff Sommers argued that our schools shortchange boys. Both sides make some good points. Coed schools do shortchange both girls *and* boys, but not primarily because the teachers are sexist or because the textbooks are biased. Coed schools will always shortchange both girls and boys to some degree, for the simple reason that girls and boys do indeed learn differently. As we've seen, the various regions of the brain develop in a different sequence in girls and boys and according to different timetables. You can't customize a school for one sex without putting the other at a disadvantage any more than you can sing the same musical note both loud and soft at the same time. Andrew Hunter, a veteran teacher who has taught at coed schools as well as at single-sex schools, says that "teaching in a coed classroom is like teaching two classes at once."[13]

You can reverse this bad karma by separating the sexes. A boys-only French language class is remarkably different from a coed French class. In a coed French class, all too often the only boys who make any attempt to speak in a French accent are the geeks. In an all-boys language class, all the boys compete to see whose accent is the best. "There may be a subtle and invidious pressure towards gender stereotyping in coed schools," says Mr.

Hunter. "Girls tend to be cautious about going into subjects or activities which are thought of as essentially boys' things, while in boys' schools boys feel free to be themselves and develop, to follow their interests and talents in what might be regarded as non-macho pursuits—music, arts, drama." Rick Melvoin, head of the Belmont Hill School (an all-boys school in Massachusetts) agrees. The all-boys setting "frees up boys from typecasting and stereotyping of what it means to be male." Melvoin says that at his school, a boy who sings in the glee club or performs in a school play isn't regarded as any less masculine than the boy who prefers playing football or soccer. Brian Buckley, an art teacher at the Roxbury Latin school, another all-boys school, has a similar perspective. "At the coed school where I used to teach, girls took the lead in art," he says. "But here, boys are not intimidated. Many top athletes excel in art at Roxbury Latin."[14]

Here's the paradox: coed schools tend to *reinforce* gender stereotypes, whereas single-sex schools can *break down* gender stereotypes. There is now very strong evidence that girls are more likely to take courses such as computer science and physics in girls-only schools than in coed schools.[15] Boys in single-sex schools are more than twice as likely to study art, music, foreign languages, and literature as boys of equal ability attending comparable coed schools.[16]

The benefits of single-sex education go beyond academics. Consider for example the James Lyng High School, a public high school in a low-income neighborhood of Montreal. Five years ago principal Wayne Commeford reinvented his school as a single-sex academy. Girls were assigned to girls-only classes. Boys were assigned to boys-only classes. Since that change, absenteeism has dropped by two-thirds, scores on standardized tests have improved by fifteen percentile ranks, and the rate at which kids are going on to college has nearly doubled. That's all well and good, but I want to share with you something that Mr. Commeford recently told me, something that hasn't appeared in any news report on Lyng High, namely, that the rate of teenage pregnancy decreased dramatically after the change to the single-sex format: from an average of about fifteen girls per year before the change to about two girls per year now.

At every girls' school I've visited, the teachers, administrators, counselors, and especially the students have all agreed on one thing: the rate of unwanted teenage pregnancy is much lower at their all-girls school than it is at any nearby coed school, public or private. Of course, at most schools it's hard to say which came first, the chicken or the egg. Is the rate of unwanted teenage pregnancy lower at the girls' schools because girls who wouldn't have gotten pregnant anyway choose to attend all-girls schools? Or is there something about girls' schools that makes teenage pregnancy less likely? The story of Lyng High suggests the latter. After all, the student body at Lyng High didn't change, the curriculum didn't change, the teachers didn't change, and the school's budget didn't change: but just by changing to the single-sex format, the rate of teenage pregnancy dropped.

Why is teenage pregnancy less likely when girls attend girls-only schools? You might guess that girls at girls-only schools are less likely to date boys; but that guess is likely to be wrong. The best research we have indicates that girls at girls' high schools are no less likely to date than girls at coed high schools are.[17] My own observation is that girls at girls' schools are more likely to go out on *dates* with boys, whereas girls at coed schools are more likely to *hook up* with boys.

Remember what we discussed in chapter 6 about how young teens pair off. When teens at coed schools form romantic relationships, they do so less on the basis of individual characteristics and more on the basis of where the teenager stands in the clique. The most popular boy in the group goes out with the most popular girl, and so on. Think about the implications of that pairing off. At a coed school, your daughter's boyfriend will be part of her circle of friends, the people she hangs out with. Her boyfriend's friends become her friends, too. They all do stuff together, go places together. If her boyfriend dumps her, her whole social network is at risk. So if the other girls in her group are having sex with their boyfriends, it's hard for her to say no. At a coed school, for a girl to say no to her boyfriend not only jeopardizes her relationship with her boyfriend, it jeopardizes her entire social identity at school.

At a single-sex school, though, even if your daughter does have a boyfriend, her group of friends at the girls' school is likely to be separate from the group her boyfriend hangs out with. Most of her friends at school may be only vaguely aware that she even has a boyfriend. They see that boyfriend maybe once or twice a month at parties, not every day at school. So it's easier for your daughter to say no to her boyfriend. She has more autonomy over her sexual decision-making. It's easier for her to contemplate life without the boyfriend. She knows that if she dumps her boyfriend, she will still be able to sit with the same girls at lunch, still hang with the same group during study hall.

Bottom line: for better or worse, girls at single-sex schools appear to have at least as many heterosexual relationships as girls at coed schools. But girls in single-sex schools have more autonomy in those relationships, and—as one result—are less likely to experience an unwanted pregnancy.

"But we live and work in a coed world," some critics respond. "If education is about training kids for the coed world, shouldn't education be conducted in a coed environment?" Seems like a reasonable point. But consider the results of a fascinating study conducted in Northern Ireland. In some neighborhoods in Belfast, girls may be assigned either to a coed public school or to a single-sex public school. Two psychologists went to Belfast to study the self-esteem of girls at different schools. There were no socioeconomic or educational differences between the two groups. These researchers asked the girls all sorts of questions: Are you a good student? Do your parents have good jobs? Are you good at sports? Do you think you're pretty? Do you have lots of friends?

The researchers then correlated each girl's answers with that girl's self-esteem, as measured by a separate inventory. They found that at *coed* schools, you don't need to ask a dozen questions to predict the girl's self-esteem. You have to ask only one question: "Do you think you're pretty?" If she answers yes, then her self-esteem is high. It doesn't matter if she is failing all her classes, if her parents are out of work, if she's no good at sports. If a girl at a coed school thinks she's pretty, her self-esteem is great. Conversely, and more darkly: if a girl at a coed school answers no, then her self-esteem is low. It doesn't matter if she is a straight-A student, if her parents have great jobs, if she is an ace soccer player. If a girl at a coed school thinks she's ugly, then her self-esteem is in the toilet. For girls at coed schools, the most important issue is how you *look*, not who you are or what you can do. For girls at single-sex schools, self-esteem is a more complex product of school performance, social experience, family income, and other factors. Personal appearance is in the mix, but it's only one factor out of many.[18]

Think about your own life, your own situation. I'm going to assume that you're over twenty-five years of age. Is personal appearance important to you? Sure it is. But personal appearance is not the only factor determining your self-esteem—not if you're living in the real world. If you look great but you don't have a job, or any friends you can really count on, or a loving spouse or partner, then you're not happy. Conversely, if you are overweight and don't win any beauty contests, but you've got a good job, you've got friends who really care, and you've got fun things to do with your partner on the weekend, then life is good. In the real world of adult life, personal appearance matters, but it's not the *only* thing that matters. It's not the most important thing. In real life the most important thing is not how you *look* but who you *are*. In that sense, in the sense that counts, single-sex schools are more like the real world than coed schools are.

The Belfast study isn't the first or only one to show that in the ways that matter, single-sex schools may provide better preparation for the real world than coed schools do. Johns Hopkins sociologist James Coleman made the same discovery forty years ago, interviewing students at single-sex and coed high schools in the United States. Coleman found that at coed schools, kids were most concerned with who was the best-looking, who was the most popular, and (for the boys) who was best in sports. He concluded that the adolescent culture of coed schools exerts "a rather strong deterrent to academic achievement." When asked about their career aspirations, girls at coed schools daydreamed out loud about becoming a fashion model or an actress. Girls at single-sex schools talked about preparing for a career either in business or in the sciences. "It is commonly assumed that it is 'better' for boys and girls to be in school together," he wrote, "if not better for their academic performance, then at least better for their social development and adjustment. But this may not be so. Coeducation may be inimical to *both* academic achievement *and* social adjustment. . . . Just putting boys and girls together in the same school is not necessarily the 'normal, healthy' thing to do. It does not necessarily promote adjustment to life. It may promote, as indicated by these data, *mal*adjustment to life after school."[19]

Beyond Pink and Blue

I recently visited the Clear Water Academy, a private school in Calgary. In the fall of 2003 the school's leadership reinvented the school as a dual academy: girls in one wing, boys in another. All classes and activities became single-sex—including the school band.

During all the years that the school was coed, the trumpet players were always boys and the flute players were always girls. That didn't happen because the band instructor told the boys to play trumpet and the girls to play flute. It happened because whenever girls and boys are together, their behavior inevitably reflects the larger society in which they live. In North America, boys aren't supposed to play the flute—at least not when there are girls around.

Once the school's format was changed to single-sex, though,

the gender stereotypes crumbled away. "If we're going to have a band, some of you boys are going to have to switch to the flute," the bandleader said to his woodwind players. Several boys volunteered. Likewise, a handful of girls offered to learn to play the trumpet. Had the band remained coed, it's doubtful whether those girls would ever have taken up the trumpet or if any of those boys would ever have picked up a flute.

Some of those kids are getting pretty good with their new instrument. Boys who choose to play the trumpet in a coed ensemble sometimes have difficulty understanding what ensemble playing is all about: blending the sound of your instrument in with everybody else. Some boys play their trumpet too loudly. On the other hand, you often have to coax girl flute players to play their flute loudly enough.

In the single-sex format, those gender-typical traits—which had been liabilities—become assets. Girls who play the trumpet are less likely than boys to try to drown out everybody else. Boys who play the flute don't need much encouragement to play their instrument as loudly as they can.

I was so impressed by what was happening at this Calgary school that immediately upon my return home, I ordered biographies of James Galway and Jean-Pierre Rampal, two of the greatest flute players of the past century—and both of them were men. Sure enough, both men learned to play the flute in all-boy ensembles: James Galway in Belfast, and Jean-Pierre Rampal in Marseilles.[20] Had those men been born and raised in North America and attended only coed schools, it's unlikely that they would ever have touched a flute. And the world would have been poorer for it.

We all want our children to grow up to be courageous and self-confident—attributes that are traditionally considered masculine. But we also want them to be nurturing, thoughtful, and good listeners—attributes traditionally seen as feminine. We want every child to grow up to be an adult who is comfortable expressing both feminine and masculine attributes, whatever is appropriate for the situation. The old-school social reformers of the 1970s believed that the best way to create androgynous adults would be to raise androgynous children. Looking back, we can understand that belief, but we can also see that it was naive and uninformed. The best way to raise your son to be a man who is caring and nurturing is to let him first of all *be a boy*. "You can't be at home everywhere until you are at home *somewhere*," Johnetta Coles said recently.[21] Once your son is sure of who he is, he'll be more confident, more able to explore gender-atypical ways of learning and listening. Remember that boys who attend single-sex schools are more than twice as likely to study art, music, drama, foreign languages, and similar subjects than are boys who attend coed schools. Recently some have even suggested that boys who attend single-sex schools are better listeners and don't try as hard to seem "macho" compared with boys who attend coed schools.[22]

In 2003 a group of distinguished scholars sponsored in part by the Dartmouth Medical School issued a report describing how girls and boys are hardwired to be different, and how our society's neglect of gender differences has caused great harm. One out of four teenagers is at serious risk of not achieving a productive adulthood, according to this report. Half of our teenagers have used illegal drugs. Adults need to get serious about the question of gender, the report concluded. "The need to attach social significance and meaning to gender appears to be a human universal," they wrote, and one that "deeply influences well-being."[23]

These scholars acknowledged that many educators continue to view gender not as an innate biological characteristic but as a socially constructed role. After reviewing the evidence, these experts concluded that such a perspective is "seriously incomplete." Gender "runs deeper, near to the core of human identity and social meaning—in part because it is biologically primed and connected to differences in brain structure and function, and in part because it is so deeply implicated in the transition to adulthood."[24]

The transition to adulthood. More than in any other realm, that's where our society lets kids down. We offer our children no guidance about what it means to be an adult woman or an adult man. No other culture has ever abandoned young people making the transition to a *gendered* adulthood as completely as the twenty-first-century postindustrial societies of North America, Western Europe, and Australia/New Zealand.

In traditional societies the transition to a gendered adulthood is a matter of great importance, observed with ceremonies and rituals that are markedly different for girls and boys—so the Dartmouth Medical School report observes. Female rites of passage "tend to celebrate entry into womanhood . . . For young women, many world rituals suggest that with menarche comes heightened introspective powers, greater spiritual access, and an enriched inner life. . . . Male rites of passage are often more punishing, typically involving suffering and endurance. Such rituals seek to help the boy connect with spiritual and mythic meaning and totemic sponsorship from which he will draw strength to control his own aggression and to direct it toward the pro-social goals of his community."[25]

I'm suggesting that we need more single-sex activities that transcend the generations, for both girls and boys. But what would such activities look like? We can't go back to the sewing circles of the 1930s.

Remember Cyndi Lauper? She had some big hits in the 1980s, including "Girls Just Want to Have Fun" and "Time after Time." Lauper recently told journalist Steve Inskeep that her singing was motivated by a desire to make a difference in people's lives, to perform a public service in her own way. Inskeep responded, "When you refer to public service and trying to sing songs that make a difference in people's lives—don't take this the wrong way—but 'Girls Just Want to Have Fun' is not the first song that would come to somebody's mind."

"That's because you're not a woman, Steve," Lauper answered without hesitation. "[That song] was the first song with a woman who brought her mother into it and brought three generations of women together. It was the first time at a concert that you could go and see grandmothers wearing their rhinestones, mothers having their hair spray-painted on one side, and girls dressed up as little scary versions of me. *I brought three generations of women together* under the guise of having a good time, which is not a bad thing. Because really and truly, it's a practice, it's a life practice to walk joyfully through life."[26]

Maybe a few of our cultural icons might follow Cyndi Lauper's lead and offer single-sex concerts. We're already seeing a resurgence of single-sex fitness clubs such as Curves. Religious communities are rediscovering the power of single-sex gatherings with groups such as the all-male Promise Keepers, although critics have expressed concern about the gender stereotypes promulgated by such meetings.

One hundred years from now, scholars may look back at the disintegration of early twenty-first-century culture and conclude that a fundamental cause for the unraveling of our social fabric was the neglect of gender in the raising of our children—not only in our schools, but also in the disbanding of gender-separate activities across generations, and in the near elimination of single-gender communal activities: women with girls, men with boys. I wonder what those future historians will say about how long it took us to recognize our mistake, to recognize that *gender matters.*

Hopefully the blinders are coming off at last. Our job now is to create a society that has the courage and the wisdom to cherish and celebrate the innate differences between the sexes while at the same time enabling equal opportunities for every child.

AFTERWORD

This is an exciting time to be involved in the study of gender differences. In the months since *Why Gender Matters* was originally published, I've had the opportunity to talk with many teachers who are using the book as a jumping-off point for their own investigations into how girls and boys learn. The results have been fascinating. As Ron Wallace, then principal of the Clear Water Academy in Calgary, Alberta, told me, "It's like the study of physics must have been after Einstein published his theory of relativity. So much that we thought we knew is now obsolete, and there are so many new questions that we have to explore." Questions such as: Do boys learn better sitting down or standing up? The basic principle, as presented in chapter 5, is that the right kind of stress enhances learning in boys but impairs learning in most girls. Standing up is a mild form of stress. Three months ago I observed a public elementary school classroom in Waterloo, Iowa, where teacher Jeff Ferguson was leading a class of first-grade boys. Mr. Ferguson had made sitting optional in his all-boy classroom. One boy was sitting. The boy next to him was standing. The next boy was crouching under his desk, and behind him a boy was slowly twirling in circles. But all those boys were paying close attention to Mr. Ferguson. And all the boys were loving that class. One of the boys kissed his paper after he finished working on the assignment. A whole class of first-grade boys, absolutely in love with school. You don't see that very often.

I've seen other elementary school classrooms where teachers waste half the class time trying to get the boys to sit down and be quiet. In a coed class, the boys have to sit because girls would be distracted by boys crouching or twirling on either side of them. But—and this may surprise you—the boy who is sitting in his chair is *not* distracted by the boy who is crouching under the desk next to him. Of course, later on these boys will have to learn to sit in a chair. But why do we have to insist that all six-year-old boys spend all their classroom time sitting down? For many six-year-old boys, that's just not developmentally appropriate. Teachers at an all-boys elementary school in Chicago told me last month that the performance of their boys improved "500 percent" after teachers removed the chairs from the classroom. "Young boys just learn better when they stand up. When they sit down, their brains shut off," one teacher told me.

Classrooms without chairs. That's the kind of new idea which makes this an exciting time to be in this field.

Gender differences made the headlines right around the time that *Why Gender Matters* was published, owing to some unwise remarks made by the president of Harvard University, Larry Summers. On January 14, 2005, Dr. Summers offered three reasons why there are so few women professors in subjects like computer science and physics. President Summers began by acknowledging that sexism probably plays some role—but he did not consider sexism to be an important factor. Second, he asserted that women make different lifestyle choices than men do. In particular (according to Dr. Summers), women with small children at home might be less willing to put in long hours at work than men are.

If he had just stopped there, he might not have gotten into much trouble. But Dr. Summers went on to say that a third factor is at work specifically with regard to subjects like computer science and physics. The third factor, the esteemed professor said, has to do with innate differences in "intrinsic aptitude."[1] In other words—according to the president of Harvard University—women just don't have the brains to excel in physics.

Had those same remarks been made by some other public person—say, by a conservative politician—they might have attracted little notice. But when the president of Harvard University says that women are innately less capable in science, a firestorm is sure to erupt. On the conservative end of the spectrum, commentators such as Linda Chavez and Cathy Young sprang to Summers's defense. They suggested that because little boys prefer to play with trucks rather than dolls, boys are destined to be better at physics. They also invoked the idea that boys are more variable than girls: so just as mental retardation is more common among boys than girls, so too is genius more common among boys than girls (according to these commentators).[2] At the other end of the spectrum, the majority of the Harvard faculty of arts and sciences rose in anger to denounce their president. One Harvard physics professor said it was "crazy" to suggest any hardwired or innate difference between the brains of women and men.[3] On the Ides of March, 2005, the faculty voted that Caesar must die: or at least, he should resign.[4]

In fact, both sides of this debate got it wrong. The outraged liberals were demonstrably wrong on the facts when they asserted that there are no hardwired differences of consequence between male and female brains. But Dr. Summers was wrong to suggest that *differences* imply an *order of rank*. A knife is different from a spoon. That doesn't mean that a knife is better or worse than a spoon. Girls and boys learn differently. That doesn't mean that boys are necessarily destined to be better physicists—unless physics is taught in a way that gives boys an advantage at the expense of girls.

One of the many relevant facts of which Dr. Summers was unaware is that girls attending single-sex high schools are far more likely subsequently to major in subjects like computer science and physics than are girls who attend coed high schools.[5] He also showed no knowledge of a classic study showing that women who attend women's colleges are at least three times more likely subsequently to earn a Ph.D. in subjects like computer science and physics, compared to women who attend coed universities. Mount Holyoke College has graduated more women who have gone on to earn Ph.D.s in physics than Harvard has.[6]

If Dr. Summers were right—if women were *innately* less capable of learning physics—then it wouldn't matter which type of school or college they went to. The fact that a single-sex school can improve girls' performance in these subjects so dramatically suggests that *the way physics is taught,* not brain ability, is the key to understanding the underrepresentation of women in these subjects.

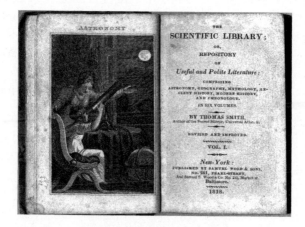

Historian Kim Tolley has shown that throughout the 1800s, girls routinely outperformed boys in subjects like physics and astronomy. During the same era, boys seemed more able to learn foreign languages than girls were. The differences in performance were enormous. Girls routinely outscored the boys by wide margins—70 percent of girls passing compared with only 30 percent of boys passing—when girls and boys took the same physics exam. These differences were seen throughout the United States, in all social strata, from elite private schools to schools for orphans and Indians. The differences in performance were so universal—favoring girls in science, and boys in foreign languages—that educators in the 1800s had a saying, "Science for the Ladies, Classics for Gentlemen."[7]

What was going on?

One part of the answer is that subjects such as physics and astronomy were taught very differently in the 1800s, even when the actual facts being covered were the same as they are today. Force diagrams, and Newton's laws, haven't changed in the past 150 years; but the way those subjects are taught has changed dramatically. In the 1800s, the emphasis was on *understanding*: How is the universe put together? What laws govern the movement of objects in space and on the earth? Learning physics was considered to be a way of understanding the mind of God, and therefore was seen as a pious activity suitable for young women. (Indeed, in the early 1800s, physics was often referred to as "natural theology.") Physics textbooks of that era showed adult women instructing young girls in the use of scientific instruments such as a telescope. The message of that picture, for a young woman of the time, was: "You belong here. Physics is an appropriate subject for you to study."

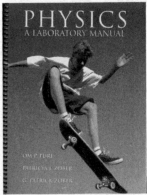

Photograph © Karl Weatherly, 2005

Contrast that picture with the typical photograph in a twenty-first-century physics textbook. The emphasis now is on extreme skateboarding, bullets, and bombs. There is remarkably little attempt to show any girl-friendly activities. If you're a girl who's not into extreme skateboarding and who doesn't see the point of shooting an apple with a high-velocity bullet (see the picture below), the unspoken message conveyed by these pictures is: "You don't belong here. Physics is about blowing things

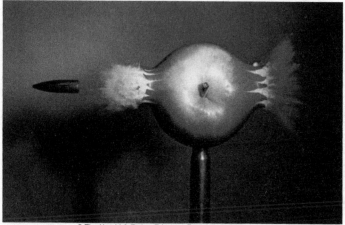

© The Harold & Esther Edgerton Foundation, 2005, courtesy of Palm Press, Inc.

up. Physics is about extreme sports. If you're not into that stuff, maybe you should take some other subject."

In math and science, it's often possible to cover the same topic in two different ways: a girl-friendly way and a boy-friendly way. I gave one example of both approaches in chapter 5, in teaching Fibonacci numbers. Educational researchers Anat Zohar and David Sela found that the same is true of physics. Talking about bombs and bullets and collisions is a good way to teach physics to boys. And that's the way it's usually taught.

A football guard with a mass of 100 kilograms, running

at a speed of 2 meters per second, collides head-on with a
quarterback who is standing, looking for a receiver. The quarter-
back's mass is 80 kilograms. Assuming a perfectly inelastic
collision and frictionless flight after the collision, describe the
motion of the guard and quarterback immediately after the
collision.

That works fine for boys. But Zohar and Sela found that simply
plugging numbers into formulae was unsatisfying for most of
the girls in the AP physics classes they surveyed. The girls were
more interested in knowing *why:* Why, for example, is the formula describing the gravitational force between two objects in-
versely proportional to the *square* of the distance between them?
Why isn't it proportional to the cube, or the fourth power?[8]
When you try to answer that question, you'll find that you
can teach physics without ever talking about football players
or skateboards. You can start with questions like these, questions that focus on the *why.* The late Nobel Laureate Richard
Feynman did precisely that in his introductory physics textbooks. You won't find many bombs or collisions in the
Feynman textbooks, but you'll find lots of explanations for why
the universe is made the way it is. You can teach physics either
way, the Feynman way or the bombs-and-bullets way, with the
same computational rigor; but it's hard to teach it *both* ways in
the same classroom, and if you emphasize one approach rather
than the other, you favor one gender at the expense of the
other. The most equitable solution may be to offer a girls' class
and a boys' class.

In the middle of the Larry Summers brouhaha, a group of
Harvard women calling themselves WISHR (Women in Science
at Harvard-Radcliffe) suggested that perhaps part of the solution
might include offering science classes for women only.[9] The
Harvard Crimson published a blistering editorial in response.
Commenting on WISHR's suggestion that women and men
learn differently, and therefore might benefit from single-sex

classes, the *Crimson* replied that "if that were accepted, then there ought to be special sections for women in every field, not just science. Indeed, we might as well return to single-sex education at Harvard. And Radcliffe."[10]

Maybe bringing back Radcliffe wouldn't be such a bad idea.

President Summers has announced that Harvard will devote $50 million to encouraging women faculty to come to Harvard.[11] I am not optimistic that such a measure will accomplish much, aside from possibly cooling the fire of those calling for Larry Summers's ouster. Last year, only 10 percent of high school seniors taking the AP examination in computer science were girls.[12] No amount of money spent by Harvard to hire women faculty away from other universities is likely to raise the percentage of high school girls studying computer science. What are needed are measures to encourage more girls to explore their potential, particularly in math and science. A wider availability of single-sex classrooms at the high school level might be a sensible place to start.

Only a few days after President Summers made his inflammatory comments about women's purported inability to excel in science, Mark Bauerlein of the National Endowment for the Arts, along with his colleague Sandra Stotsky, published an important article about what teenagers do in their spare time. Twenty years ago, many teenage boys used to read for fun. That may be hard for today's parents to believe, but it's true. That's no longer the case, according to the NEA study. The gender gap in reading—favoring girls at the expense of boys—has grown from a small gap to a yawning chasm. "What was formerly a moderate difference is fast becoming a decided marker of gender identity: Girls read; boys don't," announced Bauerlein and Stotsky. They concluded that *the neglect of gender differences* in what girls and boys like to read is at least partly to blame. "The K-12 literature curriculum may in fact be contributing to the problem," they wrote, citing data showing that "by the time they go on to high school, boys have lost their interest in reading . . ." Bauerlein and Stotsky see boys as victims of a feminized curriculum that has neglected the natural interests and inclinations of boys in the misguided pursuit of political correctness and "diversity."[13] *Huckleberry Finn* and *For Whom the Bell Tolls* have been replaced by *The Color Purple* and *Beloved*. Ernest Hemingway has been replaced by Toni Morrison. It's not a question of which author is "better." Both Ernest Hemingway and Toni Morrison won the Nobel Prize in Literature. "Better" has no meaning unless you ask "better for whom?" Ernest Hemingway's books are boy-friendly, while Toni Morrison's books are girl-friendly. I've heard some teachers respond that we need to stretch the boys' imaginations, to encourage boys to read something that isn't boy-friendly. But surely such a suggestion violates every rule of pedagogy. If a child is having problems riding a tricycle, putting that child on a bicycle is not likely to be helpful. If boys aren't reading, assigning them texts that don't fit their interests is likely to have the effect of driving them further away from literature, not bringing them closer in.

The NEA survey highlighted one aspect of a much broader phenomenon: boys are disengaging from school. More boys are dropping out of school, and a smaller proportion of boys are going on to college.[14] Young men who do attend college are less likely to earn a diploma, and those men who do earn a college diploma are now less likely than women are to go on to graduate school.[15] At the graduate level, there has been a significant drop in the number of American men earning Ph.D.s in math and science, and American women have not stepped in to fill the breach. Looking at men and women combined, the number of Americans earning degrees in engineering has dropped 8 percent since 1990, despite the rising demand for engineers; the number of Americans earning degrees in math has dropped 22 percent over the same period.[16]

The gap is being filled by foreign students. In 2005 the majority of Ph.D.s earned in math and science at American universities were awarded to non-Americans. "One has only to attend the graduation ceremonies and see embarrassed provosts attempting to pronounce the names of the Indian, Chinese, Nigerian, and Middle Eastern students receiving higher degrees to realize what an impact these foreign students have had . . . Their presence has hidden the fact that fewer than half of those leaving our excellent graduate schools with higher degrees are American-born," wrote James Gallagher in an essay suggesting that the decline in the numbers of Americans studying advanced math and science may adversely affect national security.[17]

Do you see the common element underlying these two stories, the Larry Summers story about the underrepresentation of girls in math and science and the NEA survey showing that boys no longer like to read? In both cases, the problem derives in part from a neglect of gender differences. Thirty years ago, teachers didn't hesitate to recommend books on the basis of a student's gender. Boys were encouraged to read Robert Louis Stevenson and Ernest Hemingway. Girls were encouraged to read Jane Austen, Willa Cather, and Carson McCullers. Today, such gender-specific advice is often labeled reactionary and stereotyped, if not downright sexist. But *the neglect of gender differences does not break down gender stereotypes;* ironically, neglecting hardwired gender differences more often results in a *reinforcement* of gender stereotypes. The end result of thirty years of neglect of gender differences is a generation of boys who hate to read.

Parents and teachers need to be more aware of the new research we've considered in this book. Teachers must understand that girls and boys learn differently. Teachers must be given more opportunities to learn how to use gender-specific teaching strategies to get the best out of every student. If that happens, the odds are good that we'll have more girls who excel in math and science, and more boys who love to read. It's not too late to make a change.

A SEMANTIC NOTE ON "SEX" AND "GENDER"

Here is the official line on the correct usage of "sex" and "gender," according to a 2001 monograph published by the National Academies:[1]

- *Sex* is a dichotomous biological variable. Humans are either female or male.
- *Gender* is a continuous variable. Gender is socially constructed. Humans can be mostly feminine, mostly masculine, or anything in between.

Those are the National Academies' rules for using the words "sex" and "gender." I have two problems with the rules. First, I don't agree that gender is socially constructed. The monograph notes that there is wide variety within one sex with regard to individuals' presentation of gender traits. Some men are more feminine than masculine; some women are more masculine than feminine. The authors of the monograph[2] conclude that because there is variation in gender presentation among members of one sex, gender must be socially constructed.

That doesn't follow. To give a blunt counterexample: some overweight men have large breasts. Most men have small breasts. Women also show substantial variation in breast size: some are large and some are small. The average woman has larger breasts than the average man, but there's lots of overlap. The fact that there are large variations in breast size within each sex does not mean that the size of a woman's breasts is socially constructed. Likewise, the fact that there are gender variations in other parameters does not mean that those variations are socially constructed. To some extent they may be. A central argument of this book is that for the past three decades, the influence of social and cognitive factors on gender traits has been systematically overestimated while innate factors have been neglected.

The second problem I have with the rules is that they lead to confusion and ambiguity. Consider one sentence from chapter 6: "Girls often become more concerned with femininity as gender becomes more salient." In that sentence I'm trying to convey the idea that in the middle school years, many girls become more aware of their female identity and more concerned with their own femininity.

Now imagine the same sentence with "gender" replaced by "sex," in accordance with the official guidelines: "Girls often become more concerned with femininity as sex becomes more salient." The meaning is changed completely. Now the sentence seems to suggest that girls are becoming more aware of sex as in "sexual activity," which is not what I was trying to say.

In this book I have chosen whichever word—"sex" or "gender"—that seemed best suited in each context to minimize confusion and maximize clarity.

HOW FEMININE ARE YOU?

Write down your answers to each of these ten questions. Then score your quiz. To find out how *masculine* you are, turn to page 268 for that quiz. Remember that feminine and masculine are independent variables: you can be feminine, or masculine, or both feminine and masculine (*androgynous*), or neither feminine nor masculine (*undifferentiated*).

These quizzes are most accurate for North American children ages eleven through eighteen.[3]

1) The smell of musk is best described by which of the following words:

  A) musty   B) sour   C) bitter   D) pungent
  E) I have no idea

2) When other people say nice things about me, it makes me feel good.

  A) true
  B) false: I really don't care what other people say about me

3) Endive is:

  A) something like grapefruit   B) something like lettuce
  C) something like oregano   D) something like broccoli

4) I feel shy around new people . . .

    A) often   B) sometimes   C) almost never

5) The color ocher is most similar to . . .

    A) brown   B) yellow   C) green   D) blue

    E) I have no idea

6) A person might use a serger to . . .

    A) tidy up the kitchen   B) dust behind the curtains

    C) decorate a cake   D) hem a dress   E) I have no idea

7) I try to make an effort to present myself as a cheerful person, even when I'm not feeling cheerful . .

    A) often   B) occasionally   C) seldom or never

8) I can tell when someone else needs help . . .

    A) most of the time   B) sometimes   C) not very often

9) People can fool me into believing things that aren't true—

    A) almost never   B) more often than I like to admit

10) If someone I know feels sad, I . . .

    A) will probably feel sad, too, and will want to help them.

    B) will want to help them, but probably won't feel sad.

    C) won't feel sad, and won't try to help unless specifically asked to do so.

Scoring the Questionnaire

Please remember: the point of these questionnaires is to help you understand that a person can be *both* feminine *and* masculine—or, for that matter, *neither* feminine *nor* masculine. These questionnaires may also help you see how a girl could be masculine, or a boy feminine.

    Add up your score:

1) The smell of musk is best described by which of the following words:

>Give yourself one point if you answered D, pungent.
>
>Zero points for any of the other answers.

2) When other people say nice things about me, it makes me feel good.

>Give yourself one point if you answered A, true.
>
>Zero points for answer B.

3) Endive is:

>Give yourself one point if you answered B, something like lettuce.
>
>Zero points for any of the other answers.

4) I feel shy around new people . . .

>Give yourself one point if you answered A, often.
>
>Zero points for answers B or C.

5) The color ocher is most similar to . . .

>Give yourself one point if you answered B, yellow.
>
>Zero points for any of the other answers.

6) A person might use a serger to . . .

>Give yourself one point if you answered D, hem a dress.
>
>Zero points for any of the other answers.

7) I try to make an effort to present myself as a cheerful person . . .

>Give yourself one point if you answered A, often.
>
>Zero points for answer B, occasionally.
>
>Subtract one point for answer C, seldom or never.

8) I can tell when someone else needs help . . .

>Give yourself one point if you answered A, most of the time.
>
>Zero points for answer B, sometimes.
>
>Subtract one point for answer C, not very often.

9) People can fool me into believing things that aren't true—

Give yourself one point if you answered B, more often than I like to admit.

Zero points for answer A, almost never.

10) If someone I know feels sad, I . . .

Give yourself one point if you answered A, will probably feel sad, too.

Zero points for answer B, will want to help them, but probably won't feel sad.

Subtract one point for answer C, won't feel sad, and won't try to help unless specifically asked to do so.

Add up all your points (don't forget to subtract one point if appropriate for answers 7, 8, and 10).

Minus 3 to Plus 3: You are not feminine at all.

Plus 4 to Plus 6: You've earned the Katharine Hepburn award: you are moderately feminine.

Plus 7 to Plus 10: You've earned the Audrey Hepburn award: very feminine.

HOW MASCULINE ARE YOU?

Write down your answers to each of the following ten questions. Then turn to page 270 to score your quiz. Remember that feminine and masculine are independent variables: you can be feminine, or masculine, or both feminine and masculine (*androgynous*), or neither feminine nor masculine (*undifferentiated*).

These quizzes are most accurate for North American children ages eleven through eighteen.[4]

1) When somebody has to take charge of things,
   A) I put myself forward more often than not
   B) I usually wait for someone else to take the lead

2) Talking about cars, "camber" refers to
   A) the transfer of power from the transmission to the driveshaft
   B) the ability of the car to hold the road, to handle sharp corners without slipping
   C) the angle at which the tires intersect the road .
   D) the delivery of fuel from the fuel injector to the engine
   E) I have no idea

3) It's easy for me to make up my mind about things, even before I know all the facts . . .

   A) most of the time   B) sometimes   C) not very often

4) If I have to do something I've never done before, I'd rather try to figure out how to do it on my own first, even if I have to work at it for an hour, before I ask someone else to show me how to do it.

   A) true   B) false; I'm comfortable asking others for help

5) When I'm playing a game, I often get upset if I don't win.

   A) true   B) false

6) I can get people to do what I want them to do, even when they don't want to.

   A) most of the time   B) sometimes   C) not very often

7) I think I would look better if I gained ten pounds of muscle.[5]

   A) true   B) false

8) When I'm reading, I prefer

   A) a quiet room, so I can concentrate better and not be distracted

   B) music or TV playing in the background, but not too loud. I don't like it *too* quiet

   C) I don't care—makes no difference whether there's noise or not

   D) Not applicable. I don't read much

9) If I want to do something, and a knowledgeable acquaintance tells me that it might be dangerous or risky,

   A) I'll probably go ahead with it anyway

   B) I might change my plans

   C) Not applicable—I don't usually do things that people would consider risky or dangerous

10) I'm smarter than you would guess if you knew just my grades in school.

   A) True   B) False

Scoring the Questionnaire

Add up your score:

1) When somebody has to take charge of things,

   Give yourself one point if you answered A, I put myself forward more often than not.

   Zero points for answer B, I usually wait for someone else to take the lead.

2) Talking about cars, "camber" refers to

   Give yourself one point for answer C, the angle at which the tires intersect the road.

   Zero points for all other answers.

3) It's easy for me to make up my mind about things, even before I know all the facts . . .

   Give yourself one point if you answered A, most of the time.

   Zero points for B and C.

4) If I have to do something I've never done before, I'd rather try to figure out how to do it on my own first, even if I have to work at it for an hour, before I ask someone else . . .

   Give yourself one point if you answered A, true.

   Zero points for B.

5) When I'm playing a game, I often get upset if I don't win.

   Give yourself one point for A, true. No points for B, false.

6) I can get people to do what I want them to do, even when they don't want to.

   Give yourself one point for A, most of the time.

   No points for B or C.

7) I think I would look better if I gained ten pounds of muscle.

   Give yourself one point if you answered A, true.

8) When I'm reading, I prefer

Give yourself one point if you answered either C, I don't care—makes no difference whether there's noise or not, or D, Not applicable. I don't read much.

No points for A or B.

9) If I want to do something, and a knowledgeable acquaintance tells me that it might be dangerous or risky,

Give yourself one point if you answered A, I'll probably go ahead with it anyway.

No points for B. Subtract one point if you answered C, I don't usually do things that people would consider risky.

10) I'm smarter than you would guess if you knew just my grades in school.

Give yourself one point for A, True.

No points for B, False.

Add up all your points (don't forget to subtract one point if appropriate for answer 9).

Minus 1 to Plus 3: You are not masculine at all.

Plus 4 to Plus 6: You've earned the John Ritter award: you are moderately masculine.

Plus 7 to Plus 10: You've earned the Clint Eastwood award: you are very masculine.

ACKNOWLEDGMENTS

My greatest debt is to the parents and children who have chosen me as their family doctor over the past fifteen years. It's a great privilege to be a family doctor: an extraordinary intimacy to follow the same child from the newborn nursery through toddlerhood, through childhood and into adolescence. Because I've lived and worked in the same small town for fifteen years, some of the children I first saw as babies are teenagers now. I've seen the results of different parenting styles firsthand in two-thousand-plus children. If there's anything useful in this book, it's thanks most of all to the children and parents who have walked through my office doors over those years.

Among teachers and school administrators, my deepest gratitude goes to Christopher Wadsworth, director of the International Boys' Schools Coalition, for encouraging me to share what I've learned about differences in how girls and boys learn. I am also grateful to these educators whose specific suggestions and contributions made this book better: Trent Anderson, Douglas Blakey, Wayne Commeford, Deidre Cryor, Betsey Downes, Sr. Anne Dyer, Gerald Grossman, Poppy Keras, Gail Lewis, Richard McPherson, James Power, Angela Romano, George Smitherman, Dr. Peggy Stark, Daren Starnes, Christina Sullivan, Agnes Underwood, Amy Van Dragt, Sr. Anne Wachter, Ron Wallace, and Benjamin Wright.

I sent chapters from this book out to many of the researchers whose works I cite. Thanks to Professor Simon Baron-Cohen for corrections and additions to my discussion of his extraordinary work with newborn babies. Kenji Kansaku, now at the National Institutes of Health, helped me understand his work on sex differences in brain blood flow and also provided me with references of which I had been unaware. Other academicians who offered correction and clarification include Shelley Taylor, Deborah Yurgelun-Todd, Barbara Cone-Wesson, Jerome Kagan, Pat Sexton, Edwin Lephart, Yasumasa Arai, and Marquis Vawter. Thanks also to Cornell professor John Bishop for providing me with unpublished data from his study of what's "cool" for middle school girls and boys.

Special thanks to my friend and neighbor Dr. James "Dee" Higley of the National Institutes of Health Primate Research Center. Dr. Higley has always been willing to lend an educated ear to my musings on gender differences and has clued me in to many sources in the primate literature of which I would otherwise have been unaware. When I shared some of this manuscript with him, he went far beyond the call of duty, asked to see more chapters, and provided suggestions for improving both the substance and style of the manuscript.

Professor Sandra Witelson of McMaster University, one of the world's leading experts in human neuroanatomy, was kind enough to meet with me personally to discuss sex differences in the human brain. We kept talking after we left the restaurant, and kept on talking, past midnight, in the hallway of our hotel. We didn't stop until another guest came out to complain about the noise we were making. Professor Witelson truly helped bring my understanding of these complex issues up to speed.

Three years ago I sent a proposal for a book about girls and boys to literary agent Felicia Eth. Over those three years, Felicia has been a knowledgeable guide, gently pruning here, encouraging there, always patiently waiting for my ideas to come to blossom rather than pushing her own. My editor at Doubleday, Adam Bellow, should get a prize for an extraordinarily careful reading of the manuscript and for many helpful suggestions on literary matters large and small.

My mother, Dr. Janet Sax, inspired my interest in gender differences as a child, with stories across the dinner table from her pediatric practice about differences in girls' and boys' behavior. My father, Harry Sax, has encouraged me at every step of this project.

Finally, many thanks to my wife, Katie, for tolerating the all-nighters without complaint, and for always managing to look interested when I insisted on telling her the latest news about hermaphrodite birds.

SOURCE NOTES

For tips on how to obtain the complete text of references listed here, please go to www.genderdifferences.org/original-sources.htm.

Chapter 1: Differences

1. Shelley Taylor, *The Tending Instinct* (New York: Henry Holt, 2002), p. 5.
2. All stories in this book are factual. I have changed names and some identifying details to protect my patients' privacy. In some cases I have combined elements from different patients' stories to create a single story.
3. John Corso, "Age and Sex Differences in Thresholds," *Journal of the Acoustical Society of America*, 31:489–507, 1959; also John Corso, "Aging and Auditory Thresholds in Men and Women," *Archives of Environmental Health*, 6:350–356, 1963.
4. Leonard Sax and Kathleen Kautz, "Who First Suggests the Diagnosis of Attention-Deficit Hyperactivity Disorder? A Survey of Primary-Care Pediatricians, Family Physicians, and Child Psychiatrists," *Annals of Family Medicine*, 1:171–74, 2003.
5. Anne Fausto-Sterling, *Sexing the Body: Gender Politics and the Construction of Sexuality* (New York: Basic Books, 2000), pp. 31, 3.
6. Claudia Dreifus, "Anne Fausto-Sterling: Exploring What Makes Us Male or Female," *New York Times*, January 2, 2001, p. F3. See also Courtney Weaver, "Birds Do It," *Washington Post*, March 26, 2000, p. X6; and Marc Breedlove, "Sexing the Body," *New England Journal of Medicine*, 343:668, 2000.

7. Susan Hoy Crawford, *Beyond Dolls and Guns: 101 Ways to Help Children Avoid Gender Bias* (Portsmouth, NH: Heinemann, 1995). See also *William's Doll* by Charlotte Zolotow (New York: Harper & Row, 1972).

8. When Hugh Lytton and David Romney reviewed 172 studies involving 28,000 children, they found no evidence that parents' child-rearing has any measurable effect on the gender-typical behavior of their children. Boys who are encouraged to play with dolls do not grow up to be any more nurturing than boys who play with trucks or guns. See their paper, "Parents' Differential Socialization of Boys and Girls: A Meta-Analysis," *Psychological Bulletin*, 109:267–96, 1991.

9. These figures come from *Time* magazine's report on teenage drinking and drug use, "Women on a Binge," April 1, 2002, pp. 58–59.

10. National Research Council, "Characteristics of Underage Drinking," in *Reducing Underage Drinking: A Collective Responsibility* (Washington, DC: National Academies Press, 2004), p. 49.

11. According to the FBI's Uniform Crime Report for 2003, the number of boys arrested for drug abuse violations increased from 65,051 in 1993 to 98,383 in 2002, an increase of 51 percent. In 2002, 18,398 girls were arrested for drug abuse violations: i.e., more than five boys were arrested for every girl (98,383/18,398 = 5.35). See Table 33 in FBI report, "Ten Year Arrest Trends," p. 239, online at www.FBI.gov/ucr/cius_02/4sectionfour.pdf.

12. A well-documented review of this phenomenon is provided by the cover story for *Business Week* magazine, May 26, 2003, "The New Gender Gap," by Michelle Conlin (pp. 74–84). See also Thomas Newkirk's report for *Education Week*, "The Quiet Crisis in Boys' Literacy," September 10, 2003.

13. U.S. Department of Education, *Educational Equity for Girls and Women* (Washington, DC: U.S. Government Printing Office, 2000), p. 18.

14. For more information about gender gaps in the United Kingdom, Australia, New Zealand, and Canada, please go to www.genderdifferences.org/gendergaps.htm.

15. Department of Education, National Center for Education Statistics, *Projection of Education Statistics To 2011*, chapter 4, "Earned Degrees Conferred." The department projects that in May–June 2011, 568,000 men will be awarded bachelor's degrees compared with 824,000 women. That works out to 59.2 percent of degrees being awarded to women. You can access this report online at http://nces.ed.gov/pubs2001/proj01/chapter4.asp.

16. These examples come from Michelle Conlin's cover story for *Business Week* magazine, May 26, 2003, "The New Gender Gap," pp. 74–84.

17. See the study conducted by the Center for Labor Market Studies at Northeastern University, "The Hidden Crisis in the High School Dropout Problems of Young Adults in the U.S.: Recent Trends in Overall School Dropout Rates and Gender Differences in Dropout Behavior." The study can be downloaded at www.businessroundtable.org/document.cfm/914. Recent reports have shown that some school districts "fudge" their graduation rates, for example, by coding dropouts as having transferred to other school districts or to a GED program. Such transfers don't count as dropouts. The *New York Times* published a series of three articles in 2003 on this phenomenon. See Tamar Lewin and Jennifer Medina, "To Cut Failure Rate, Schools Shed Students," *New York Times*, July 31, 2003, p. A1; and also Tamar Lewin and Jennifer Medina, "High School Under Scrutiny for Giving Up on Its Students," *New York Times*, August 1, 2003, p. A1; and also Tamar Lewin, "Education: The Pushouts," *New York Times*, August 3, 2003, sec. 4, p. 2. See also Diana Jean Schemo's article "Houston Punishes Former Principal in Undercount of Dropouts," *New York Times*, August 30, 2003, p. A11.

18. The number of schools offering single-sex educational options increased from 27 in the fall of 2001 to more than 140 in the fall of 2004. You can access a list of American schools offering such options at www.singlesexschools.org.

19. You can learn more about the worldwide resurgence of single-sex education at www.singlesexschools.org. More information about the bipartisan alliance between Senator Hutchison and Senator Clinton on single-sex education is available at www.singlesexschools.org/odd_couple.html.

Chapter Two: Female Brains, Male Brains

1. Gaya Aranoff and Jennifer Bell, "Endocrinology and Growth in Children and Adolescents," in Marianne Legato, ed., *Principles of Gender-Specific Medicine* (New York: Academic Press [Elsevier], 2004), p. 12. Dr. Aranoff directs endocrine testing for the Department of Pediatrics at Columbia University Medical Center. Dr. Bell is a lecturer in pediatric endocrinology at the Columbia College of Physicians and Surgeons.

2. Walter Riese, *A History of Neurology* (New York: MD Publications, 1959),

chapter 4, "History of the Doctrine of Cerebral Localization," pp. 73–117.

3. Herbert Lansdell, "Sex Differences in Hemispheric Asymmetries of the Human Brain," *Nature*, 203:550, 1964.

4. For a review of studies from the 1960s and 1970s demonstrating that the male brain is more asymmetric than the female brain, particularly with regard to language functions, see Jeannette McGlone's review, "Sex Differences in Human Brain Asymmetry: A Critical Survey," *Behavioral and Brain Sciences*, 3:215–263, 1980. For a more recent update using next-generation technology, see the paper by Ruben Gur, Bruce Turetsky, and associates, "Sex Differences in Brain Gray and White Matter in Healthy Young Adults: Correlations with Cognitive Performance," *Journal of Neuroscience*, 19:4065–4072, 1999, especially figure 3, p. 4068.

5. These figures are drawn from Jeannette McGlone's review (see the previous note for the full reference), pp. 218–19; see also Table I, p. 232 in the same citation.

6. Norm Geschwind and A. M. Galaburda, "Cerebral Lateralization: Biological Mechanisms, Associations, and Pathology," *Archives of Neurology*, 42:428–59, 1985.

7. Arthur Arnold and Paul Burgoyne, "Are XX and XY Brain Cells Intrinsically Different?" *Trends in Endocrinology and Metabolism*, 15:6–11, 2004. For more about the hermaphrodite finch, see Robert Agate and associates, "Neural, Not Gonadal, Origin of Brain Sex Differences in a Gynandromorphic Finch," *Proceedings of the National Academies of Science*, 100:4873–78, 2003.

8. Marquis Vawter and associates, "Gender-Specific Gene Expression in Postmortem Human Brain: Localization to Sex Chromosomes," *Neuropsychopharmacology*, 29:373–84, 2004. If this topic interests you, you can learn more at www.genderdifferences.org/chromosomes.htm.

9. Traditionally, molecular biologists have believed in the doctrine of "X-inactivation." According to that doctrine, one of the two X chromosomes in females is inactivated, so that females and males receive the same "dose" of X-chromosome genes. While that doctrine remains largely valid for organs such as the liver and spleen, there is now overwhelming evidence that the doctrine of X-inactivation is routinely violated in the brain. In other words, many X chromosome genes are transcribed in female brain tissue twice as much as in male brain tissue. The brain may well be the most sexually dimorphic organ after the gonads. For starters, see the paper by Jun Xu, Paul Burgoyne, and Arthur

Arnold, "Sex Differences in Sex Chromosome Gene Expression in the Mouse Brain," *Human Molecular Genetics*, 11:1409–19, 2002.

10. Janel Caine, "The Effects of Music on the Selected Stress Behaviors, Weight, Caloric and Formula Intake, and Length of Hospital Stay of Premature and Low Birth Weight Neonates in a Newborn Intensive Care Unit," Master's thesis, Florida State University, 1989 (unpublished). If you go to the Robert Manning Strozier Library at FSU, the call number for Janel Caine's thesis is ML/3920/C34/1989.

11. Janel Caine, "The Effects of Music on the Selected Stress Behaviors, Weight, Caloric and Formula Intake, and Length of Hospital Stay of Premature and Low Birth Weight Neonates in a Newborn Intensive Care Unit," *Journal of Music Therapy*, 28:180–92, 1991.

12. Jayne Standley, "The Effect of Music and Multimodal stimulation on Physiologic and Develomental Responses of Premature Infants in Neonatal Intensive Care," *Pediatric Nursing Journal*, 21:532–39, 1998.

13. My remarks in this paragraph are drawn from two studies. The first, chronologically, is: Barbara Cone-Wesson and Glendy Ramirez, "Hearing Sensitivity in Newborns Estimated from ABRs to Bone-Conducted Sounds," *Journal of the American Academy of Audiology*, 8:299–307, 1997. The second is: Yvonne Sininger, Barbara Cone-Wesson, and Carolina Abdala, "Gender Distinctions and Lateral Asymmetry in the Low-Level Auditory Brainstem Response of the Human Neonate," *Hearing Research*, 126:58–66, 1998. The fact that girl babies have a more sensitive threshold for very quiet sounds does not by itself *prove* that girls hear better than boys when the sound is louder; however, an earlier investigation by a European team found that girl babies do in fact have a brisker, faster acoustic brain response than boy babies do, for medium-amplitude sounds similar to normal conversation. See Giuseppe Chiarenza, Giulia D'Ambrosio, and Adriana Cazzullo, "Sex and Ear Differences of Brain-Stem Acoustic Evoked Potentials in a Sample of Normal Full-Term Newborns," *Electroencephalography and Clinical Neurophysiology*, 71:357–66, 1988.

14. If you play a 4-kHz tone on a tone generator, you'll hear a very high pitch. Why are such high-frequency sounds so important for understanding speech? The answer is that distinguishing one consonant from another often involves that frequency range. For instance, consider the words "like" and "light." If you do spectral analysis of the sound energy when someone says those two words, you'll find that the difference in sound energy between "like" and "light" is almost entirely up in the 4-kHz range and higher.

15. Jane Cassidy and Karen Ditty, "Gender Differences among Newborns on a Transient Otoacoustic Emissions Test for Hearing," *Journal of Music Therapy*, 37:28–35, 2001.

16. For more information about innate gender differences in hearing, please go to www.genderdifferences.org/hearing.htm.

17. Professor Corso's classic work (see note 3, ch. 1) demonstrated that the female superiority in hearing at frequencies above 2 kHz gets larger as kids progress through adolescence and into adulthood and indeed throughout adult life. For more information about how gender differences in hearing change with age, please go to www.genderdifferences.org/hearing.htm.

18. Actually, the girl is going to experience her father's voice as being more than 100 times louder in amplitude than what the father himself is experiencing. Corso (1959) found that the threshold for a 3-kHz tone for a 43-year-old man was 30.5 decibles (dB), while the threshold for a 3-kHz tone for an 18-year-old girl was 7.3 dB. That's a difference of 23.2 dB (30.5 - 7.3 = 23.2). A difference of 23.2 dB corresponds to more than a hundredfold difference in the amplitude of the sound. If you're a little rusty on this, recall the definition of decibels (dB):

    Sound in dB = 10 log [amplitude/reference].

    23.2/10 = 2.32, so a 30.5 decibel sound has an amplitude that is $10^{2.32}$ times louder, or > 100-fold louder, than a 7.3 dB sound.

    What if the girl's 43-year-old *mother* spoke to her? In that case, the threshold for a 3-kHz tone for a 43-year-old woman is 13.7 dB, much closer to the girl's threshold. Result: middle-aged women are likely to speak in a more appropriate tone of voice to their daughters than are middle-aged men.

19. Colin Elliott, "Noise Tolerance and Extraversion in Children," *British Journal of Psychology*, 62(3):375–80, 1971.

20. Many studies provide support for this statement. Start by reading Judith Hall's classic and scholarly book *Nonverbal Sex Differences* (Baltimore: Johns Hopkins University Press, 1985). For a more recent review, see Erin McClure's authoritative article, "A Meta-Analytic Review of Sex Differences in Facial Expression Processing and Their Development in Infants, Children, and Adolescents," *Psychological Bulletin*, 126:424–53, 2000.

21. Jennifer Connellan, Simon Baron-Cohen, and associates, "Sex Differences in Human Neonatal Social Perception," *Infant Behavior & Development*, 23:113–18, 2000. The quotation comes from page 114.

22. Ehud Kaplan and Ethan Benardete, "The Dynamics of Primate Retinal

Ganglion Cells," *Progress in Brain Research*, 134:17–34, 2001. See also Claire Meissirel and associates, "Early Divergence of Magnocellular and Parvocellular Functional Subsystems in the Embryonic Primate Visual System," *Proceedings of the National Academy of Sciences*, 94:5900–5905, 1997.

23. Tamas Horvath and K. C. Wikler, "Aromatase in Developing Sensory Systems of the Rat Brain," *Journal of Neuroendocrinology*, 11:77–84, 1999.

24. See Alexandra Wickham and associates, "Identification of Androgen, Estrogen, and Progesterone Receptor mRNAs in the Eye," *Acta Ophthalmologica Scandinavica*, 78:146–53, 2000. See also Sandra Ogueta and associates, "Estrogen Receptor in the Human Eye: Influence of Gender and Age on Gene Expression," *Investigative Ophthalmology and Visual Science*, 40:1906–11, 1999.

25. David Salyer, Edwin Lephart, and associates, "Sexual Dimorphism and Aromatase in the Rat Retina," *Developmental Brain Research*, 126: 131–36, 2001.

26. Megumi Iijima, Osamu Arisaka, Fumie Minamoto, and Yasumasa Arai, "Sex Differences in Children's Free Drawings," *Hormones and Behavior*, 40:99–104, 2001.

27. William Overman and associates, "Cognitive Gender Differences in Very Young Children Parallel Biologically Based Cognitive Gender Differences in Monkeys," *Behavioral Neuroscience*, 110:673–84, 1996.

28. Gerianne Alexander and Melissa Hines, "Sex Differences in Response to Children's Toys in Nonhuman Primates," *Evolution & Human Behavior*, 23:467–79, 2002.

29. Megumi Iijima, Osamu Arisaka, Fumie Minamoto, and Yasumasa Arai, "Sex Differences in Children's Free Drawings," *Hormones and Behavior*, 40:99–104, 2001.

30. Chris Boyatzis and Julie Eades, "Gender Differences in Preschoolers' and Kindergartners' Artistic Production and Preference," *Sex Roles*, 41:627–38, 1999. See also I. Kawecki, "Gender Differences in Young Children's Artwork," *British Educational Research Journal*, 20:485–90, 1994. See also the paper by Iijima et al., "Sex Differences," in the previous note.

31. Donna Tuman, "Sing a Song of Sixpence: An Examination of Sex Differences in the Subject Preference of Children's Drawings," *Visual Arts Research*, 25:51–62, 1999.

32. The most definitive paper in this regard was published by Deborah Saucier and associates, "Are Sex Differences in Navigation Caused by

Sexually Dimorphic Strategies or by Differences in the Ability to Use the Strategies?" *Behavioral Neuroscience*, 116:403–10, 2002. We will consider their paper at some length in chapter 5. See also N. Sandstrom, J. Kaufman, and S. A. Huettel, "Males and Females Use Different Distal Cues in a Virtual Environment Navigation Task," *Brain Research: Cognitive Brain Research*, 6:351–60, 1998.

33. Jennifer Kersker, Melissa Epley, and Josephine Wilson, "Sex Differences in Landmark Learning by Children Aged 5 To 12 Years," *Perceptual and Motor Skills*, 96:329–38, 2003.

34. Georg Grön, Matthias Riepe, and associates, "Brain Activation during Human Navigation: Gender-Different Neural Networks as Substrate of Performance," *Nature neuroscience*, 3:404–8, 2000.

35. John Colapinto, *As Nature Made Him: The Boy Who Was Raised as a Girl* (New York: HarperCollins, 2001).

36. Lisa Serbin and associates, "Gender Stereotyping in Infancy: Visual Preferences for and Knowledge of Gender-Stereotyped Toys in the Second Year," *International Journal of Behavioral Development*, 25:7–15, 2001.

37. Anne Campbell and associates, "Infants' Visual Preference for Sex-Congruent Babies, Children, Toys and Activities: A Longitudinal Study," *British Journal of Developmental Psychology*, 18:479–98, 2000.

38. Anne Campbell and associates, "Sex-Typed Preferences in Three Domains: Do Two-Year-Olds Need Cognitive Variables?" *British Journal of Psychology*, 93:203–17, 2002.

39. Gerianne Alexander and Melissa Hines, "Sex Differences in Response to Children's Toys in Nonhuman Primates," *Evolution & Human Behavior*, 23:467–79, 2002.

40. If you're interested in gender differences in play, please go to www.genderdifferences.org/playfighting.htm.

41. Michael Meaney and William Beatty, "Sex Dependent Effects of Amygdalar Lesions on the Social Play of Prepubertal Rats," *Physiology and Behavior*, 26:467–72, 1981.

42. William Killgore, Mika Oki, and Deborah Yurgelun-Todd, "Sex-Specific Developmental Changes in Amygdala Responses To Affective Faces," *NeuroReport*, 12:427–33, 2001. The same group reported in a subsequent paper that the functional significance of amygdala activation in women appears to be different than in men. Specifically, they found that "males and females showed *opposite* patterns of lateralized amygdala signal intensity changes in response to happy faces." William Killgore and Deborah Yurgelun-Todd, "Sex Differences in Amygdala

Activation during the Perception of Facial Affect," *NeuroReport*, 12:2543–47, 2001. The quotation is from the caption for Figure 2, p. 2546; emphasis added.

43. Frank Schneider, Ute Habel, and associates, "Gender Differences in Regional Cerebral Activity during Sadness," *Human Brain Mapping*, 9:226–38, 2000.

44. Tor Wager and associates reviewed every study published between 1992 and 2002 that concerned brain areas activated by emotion. Although the character of brain activation varied depending on details of the experimental situation, one general finding was that emotions are processed in male brains differently than in female brains. Emotions are processed in male brains in more focal and lateralized regions (i.e., in the left hemisphere *or* the right hemisphere, but not both), whereas emotions are processed in female brains more globally and bilaterally. See Tor Wager, Luan Phan, Israel Liberzon, and Stephan Taylor, "Valence, Gender, and Lateralization of Functional Brain Anatomy in Emotion: A Meta-Analysis of Findings from Neuro-Imaging," *Neuro-Image*, 19:513–31, 2003.

45. The best-selling book in this genre is *Raising Cain: Protecting the Emotional Life of Boys*, by Daniel Kindlon and Michael Thompson (New York: Ballantine, 2000). See also Peter Sharp's *Nurturing Emotional Literacy: A Practical Guide for Teachers, Parents, and Those in the Caring Professions* (London: David Fulton Publishers, 2001).

46. Kenneth Rowe, "What Really Matters: Exploring the Evidence for Factors Affecting Girls' and Boys' Experiences and Outcomes of Schooling." Paper presented at the Boys' Education and Beyond Conference, Fremantle, Western Australia, November 2001.

47. Dr. Möbius's book was reissued in 1990 in a critical edition edited by Susanne Wäckerle, published by Matthes & Seitz, Munich, in 1990. The original title is *Über den physiologischen Schwachsinn des Weibes*. At this writing (September 2004), the book is available at German-language online bookstores such as www.buecher.de and www.amazon.de. I suspect it is purchased as a gag gift for women when they graduate from college. Unfortunately, it has never been translated into English.

48. Scientists at the National Institutes of Health have found that the blood flow in a female's brain is not only richer than that in a male brain, it is directed more to the cerebral cortex, the most "advanced" area of the brain, whereas the blood flow in a male's brain is directed toward more phylogenetically primitive areas in the base of the brain. See Mark Willis, Terence Ketter, and associates, "Age, Sex, and Laterality

Effects on Cerebral Glucose Metabolism in Healthy Adults," *Psychiatry Research Neuroimaging*, 114:23–37, 2002. Japanese neuroscientists led by Kenji Kansaku found dramatic sex differences in brain blood flow, with more bilateral flow in females—at least for language tasks—while males have flow more to just one side of the brain or the other. See Kenji Kansaku, Akira Yamaura, and Shigeru Kitazawa, "Sex Differences in Lateralization Revealed in the Posterior Language Areas," *Cerebral Cortex*, 10:866–72, 2000.

49. See for example Theodore Rabinowicz and associates, "Structure of the Cerebral Cortex in Men and Women," *Journal of Neuropathology and Experimental Neurology*, 61:52, 2002. See also María Elena Cordero and associates, "Sexual Dimorphism in Number and Proportion of Neurons in the Human Median Raphe Nucleus," *Developmental Brain Research*, 124:43–52, 2000.

50. For example, with respect to navigation and geometrical tasks, we will find that females use the cerebral cortex, whereas males use the hippocampus.

51. Ahmet Akgün, Mukadder Okuyan, and Şükrücan Baytan, "Relationship between Nonverbal IQ and Brain Size in Right- and Left-Handed Men and Women," *International Journal of Neuroscience*, 113:893–902, 2003.

52. Deborah Yurgelun-Todd, William Killgore, and A. D. Young, "Sex Differences in Cerebral Tissue Volume and Cognitive Performance during Adolescence," *Psychological Reports*, 91:743–57, 2002.

53. Siobhan Hutchinson, Leslie Hui-Lin Lee, Nadine Gaab, and Gottfried Schlaug, "Cerebellar Volume of Musicians," *Cerebral Cortex*, 13:943–49, 2003.

54. This legendary December 1989 action of the BLO received widespread press coverage, including a story by Brigitte Greenberg for the Associated Press, "The Barbie Liberation Organization Strikes." You can read Greenberg's story at http://www.etext.org/Zines/UnitCircle/uc3/page10.html.

55. Katherine Green and Malcolm Gynther, "Blue Versus Periwinkle: Color Identification and Gender," *Perceptual and Motor Skills*, 80:27–32, 1995.

56. Deborah Tannen, *You Just Don't Understand: Women and Men in Conversation*, rev. ed. (New York: HarperCollins, 2001), p. 245.

57. Bente Pakkenberg, Dorte Pelvig, and associates, "Aging and the Human Neocortex," *Experimental Gerontology*, 38:95–99, 2003. See also the earlier paper by Bente Pakkenberg and Hans Jørgen Gundersen, "Neocortical Neuron Number in Humans: Effect of Sex and Age," *Journal of Comparative Neurology*, 384:312–20, 1997.

58. In chapter 9, we'll review evidence supporting this statement.

59. Letitia Anne Peplau, "Human Sexuality: How Do Men and Women Differ?" *Current Directions in Psychological Science*, 12:37–44, 2003.

60. David Schmitt and 118 (!) other authors, "Universal Sex Differences in the Desire for Sexual Variety: Tests from 52 Nations, 6 Continents, and 13 Islands," *Journal of Personality and Social Psychology*, 85:85–104, 2003. Emphasis added.

Chapter Three: Risk

1. The full translation of this passage from Nietzsche's *Die Fröhliche Wissenschaft*, section 283, is: "The secret to harvesting the greatest fruitfulness and the most fun from life, is: *to live dangerously*. Build your cities on the slopes of Vesuvius! Send your ships into unknown seas! Live at war with your peers and with yourselves!" The translation is my own. The emphasis is in the original.

2. See Richard Sorrentino, Erin Hewitt, and Patricia Raso-Knott, "Risk-taking in Games of Chance and Skill: Informational and Affective Influences on Choice Behavior," *Journal of Personality and Social Psychology*, 62(3):522–33, 1992.

3. This phenomenon is seen with young girls and boys just as it is seen with adults. Psychologists David Miller and James Byrnes demonstrated this effect with third-, fifth-, and seventh-graders in their paper, "The Role of Contextual and Personal Factors in Children's Risk Taking," *Developmental Psychology*, 33(5):814–23, 1997.

4. See for example Paul Poppen, "Gender and Patterns of Sexual Risk Taking in College Students," *Sex Roles*, 32:545–55, 1995. See also Debra Murphy, Mary Jane Rotheram-Borus, and Helen Reid, "Adolescent Gender Differences in HIV-Related Sexual Risk Acts, Social-Cognitive Factors and Behavioral Skills," *Journal of Adolescence*, 21:197–208, 1998.

5. Barbara Morrongiello and Tess Dawber, "Toddlers' and Mothers' Behaviors in an Injury-Risk Situation: Implications for Sex Differences in Childhood Injuries," *Journal of Applied Developmental Psychology*, 19(4):625–39, 1998.

6. William Pickett and associates, "Multiple Risk Behavior and Injury: An International Analysis of Young People," *Archives of Pediatrics and Adolescent Medicine*, 156:786–93, 2002.

7. Anna Waller, Susan Baker, and Andrew Szacka, "Childhood Injury Deaths: National Analysis and Geographic Variations," *American Journal of Public Health*, 79:310–15, 1989.

8. Barbara Morrongiello, "Children's Perspectives on Injury and Close-Call Experiences: Sex Differences in Injury-Outcome Processes," *Journal of Pediatric Psychology*, 22(4):499–512, 1997.

9. Lizette Peterson, Tammy Brazeal, Krista Oliver, and Cathy Bull, "Gender and Developmental Patterns of Affect, Belief, and Behavior in Simulated Injury Events," *Journal of Applied Developmental Psychology*, 18:531–46, 1997.

10. Jonathan Howland and associates, "Why Are Most Drowning Victims Men? Sex Differences in Aquatic Skills and Behaviors," *American Journal of Public Health*, 86(1):93–96, 1996.

11. Epidemiologist Dr. Thomas Songer had not expected to find gender differences in the risk of death during thunderstorms; he was surprised by his findings. His report was described in an article by Dana Fritsch, "Men More Likely to Die in Thunderstorms Than Women," carried on the Reuters news wire, April 28, 2003.

12. Barbara Morrongiello, Corina Midgett, and Kerri-Lynn Stanton, "Gender Biases in Children's Appraisals of Injury Risk and Other Children's Risk-Taking Behaviors," *Journal of Experimental Child Psychology*, 77(4):317–36, December 2000.

13. Linda Marie Fedigan and Sandra Zohar, "Sex Differences in Mortality of Japanese Macaques: Twenty-One Years of Data from the Arashiyama West Population," *American Journal of Physical Anthropology*, 102(2): 161–75, 1997.

14. For a thoughtful discussion of this issue, see Patricia Sellers's article, "Power: Do Women Really Want It?" in *Fortune* magazine, October 2003, pp. 80–100.

15. Seventy-three percent is economist Linda Babcock's summary figure. You can derive your own figure by going to this link: www.census.gov/hhes/income/dinctabs.html. Click on "person." Then click on the gender and ethnicity you want to compare. For example, in 2001 the average income for all women (i.e., women from all ethnic groups) with a master's degree was $40,744, compared with $61,960 for all men who had a master's degree. Those numbers yield a figure of 65.8 percent. The gender gap is smaller for African-Americans than for other groups. The average income for African-American women with a master's degree was $41,286, compared with $48,772 for African-American men with a master's degree, yielding a gender gap of 84.6 percent.

16. For a thorough, unbiased review, see Judith Fields and Edward Wolff, "Interindustry Wage Differentials and the Gender Wage Gap," *Industrial and Labor Relations Review*, 49:105–20, 1995. For a more re-

cent update, focusing on middle-class managerial jobs, see Cheri Ostroff and Leanne Atwater, "Does Whom You Work with Matter? Effects of Referent Group Gender and Age Composition on Manager's Compensation," *Journal of Applied Psychology*, 88:725–40, 2003.

17. Linda Babcock and Sara Laschever, *Women Don't Ask: Negotiation and the Gender Divide* (Princeton: Princeton University Press, 2003).

18. Margrét Pála Ólafsdóttir, "Kids Are Both Girls and Boys in Iceland," *Women's Studies International Forum*, 19(4):357–69, 1996.

19. Wendy Mogel, *The Blessing of a Skinned Knee* (New York: Penguin, 2001).

Chapter Four: Aggression

1. Gen. George S. Patton spoke these words in a 1944 speech to the 3rd Army. The full passage reads: "You are here today for three reasons. First, because you are here to defend your homes and your loved ones. Second, you are here for your own self-respect, because you would not want to be anywhere else. Third, you are here because you are real men and all real men like to fight."

2. Romanowski made this comment during the pregame show on ESPN before the season opener, September 7, 2003. Lest you think only teenage boys talk like this, consider that Romanowski was thirty-seven years old when he made this remark.

3. Rachel Simmons, *Odd Girl Out: The Hidden Culture of Aggression in Girls* (New York: Harcourt, 2002), p. 75.

4. Section 116 from *Jenseits von Gut und Böse* [Beyond Good & Evil]. The literal translation would be: "Our great moments come when we find the courage to rechristen our evil as the best within us." I have re-phrased the plural as a singular.

5. See two articles by Janet Lever: "Sex Differences in the Games Children Play," *Social Problems*, 23:478–87, 1976, and "Sex Differences in the Complexity of Children's Games," *American Sociological Review*, 43:471–83, 1978.

6. Quoted in Deborah Blum's book *Sex on the Brain: The Biological Differences between Men and Women* (New York: Penguin, 1998), pp. 73–74.

7. Tracy Collins-Stanley, Su-lin Gan, Jessy Hsin-Ju, and Dolf Zillman, "Choice of Romantic, Violent, and Scary Fairy-Tale Books by Preschool Girls and Boys," *Child Study Journal*, 26(4):279–302, 1996.

8. Kai Klitzing, Kimberly Kelsay, Robert Emde, JoAnn Robinson, and

Stephanie Schmitz, "Gender-Specific Characteristics of 5-Year-Olds' Play Narratives and Associations with Behavior Ratings," *Journal of the American Academy of Child and Adolescent Psychiatry*, 39:1017–23, 2000.

9. David Perry, Louise Perry, and Robert Weiss, "Sex Differences in the Consequences that Children Anticipate for Aggression," *Developmental Psychology*, 25(2):312–19, 1989.

10. See for example Sheri Berenbaum and Elizabeth Snyder, "Early Hormonal Influences on Childhood Sex-Typed Activity and Playmate Preferences," *Developmental Psychology*, 31(1):31–42, 1995. See also Sheri Berenbaum and Melissa Hines, "Early Androgens Are Related To Childhood Sex-Typed Toy Preferences," *Psychological Science*, 3:203–6, 1992.

11. Anna Servin, Anna Nordenström, Agne Larsson, and Gunilla Bohlin, "Prenatal Androgens and Gender-Typed Behavior: A Study of Girls with Mild and Severe Forms of Congenital Adrenal Hyperplasia," *Developmental Psychology*, 39:440–50, 2003.

12. If you're interested in sex differences in playfighting, please go to www.genderdifferences.org/playfighting.htm.

13. Maria Van Noordwik and associates, "Spatial Position and Behavioral Sex Differences in Juvenile Long-Tailed Macaques," in Michael Pereira and Lynn Fairbanks, *Juvenile Primates* (New York: Oxford University Press, 2002), pp. 77–84.

14. Carolyn Crockett and Theresa Pope, "Consequences of Sex Differences in Dispersal for Juvenile Red Howler Monkeys," in ibid., pp. 104–18; see especially "Infant Care by Juvenile Females," pp. 112–13. See also David Watts and Anne E. Pusey, "Behavior of Juvenile and Adolescent Great Apes," in ibid., pp. 148–72, especially "Alloparenting," p. 162.

15. N. Bolwig, "A Study of the Behaviour of the Chacma Baboon," *Behaviour*, 14:136–63, 1959.

16. Jennifer Lovejoy and Kim Wallen, "Sexually Dimorphic Behavior in Group-Housed Rhesus Monkeys at 1 Year of Age," *Psychobiology*, 16:348–56, 1988.

17. Chris Pryce, Max Dobeli, and Robert Martin, "Effects of Sex Steroids on Maternal Motivation in the Common Marmoset," *Journal of Comparative Psychology*, 107:99–115, 1993.

18. Michael Meaney, Elizabeth Lozos, and Jane Stewart, "Infant Carrying by Nulliparous Female Vervet Monkeys," *Journal of Comparative Psychology*, 104:377–81, 1990.

19. See for example Dario Maestripieri and Suzanne Pelka, "Sex Differences in Interest in Infants across the Lifespan: A Biological Adaptation for Parenting?" *Human Nature*, 13:327–44, 2002.

20. When psychologists Hugh Lytton and David Romney reviewed 172 studies involving 28,000 children, they found no evidence that parents' child-rearing has any measurable effect on the gender-typical behavior of their children. See their paper, "Parents' Differential Socialization of Boys and Girls: A Meta-Analysis," *Psychological Bulletin*, 109:267–96, 1991.

21. Michael Meaney, Elizabeth Lozos, and Jane Stewart, "Infant Carrying by Nulliparous Female Vervet Monkeys," *Journal of Comparative Psychology*, 104:377–81, 1990.

22. See for example the article by Jane Goodall and her associates in the *American Journal of Physical Anthropology*, "Patterns of Predation by Chimpanzees on Red Colobus Monkeys in Gombe National Park, 1982–1991," 94:213–28, 1994. They found that adolescent male and adult male chimps often kill colobus monkeys. The anthropologists never saw an *adolescent* female chimp kill a monkey, and even adult female chimps rarely killed monkeys. The anthropologists identified fifteen different male chimps each of whom killed three or more monkeys, and nine male chimps each of whom killed more than ten monkeys each. One male killed 76 monkeys. By contrast, only two female chimps killed more than two monkeys: one female killed four monkeys, and one (an infertile female who never mated) killed ten monkeys. See their Table 3, p. 220. See also Michael Hopkin's article, "Girl Chimps Learn Faster than Boys," *Nature*, April 15, 2004, online at http://www.nature.com/nsu/ 040412/040412-6.html. In this article, primatologist Andrew Whiten is quoted as saying, "While termites are a valuable food for females, males often catch larger animals such as monkeys. Their rough-and-tumble play may be a way to hone their hunting skills."

23. J. Dee Higley, "Aggression," in Dario Maestripieri, ed., *Primate Psychology* (Cambridge, Mass.: Harvard University Press, 2003), pp. 17–40. See also the forthcoming paper by Christina Barr, Michelle Becker, and J. Dee Higley, "Early Life Events as Predictors of Aggression and Violence in the Adult."

24. See the *New York Times*, "Schools Move to Restrict Dodgeball," May 6, 2001, p. 42, (no byline); and also Marc Fisher, "Skittish Schools Need to Take a Recess," *Washington Post*, November 23, 2003, p. C1; and also Sophia Dembling's essay, "The Tyranny of Dodgeball," online at http://www.drwoolard.com/peinnews2/ tyranny.htm.

25. Marc Fisher, "Skittish Schools Need to Take a Recess," *Washington Post*, November 23, 2003, p. C1.

26. John Gehring, "Snowball's Chance," *Education Week*, January 21, 2004, p. 9.

27. This line is a quotation from the *Epistles* of Horace (I, 10). The original Latin is *Naturam expellas furca, tamen usque recurret.*

28. Cited in Patricia Cayo Sexton, *The Feminized Male* (New York: Random House, 1969), p. 3.

29. Adam Bellow, *In Praise of Nepotism: A Natural History* (New York: Doubleday, 2003), pp. 341–42.

30. Albert Beveridge, *Abraham Lincoln, 1809–1859* (Boston: Houghton-Mifflin, 1928), pp. 120–21.

31. Adam Bellow, *In Praise of Nepotism: A Natural History* (New York: Doubleday, 2003), p. 342.

32. The interview with Volker Morawe and Tilman Reiff was broadcast on the NPR program *On the Media*, June 27, 2003. The transcript is online at http://www.wnyc.org/onthemedia/transcripts_062703_painstation.html.

33. For a review of sex differences in stress-induced analgesia, see Wendy Sternberg and Melissa Wachterman, "Experimental Studies of Sex-Related Factors Influencing Nociceptive Responses: Nonhuman Animal Research," pp. 71–88, in the monograph *Sex, Gender, and Pain*, edited by Roger Fillingim, published by the International Association for the Study of Pain (Seattle, 2000).

34. To learn more about pregnancy-induced analgesia, start with the review by Alan Gintzler and Nai-Jiang Liu, "Ovarian Sex Steroids Activate Antinociceptive Systems and Reveal Gender-Specific Mechanisms," pp. 89–108, in ibid.

35. D. Sarkar and associates, "Sex Difference in Response to Alphaxalone Anaesthesia May Be Oestregen Dependent," *Nature*, 298:270–72, July 15, 1982.

36. Igor Mitrovic and associates, "Contribution of GIRK2-Mediated Postsynaptic Signaling in Opiate and Alpha2-Adrenergic Analgesia and Analgesic Sex Differences," *Proceedings of the National Academy of Sciences*, 100(1):271–76, January 7, 2003. See also Y. A. Blednov and associates, "A Pervasive Mechanism for Analgesia: Activation of GIRK2 Channels," in ibid., pp. 277–82.

37. See Alison McCook's article for Reuters, "Why a Man's 'Ouch' Is Different Than a Woman's," December 20, 2002.

38. Shelley Taylor and associates, "Biobehavioral Responses to Stress in Females: Tend-and-Befriend, Not Fight-or-Flight," *Psychological Review*,

107:411–29, 2000. See also Dr. Taylor's book *The Tending Instinct* (New York: Henry Holt, 2002).

39. Many studies demonstrate that the female autonomic nervous system in humans is influenced more by the parasympathetic nervous system while the male autonomic nervous system is influenced more by the sympathetic nervous system. For a discussion and list of relevant references, please go to www.genderdifferences.org/autonomic.htm.

40. http://www.npr.org/features/feature.php?wfld=1119380 is the link if you'd like to listen to Alix Spiegel's report "Wrestling" online. The broadcast date was March 2, 2001, on *All Things Considered*. See also Ron Matus's article for the *South Tampa City Times*, August 2, 2002, entitled "Go Down Fighting."

41. For one example, listen to the report that aired on NPR's *Weekend Edition Sunday*, May 23, 2004, entitled "New School Phys-Ed: Aerobics, No Sports," online at http://www.npr.org/ features/feature.php? wfld=1907101. Remarkably, the conflict described in this news story was not between advocates of traditional P.E. and aerobics-centered P.E., but rather between advocates of aerobics-centered P.E. and those who insist that P.E. should be dropped altogether in favor of more time for academics, for students whose academics are in need of improvement (and wouldn't that include most students?).

42. Here are the most recent (2003) statistics from the CDC:
Percentage of boys who were overweight in 1965: 4.0%.
Percentage of boys who were overweight in 2000: 16.0%.
Source: www.cdc.gov/nchs/data/hus/tables/2003/03hus069.pdf.

43. Rachel Simmons, *Odd Girl Out: The Hidden Culture of Aggression in Girls* (New York: Harcourt, 2002), p. 75.

44. John Bishop, Matthew Bishop, Lara Gelbwasser, Shanna Green, and Andrew Zuckerman, "Nerds and Freaks: A Theory of Student Culture and Norms," in *Brookings Papers on Education Policy, 2003*, Diane Ravitch, ed. (Washington, DC: Brookings Institution Press, 2003), pp. 141–213. The quote is from page 158.

45. See the review by Jon Sutton and colleagues, "Bullying and 'Theory of Mind': A Critique of the Social Skills Deficit View of Anti-Social Behaviour," *Social Development*, 8:117–27, 1999. These authors observe that "the stereotype of a bully as a powerful but 'oafish' person with little understanding of others" may be a good description of the typical *boy* who bullies, but rarely describes the *girl* who bullies. Girls who bully "need good social cognition and theory of mind skills in order to

manipulate and organize others, inflicting suffering in subtle and damaging ways while avoiding detection themselves."

Chapter Five: School

1. Myra Sadker (now deceased) and David Sadker, *Failing at Fairness: How Our Schools Cheat Girls* (Simon & Schuster, 1994), pp. 2, 5.

2. Christina Hoff Sommers, *The War against Boys* (New York: Simon & Schuster, 2000), p. 14.

3. Ms. Woods made this comment during an interview for *60 Minutes*, October 20, 2002. Woods was asked whether boys are being shortchanged *more than* girls are. Woods responded, *"Both* girls and boys are being shortchanged." I should point out that when Woods made this comment, she did not intend her comment to be interpreted as a criticism of coeducation or an endorsement of single-sex education.

4. See Tricia Valeski and Deborah Stipek, "Young Children's Feelings about School," *Child Development*, 72:1198–1213, 2001. See also Eva Pomerantz and Jill Saxon, "Conceptions of Ability as Stable and Self-Evaluative Processes: A Longitudinal Examination," *Child Development*, 72:152–73, 2001. See also Eva Pomerantz, Ellen Altermatt, and Jill Saxon, "Making the Grade but Feeling Distressed: Gender Differences in Academic Performance and Internal Distress," *Journal of Educational Psychology*, 94(2):396–404, 2002.

5. Elizabeth Lonsdorf, Lynn Eberly, and Anne Pusey, "Sex Differences in Learning in Chimpanzees," *Nature*, 428:715–16, 2004.

6. Eva Pomerantz, Ellen Altermatt, and Jill Saxon, "Making the Grade but Feeling Distressed: Gender Differences in Academic Performance and Internal Distress," *Journal of Educational Psychology*, 94(2):396–404, 2002. The quotation is from page 402.

7. This observation—that girls' friendships are face-to-face, while boys' friendships are shoulder-to-shoulder—has been made by many scholars, most accessibly by Deborah Tannen, *You Just Don't Understand: Women and Men in Conversation*, rev. ed. (New York: HarperCollins, 2001); and by Helen Fisher, *Why We Love: The Nature and Chemistry of Romantic Love* (New York: Henry Holt, 2004).

8. See Kathryn Dindia and Mike Allen's review of 205 studies on this topic: "Sex Differences in Self-Disclosure: A Meta-Analysis," *Psychological Bulletin*, 112:106–24, 1992.

9. See for example Deborah Belle's essay, "Gender Differences in Children's Social Networks and Supports," pp. 173–88, in the book she

edited, *Children's Social Networks and Supports* (New York: John Wiley, 1989).

10. Shelley Taylor and associates, "Biobehavioral Responses to Stress in Females: Tend-and-Befriend, Not Fight-or-Flight," *Psychological Review*, 107:411–29, 2000. The quotation comes from page 418.

11. John Bishop, Matthew Bishop, Lara Gelbwasser, Shanna Green, and Andrew Zuckerman, "Nerds and Freaks: A Theory of Student Culture and Norms," in *Brookings Papers on Education Policy, 2003*, Diane Ravitch, ed. (Washington, DC: Brookings Institution Press, 2003), pp. 141–213. The quotation is from pages 182–83.

12. 1 Samuel 18:3–4 and 23:17.

13. Elinor Burkitt spent one year observing kids in a "good" public high school in a "nice" suburb. See her book *Another Planet: A Year in the Life of a Suburban High School* (New York: HarperCollins, 2001). The quotation is from page 69. Burkitt mentions later in the same paragraph that "every once in a while, when the class deteriorated into total anarchy, some *girl* would take pity on [the teacher] and let loose a timid 'Come on, you guys.' " It is apparently usually a *girl* who seeks to come to the rescue of the beleaguered teacher.

14. See, for example, Gwendolyn Wood and Tracey Shors, "Stress Facilitates Classical Conditioning in Males, but Impairs Classical Conditioning in Females through Activational Effects of Ovarian Hormones," *Proceedings of the National Academy of Sciences*, 95:4066–71, 1998.

15. Tracey Shors and associates, "Sex Differences and Opposite Effects of Stress on Dendritic Spine Density in the Male Versus Female Hippocampus," *Journal of Neuroscience*, 21(16):6292–97, 2001.

16. Professor Shors demonstrated this fact by injecting pregnant mothers with an antitestosterone drug that crosses the placenta. Male babies born to mothers injected with the drug showed no improvement, as adults, in their learning in response to stress. They lost that characteristic as a result of their mothers' being injected with the antitestosterone drug while they were in utero. Male babies castrated at birth *did* show the male-typical beneficial effect of stress on learning—despite the fact that they couldn't make testosterone after birth. See Tracey Shors and George Miesegaes, "Testosterone in Utero and at Birth Dictates How Stressful Experience Will Affect Learning in Adulthood," *Proceedings of the National Academy of Sciences*, 99:13955–60, October 15, 2002.

17. For an introduction to this topic, begin with the review by Lawrence

Stricker, Donald Rock, and Nancy Burton, "Sex Differences in Predictions of College Grades from Scholastic Aptitude Test Scores," *Journal of Educational Psychology*, 85:710–18, 1993.

18. Reuwen Achiron, Shlomo Lipitz, and Anat Achiron, "Sex-Related Differences in the Development of the Human Fetal Corpus Callosum: *In Utero* Ultrasonographic Study," *Prenatal Diagnosis*, 21:116–20, 2001. This in utero study confirmed the findings of a previous anatomical study in which investigators examined the brains of babies who had died before birth. See M. de Lacoste and associates, "Sex Differences in the Fetal Human Corpus Callosum," *Human Neurobiology*, 5:93–96, 1986. These differences in the corpus callosum derive primarily from the fact that the female brain is more mature, further along in its development, than the male brain. In adults there are few significant differences in the corpus callosum between women and men.

19. Harriet Hanlon, Robert Thatcher, and Marvin Cline, "Gender Differences in the Development of EEG Coherence in Normal Children," *Developmental Neuropsychology*, 16(3):479–506, 1999. The quotation comes from page 502. Similar results were reported in a smaller study by A. P. Anokhin and associates, "Complexity of Electrocortical Dynamics in Children: De-velopmental Aspects," *Developmental Psychobiology*, 36:9–22, 2000.

20. Jean Christophe Labarthe, "Are Boys Better Than Girls at Building a Tower or a Bridge at 2 Years of Age?" *Archives of Diseases of Childhood*, 77:140–44, 1997.

21. Chris Boyatzis, Elizabeth Chazan, and Carol Ting, "Preschool Children's Decoding of Facial Emotions," *Journal of Genetic Psychology*, 154:375–82, 1993.

22. For a review of how the kindergarten curriculum has accelerated over the past thirty years, and how this change has been especially harmful to boys, see my paper "Reclaiming Kindergarten: Making Kindergarten Less Harmful to Boys," *Psychology of Men and Masculinity*, 2:3–12, 2001.

23. See Deborah Stipek and associates, "Good Beginnings: What Difference Does the Program Make in Preparing Young Children for School?" *Journal of Applied Developmental Psychology*, 19:41–66, 1998. See also D. Burts and associates, "Observed Activities and Stress Behaviors of Children in Developmentally Appropriate and Inappropriate Kindergarten Classrooms," *Early Childhood Research Quarterly*, 7:297–318, 1992.

24. See Tricia Valeski and Deborah Stipek, "Young Children's Feelings about School," *Child Development*, 72(4):1198–1213, 2001. Quotations

are from page 1199. See also Professor Stipek's chapter "Pathways to Constructive Behavior: Importance of Academic Achievement in the Early Elementary Grades," in the book she edited entitled *Constructive and Destructive Behavior: Implications for Family, School, and Society* (Washington, DC: American Psychological Association, 2001).

25. For a brief review, see John Holloway's article, "When Children Aren't Ready for Kindergarten," *Educational Leadership*, April 2003, pp. 89–90. See also my paper, "Reclaiming Kindergarten: Making Kindergarten Less Harmful To Boys," *Psychology of Men and Masculinity*, 2:3–12, 2001.

26. Julie Zito, Daniel Safer, Susan dos Reis, and associates, "Psychotropic Practice Patterns in Youth," *Archives of Pediatrics and Adolescent Medicine*, 157:17–23, 2003.

27. Deborah Saucier and associates, "Are Sex Differences in Navigation Caused by Sexually Dimorphic Strategies or by Differences in the Ability to Use the Strategies?" *Behavioral Neuroscience*, 116:403–10, 2002.

28. Georg Grön, Matthias Riepe, and associates, "Brain Activation during Human Navigation: Gender-Different Neural Networks as Substrate of Performance," *Nature neuroscience*, 3:404–8, 2000.

29. John O'Keefe and Lynn Nadel, *The Hippocampus as a Cognitive Map* (London: Oxford University Press, 1978).

30. See, for example, Robin Roof and Donald Stein, "Gender Differences in Morris Water Maze Performance Depend on Task Parameters," *Physiology & Behavior*, 68:81–86, 1999. See also Tara Perrot-Sinal and associates, "Sex Differences in Performance in the Morris Water Maze and the Effects of Initial Nonstationary Hidden Platform Training," *Behavioral Neuroscience*, 110:1309–20, 1996.

31. Damage to the frontal cerebral cortex impairs spatial performance in females but not males, whereas damage to hippocampal circuits impairs spatial performance in males but not in females. See Robin Roof and associates, "Gender-Specific Impairment on Morris Water Maze Task after Entorhinal Cortex Lesion," *Behavioral and Brain Research*, 57:47–51, 1993; and Bryan Kolb and Jan Cioe, "Sex-Related Differences in Cortical Function after Medial Frontal Lesions in Rats," *Behavioral Neuroscience*, 110:1271–81, 1996.

32. Trudi Hammel Garland, *Fascinating Fibonaccis: Mystery and Magic in Numbers* (Parsippany, N.J.: Pearson, 1987).

33. See, for example, A. Simpson, "Fictions and Facts: An Investigation of the Reading Practices of Girls and Boys," *English Education*, 28:268–79, 1991. An extensive review of this topic may be found in the book

edited by Myra Barrs and Sue Pidgeon, *Reading the Difference: Gender and Reading in Elementary Classrooms* (London: Centre for Language in Primary Education, 1994).

34. All quotations in this paragraph come from the article "How Teachers Can Develop Boys' Interests in Literature," in *Curriculum Update*, summer 2001, Association for Supervision and Curriculum Development, Arlington, Virginia.

35. William McDonald, personal communication, August 10, 2001.

36. Edward DeRoche, "Read All about It: The Case for Newspapers in the Classroom," *Education Week*, January 29, 2003, pp. 34, 36.

37. See, for example, Carol Dwyer and Linda Johnson, "Grades, Accomplishments, and Correlates," in *Gender and Fair Assessment*, ed. Warren Willingham and Nancy Cole (Mahwah, N.J.: Erlbaum, 1997), pp. 127–56.

38. Eva Pomerantz, Ellen Altermatt, and Jill Saxon, "Making the Grade but Feeling Distressed: Gender Differences in Academic Performance and Internal Distress," *Journal of Educational Psychology*, 94(2):396–404, 2002.

39. "Balancing the Equation: Where Are Women and Girls in Science, Engineering and Technology?" National Council for Research on Women monograph, 2001. Press release online at www.ncrw.org/research/scipress.htm.

Chapter Six: Sex

1. Joan Jacobs Brumberg, *The Body Project: An Intimate History of American Girls* (New York: Random House, 1997), p. 197.

2. Ms. Burford made these remarks on the *Oprah Winfrey Show*, October 2, 2003, rebroadcast on March 18, 2004. Transcript obtained through Lexis-Nexis.

3. After I had written this chapter, I was startled, though not really surprised, to find *precisely these words*—"I don't kiss girls on the mouth because if I'm not in a relationship why should I kiss?"—in a Kaiser Family Foundation report on teenage sexuality, online at www.kff.org/content/2002/3257/Sexsmarts web.pdf.

4. Anne Jarrell, "The Face of Teenage Sex Grows Younger," *New York Times*, April 2, 2000.

5. This paragraph is excerpted from pages 218 and 219 of *Seventeen* magazine's August 2003 survey and report on oral sex, entitled *Oral Report*. The lead author was Noelle Howey.

6. This story is taken from page 220 of *Seventeen* magazine's August 2003 survey and report on oral sex, entitled *Oral Report*. The lead author was Noelle Howey.

7. "Trends in Sexual Risk Behaviors among High School Students, United States, 1991–2001," *Morbidity and Mortality Weekly Report*, 51:856–59, 2002.

8. Lorraine Ali and Julie Scelfo with Sarah Downey and Vanessa Juarez, "Choosing Virginity," *Newsweek*, pp. 60–68, December 9, 2002.

9. Alexandra Hall, "The Mating Habits of the Suburban High School Teenager," *Boston* magazine, May 2003.

10. Dr. Kass made this remark in an interview on November 29, 2000, "Lessons in Courtship and Marriage," online at www.pbs.org/merrow/tmr_radio/pgm14/index.html.

11. This quote comes from her article, "Forget Sex in the City, Women Want Romance in Their Lives," *Washington Post*, February 9, 2003, p. B2.

12. Alexandra Hall, "The Mating Habits of the Suburban High School Teenager," *Boston* magazine, May 2003.

13. Lisa Diamond, "What Does Sexual Orientation Orient? A Biobehavioral Model Distinguishing Romantic Love and Sexual Desire," *Psychological Review*, 110:173–92, 2003.

14. Sherif Karama and associates, "Areas of Brain Activation in Males and Females during Viewing of Erotic Film Excerpts," *Human Brain Mapping*, 16:1–13, 2002.

15. Stephan Hamann, Rebecca Herman, Carla Nolan, and Kim Wallen, "Men and Women Differ in Amygdala Response to Visual Sexual Stimuli," *Nature neuroscience*, 7:411–16, 2004.

16. Letitia Anne Peplau, "Human Sexuality: How Do Men and Women Differ?" *Current Directions in Psychological Science*, 12:37–44, 2003.

17. Neil Malamuth, "Rape Proclivity among Males," *Journal of Social Issues*, 37:138–57, 1981.

18. Neil Malamuth, "Testing Hypotheses Regarding Rape: Exposure to Sexual Violence, Sex Differences, and the 'Normality' of Rapists," *Journal of Research in Personality*, 14:121–37, 1980.

19. Sarah Murnen, Carrie Wright, and Gretchen Kaluzny, "A Meta-Analytic Review of the Research that Relates Masculine Ideology to Sexual Aggression," *Sex Roles*, 46:359–75, 2002.

20. Anthony Bogaert and associates, "Intellectual Ability and Reactions to Pornography," *Journal of Sex Research*, 36:283–91, 1999.

21. Park Elliott Dietz and Barbara Evans, "Pornographic Imagery and Prevalence of Paraphilia," *American Journal of Psychiatry*,

139:1493–95, 1982. These authors concluded that "bondage and domination imagery is by far the most prevalent nonnormative imagery of current heterosexual pornography" (p. 1495).

22. J. G. Beck and A. W. Bozman, "Gender Differences in Sexual Desire: The Effects of Anger and Anxiety," *Archives of Sexual Behavior*, 24:595–612, 1995.

23. Neil Malamuth and associates, "Sexual Responsiveness of College Students to Rape Depictions: Inhibitory and Disinhibitory Effects," *Journal of Personality & Social Psychology*, 38:399–408, 1980.

24. A small minority of women *fantasize* about being raped, but there is no evidence that these women would enjoy actually *being* raped in a situation that wasn't a game, that is, in which they had no control over the rapist. Women who fantasize about being raped may themselves have been heavily exposed to the myth that women enjoy being raped. See for example the paper by Shawn Corne and associates, "Women's Attitudes and Fantasies about Rape as a Function of Early Exposure to Pornography," *Journal of Interpersonal Violence*, 7:454–61, 1992.

25. Neil Malamuth and associates, "Sexual Responsiveness of College Students to Rape Depictions: Inhibitory and Disinhibitory Effects," *Journal of Personality & Social Psychology*, 38:399–408, 1980.

26. Quoted in Seymour Feshbach and Neil Malamuth, "Sex and Aggression: Proving the Link," *Psychology Today*, November 1978, p. 112.

27. Roy Baumeister, "Gender Differences in Erotic Plasticity: The Female Sex Drive as Socially Flexible and Responsive," *Psychological Bulletin*, 126:247–74, 2000.

28. Joan Jacobs Brumberg, *The Body Project: An Intimate History of American Girls* (New York: Random House, 1997), p. 190.

29. Anne Jarrell, "The Face of Teenage Sex Grows Younger," *New York Times*, April 2, 2000.

30. Stephen Eyre and Susan Millstein, "What Leads to Sex? Adolescent Preferred Partners and Reasons for Sex," *Journal of Research on Adolescence*, 9:277–307, 1999.

31. The show was broadcast on October 2, 2003, rebroadcast on March 18, 2004. Transcript obtained through Lexis-Nexis.

32. Again, the show was the *Oprah Winfrey Show*, October 2, 2003, rebroadcast on March 18, 2004. Transcript obtained through Lexis-Nexis.

33. The survey was conducted by the Kaiser Family Foundation, online at http://www.kff.org/content/2003/3309/Sexsmarts_ Gender_Roles.pdf.

34. This report is online at www.kff.org/content/2002/3257/Sexsmartsweb.pdf.

35. Anne Jarrell, "The Face of Teenage Sex Grows Younger," *New York Times*, April 2, 2000.

36. This quote comes from Whitehead's article "Forget Sex in the City, Women Want Romance in Their Lives," *Washington Post*, February 9, 2003, p. B2.

37. Dr. Pinsky made these remarks as a guest on the NPR program "Fresh Air," September 24, 2003, online at http://freshair.npr.org. See also Dr. Pinsky's book *Cracked: Putting Broken Lives Together Again* (New York: HarperCollins, 2003), especially chapter 10, pp. 111–17.

38. Renee Sieving, Jennifer Oliphant, and Robert Blum, "Adolescent Sexual Behavior and Sexual Health," *Pediatrics in Review*, 22(12):407–16, 2002.

39. National Campaign to Prevent Teen Pregnancy, *14 and Younger: The Sexual Behavior of Young Adolescents* (Washington, DC: 2003), summarized at http://www.teenpregnancy.org/resources/reading/pdf/14summary.pdf.

40. Alexandra Hall, "The Mating Habits of the Suburban High School Teenager," *Boston* magazine, May 2003.

41. Thomas Young and Rick Zimmerman, "Clueless: Parental Knowledge of Risk Behaviors of Middle School Students," *Archives of Pediatrics and Adolescent Medicine*, 152:1137–39, 1998.

42. See, for example, Wyndol Furman and Elizabeth Wehner, "Adolescent Romantic Relationships: A Developmental Perspective," in *Romantic Relationships in Adolescence: Developmental Perspectives*, ed. Shmuel Shulman and Andrew Collins (San Francisco: Wiley/Jossey-Bass, 1997), pp. 21–36. See especially the chart and discussion on page 25.

43. A large body of scholarly work over the past thirty years demonstrates this fact. See, for example, Jason Luoma and Jane Pearson, "Suicide and Marital Status in the United States, 1991–1996," *American Journal of Public Health*, 92:1518–22, 2002; and Robin Simon, "Assessing Sex Differences in Vulnerability among Employed Parents: The Importance of Marital Status," *Journal of Health & Social Behavior*, 39:38–54, 1998; also Allan Horwitz and associates, "Becoming Married and Mental Health: A Longitudinal Study of a Cohort of Young Adults," *Journal of Marriage & the Family*, 58:895–907, 1996; and also Walter Gove, Carolyn Stile, and Michael Hughes, "The Effect of Marriage on the Well-Being of Adults," *Journal of Family Issues*, 11:4–35, 1990.

44. B. Bradford Brown, " 'You're Going Out with WHO?' Peer Group Influences on Adolescent Romantic Relationships," in Wyndol

Furman, B. Bradford Brown, and Candice Feiring, eds., *The Development of Romantic Relationships in Adolescence* (New York: Cambridge University Press, 1999), pp. 291–329.

45. Linda Perlstein, *Not Much Just Chillin': The Hidden Lives of Middle Schoolers* (New York: Farrar, Straus & Giroux, 2003), pp. 84, 43.

46. Neville Bruce and Katherine Sanders, "Incidence and Duration of Romantic Attraction in Students Progressing from Secondary to Tertiary Education," *Journal of Biosocial Science*, 33:173–84, 2001.

47. Wyndol Furman and Elizabeth Wehner, "Adolescent Romantic Relationships: A Developmental Perspective," in *Romantic Relationships in Adolescence: Developmental Perspectives*, ed. Shmuel Shulman and Andrew Collins (San Francisco: Wiley/ Jossey-Bass, 1997), pp. 23, 27.

48. National Campaign to Prevent Teen Pregnancy, *14 and Younger: The Sexual Behavior of Young Adolescents* (Washington, DC: 2003), summary at http://www.teenpregnancy.org/resources/ reading/pdf/14summary.pdf.

49. See, for example, Bradford Brown and associates, "Parenting Practices and Peer Group Affiliation in Adolescence," *Child Development*, 64:467–82, 1993. Several reports have shown a link between the closeness of the mother-daughter relationship and the likelihood of the daughter's becoming pregnant: the closer the relationship, the lower the risk of pregnancy. See Brent Miller, "Family Influences on Adolescent Sexual and Contraceptive Behavior," *Journal of Sex Research*, 39:22–26, 2002, and "Family Relationships and Adolescent Pregnancy Risk," *Developmental Review*, 21:1–38, 2001. See also Sunita Stewart and associates, "Parent and Adolescent Contributors To Teenage Misconduct in Western and Asian High School Students in Hong Kong," *International Journal of Behavioral Development*, 22:847–69, 1998.

50. See, for example, Mike Males, "Adult Liaison in the Epidemic of Teenage Birth, Pregnancy, and Venereal Disease," *Journal of Sex Research*, 29:525–45, 1992.

51. See, for example, Les Whitbeck and associates, "Early Adolescent Sexual Activity: A Developmental Study," *Journal of Marriage and the Family*, 61:934–46, 1999.

52. Donald Sabo, Kathleen Miller, and associates, "High School Athletic Participation, Sexual Behavior and Adolescent Pregnancy: A Regional Study," *Journal of Adolescent Health*, 25(3):207–16, 1999. See also (by the same group) "Athletic Participation and Sexual Behavior in Adolescents: The Different Worlds of Boys and Girls," *Journal of Health & Social Behavior*, 39(2):108–23, 1998.

53. Wendy Delany and Christina Lee, "Self-Esteem and Sex Roles among Male and Female High School Students: Their Relationship to Physical Activity," *Australian Psychologist*, 30(2):84–87, 1995. See also Karen Stein and Kristen Hedger, "Body Weight and Shape Self-Cognitions, Emotional Distress, and Disordered Eating in Middle Adolescent Girls," *Archives of Psychiatric Nursing*, 11:264–75, 1997. See also Marika Tiggemann, "The Impact of Adolescent Girls' Life Concerns and Leisure Activities on Body Dissatisfaction, Disordered Eating, and SelfEsteem," *Journal of Genetic Psychology*, 162:133–42, June 2001. Tiggemann found that girls who participate in competitive sports have substantially higher self-esteem than girls who don't. In addition, girls who competed were less likely to have eating disorders and less likely be concerned about their weight.

54. Sue Kimm and associates, "Decline in Physical Activity in Black Girls and White Girls during Adolescence," *New England Journal of Medicine*, 347:709–15, 2002.

55. James Kandy, " 'You Can Feel Them Looking at You': The Experiences of Adolescent Girls at Swimming Pools," *Journal of Leisure Research*, 32:262–80.

56. American school administrators may claim that single-sex P.E. classes violate Title IX regulations. That was true before the regulations were changed as a result of the Hutchison-Clinton amendment we discussed at the end of chapter 1. More information is available at www.SingleSexSchools.org/nprm.html.

57. Anna Engel, "Sex Roles and Gender Stereotyping in Young Women's Participation in Sport," *Feminism and Psychology*, 4:439–48, 1994.

Chapter Seven: Drugs

1. "Barbie Doll" by Marge Piercy. This poem has appeared in several anthologies, but according to Piercy's own Web page (www.margepiercy.com) it first appeared in the magazine *Moving Out* in March 1971.

2. CASA: Center on Addiction and Substance Abuse, *The Formative Years: Pathways to Substance Abuse among Girls and Young Women Ages 8–22*. In chapter 5, see the heading "Concerns about Weight and Appearance Increase Risk," on pp. 42–45. The report is online at www.casacolumbia.org.

3. Dreama Moon and associates, "Ethnic and Gender Differences and

Similarities in Adolescent Drug Use and Refusals of Drug Offers," *Substance Use and Misuse*, 34:1059–83, 1999.

4. Elisabeth Simantov, Cathy Schoen, and Jonathan Klein, "Health-Compromising Behaviors: Why Do Adolescents Smoke or Drink?" *Archives of Pediatrics and Adolescent Medicine*, 154:1025–33, 2000.

5. CASA: Center on Addiction and Substance Abuse, *The Formative Years: Pathways to Substance Abuse among Girls and Young Women Ages 8–22*. Online at www.casacolumbia.org. Quotations come from pages 5 and 75.

6. Lily McNair and associates, "Self-Esteem, Gender, and Alcohol Use," *Journal of Sex and Marital Therapy*, 24:29–36, 1998. See also Kirsti Kumpulainen and Saija Roine, "Depressive Symptoms at the Age of 12 Years and Future Heavy Alcohol Use," *Addictive Behaviors*, 27(3):425–36, 2002. Girls who had low self-esteem at age twelve were two and a half times more likely to be heavy drinkers at age fifteen than girls who had higher self-esteem at age twelve. Self-esteem was not related to heavy alcohol use in boys.

7. John Hoffmann and Susan Su, "Stressful Life Events and Adolescent Substance Use and Depression: Conditional and Gender Differentiated Effects," *Substance Use and Misuse*, 33:2219–62, 1998.

8. Suniya Luthar and Bronwyn Becker, "Privileged But Pressured? A Study of Affluent Youth," *Child Development*, 73:1593–1610, 2002.

9. See Marian Burros's *Cooking for Comfort: More Than 100 Wonderful Recipes That Are as Satisfying to Cook as They Are to Eat* (New York: Simon & Schuster, 2003).

10. National Public Radio, "Five-Year Government Ad Campaign Has Not Reduced Drug Use among American Teens," *Morning Edition*, May 16, 2002.

11. Deborah Aaron and associates, "Physical Activity and the Initiation of High-Risk Health Behaviors in Adolescents," *Medicine and Science in Sports & Exercise*, 27:1639–45, 1995.

12. CASA: Center on Addiction and Substance Abuse, *The Formative Years: Pathways to Substance Abuse among Girls and Young Women Ages 8–22*, 2003, p. 8. Online at www.casacolumbia.org.

13. Dreama Moon and associates, "Ethnic and Gender Differences and Similarities in Adolescent Drug Use and Refusals of Drug Offers," *Substance Use and Misuse*, 34:1059–83, 1999.

14. CASA: Center on Addiction and Substance Abuse, *The Formative Years: Pathways to Substance Abuse among Girls and Young Women Ages 8–22*, 2003, p. 59. The CASA report cites five studies documenting the bene-

ficial effects (with regard to decreased drug and alcohol use) of teens having dinner with their parents. Online at www.casacolumbia.org.

15. Kenneth Griffin and associates, "Parenting Practices as Predictors of Substance Use, Delinquency, and Aggression among Urban Minority Youth: Monitoring Effects of Family Structure and Gender," *Psychology of Addictive Behaviors*, 14:174–84, 2000. The protective effect of having supper together decreased the risk of delinquency for girls more than for boys. On the other hand, boys were more likely to benefit when the parameter was risk of alcohol use. With regard to smoking, boys and girls benefited equally.

Chapter Eight: Discipline

1. Many parents have expressed this sentiment to me in similar words. These exact words were quoted by Sarah Brown in her article, "Just Talking Is Not Enough," *Washington Post*, September 28, 2003, p. B7.

2. I'm referring here to "Veränderungen europäischer Verhaltens-standards im 20. Jahrhundert" (Changes in European standards of behavior in the 20th century), the opening essay in Elias's book *Studien über die Deutschen (Essays Regarding the Germans* [Frankfurt am Main: Suhrkamp, 1989]). Although Elias is writing about Europe, I find most of his comments to be equally true for North America.

3. I am simplifying Dr. Elias's argument. He was interested in the general decline of power differentials in society, not merely between parents and children, but also in the relations between men and women, in the relations between employer and employee, and in the relations between European societies and their former colonies.

4. Here are the most recent statistics from the CDC:
   Percentage of boys who were overweight in 1965: 4.0%
   Percentage of boys who were overweight in 2000: 16.0%
   Percentage of girls who were overweight in 1965: 4.5%
   Percentage of girls who were overweight in 2000: 14.5%
   Source: www.cdc.gov/nchs/data/hus/tables/2003/03hus069.pdf.

5. Quoted by Rick Reilly in his article, "The Fat of the Land," *Sports Illustrated*, September 22, 2003, p. 84.

6. Sarah Mustillo and associates, "Obesity and Psychiatric Disorder: Developmental Trajectories," *Pediatrics*, 111(4):851–59, 2003. Children who were obese were two and a half times more likely to meet criteria for "oppositional-defiant disorder" than kids who were not obese (see Table 4, p. 256).

7. Joan Jacobs Brumberg, *The Body Project: An Intimate History of American Girls* (New York: Random House, 1997), p. 201.

8. Judith Levine is the most vocal advocate of early sexuality for teens. See her book *Harmful to Minors: The Perils of Protecting Children from Sex* (University of Minnesota Press, 2002). Levine argues that it is harmful to *protect* children from sex. "Sex is a wonderful, crucial part of growing up, and children and teens can enjoy the pleasures of the body and be safe, too," she argues. She devotes a full chapter of her book to an attack on the idea of statutory rape, arguing that the existence of statutory rape laws is "a denial of female desire." She defends a twenty-one-year-old man (Dylan Healy) who had sex with a thirteen-year-old girl, on the grounds that the sex was "consensual." I respond that there can be no such thing as consensual sex between a twenty-one-year-old man and a thirteen-year-old girl, because the power balance between an adult man and a thirteen-year-old girl will always be unequal.

9. National Commission on Children, *Just the Facts: A Summary of Recent Information on America's Children and their Families* (Washington, DC: National Commission on Children, 1993), p. 115.

10. Dana Chidekel, *Parents in Charge: Setting Healthy, Loving Boundaries for You and Your Child* (New York: Simon & Schuster, 2002).

11. Paul Kropp, *I'll Be the Parent, You Be the Child* (New York: HarperCollins, 2001), p. 39.

12. Claire Hughes, Kirby Deater-Deckard, and Alexandra Cutting, " 'Speak Roughly to Your Little Boy'? Sex Differences in the Relations between Parenting and Preschoolers' Understanding of Mind," *Social Development*, 8(2):143–60, 1999.

13. See Mark Barnett, Steven Quackenbush, and Christina Sinisi, "Factors Affecting Children's, Adolescents', and Young Adults' Perceptions of Parental Discipline," *Journal of Genetic Psychology*, 157(4):411–24, 1996. These psychologists queried 663 second-graders, sixth-graders, high school students, and even college undergraduates for their opinions on different methods of parental discipline.

14. Nicole Horton, Glen Ray, and Robert Cohen, "Children's Evaluation of Inductive Discipline as a Function of Transgression Type and Induction Orientation," *Child Study Journal*, 31:71–93, 2001.

15. Martin Hoffman, "Affective and Cognitive Processes in Moral Internalization," In Diane Ruble, ed., *Social Cognition and Social Development* (Cambridge: Cambridge University Press, 1983), pp. 236–74.

16. As we discussed in chapter 4, confrontation can build a friendly relationship between males (both in our species and among other pri-

mates). Two boys who fight each other are often better friends after the fight than they were before. Likewise, a young boy may respect his father more if his father occasionally spanks him when the boy does something really outrageous. Conversely, confrontation can destroy a relationship with a girl. She may bear a grudge against you for weeks or months.

There is empirical support for the notion that spanking is harmful for girls, but may be a useful disciplinary adjunct for boys in certain circumstances. See, for example, Kirby Deater-Deckard and Kenneth Dodge, "Externalizing Behavior Problems and Discipline Revisited: Nonlinear Effects and Variation by Culture, Context, and Gender," *Psychological Inquiry*, 8:161–75, 1997.

17. Alice Miller, *For Your Own Good: Hidden Cruelty in Child-Rearing and the Roots of Violence* (New York: Farrar, Straus & Giroux, 1983). Miller originally published her book in 1980, in German, under the title *Am Anfang war Erzierher*, which we might translate as *In the Beginning There Was Upbringing*.

18. Specifically with regard to Alice Miller's claim that Hitler suffered an unusually abusive childhood that left him irredeemably scarred: scholars have demonstrated that Hitler was not beaten by his father, as conclusively as such things can be demonstrated after all the principals are deceased. Youthful contemporaries deny that Adolf's father ever struck Adolf at all. Josef Mayerhofer, a friend of Adolf's during his youth in Leonding, later said: "[Adolf's father] never touched him [Adolf]. I don't believe that he ever beat him, but he often scolded him. 'That miserable urchin!' he used to say. 'I'll bash him yet!' But his bark was worse than his bite." See Bradley Smith's book *Adolf Hitler: His Family, Childhood, and Youth*, published by the Hoover Institution Press of Stanford University in 1967. The Mayerhofer quotation is taken from page 63 of that book. See also Franz Jetzinger's *Hitlers Jugend: Phantasien, Lügen, und die Wahrheit*, published by Europa Publishers, Vienna, Austria, 1956. Jetzinger demonstrates that the notion that Hitler was beaten by his father has no evidentiary basis (see *In Leonding bei Linz*, pages 90–95, in the German original).

19. Ronald Simons, Christine Johnson, and Rand Conger, "Harsh Corporal Punishment versus Quality of Parental Involvement as an Explanation of Adolescent Maladjustment," *Journal of Marriage and the Family*, 56:591–607, 1994.

20. Jerome Kagan, *Galen's Prophecy: Temperament in Human Nature* (New York: Basic Books, 1994), p. 241.

21. Here I am paraphrasing John Rosemond in his book *Raising a Nonviolent Child* (Kansas City: Andrews McMeel, 2000), p. 71.

22. Diana Baumrind, "Necessary Distinctions," *Psychological Inquiry*, 8:176–82, 1997.

23. *Ritalin Use among Youth: Hearing before the Subcommittee on Early Childhood, Youth, and Families of the House Committee on Education and the Workforce*, 106th Cong., 2nd sess., May 16, 2000. Testimony of Terrance Woodworth, deputy director, Office of Diversion Control, Drug Enforcement Administration. Online at http://edworkforce. house.gov/hearings/106th/ecyf/ ritalin51600/woodworth.htm.

24. Michael Janofsky, "Colorado Fuels U.S. Debate over Use of Behavioral Drugs," *New York Times*, November 25, 1999, p. A1.

25. Peter Chronis, "Panel OKs Edict on Behavior Drugs," *Denver Post*, November 12, 1999, p. B1.

26. Milt Freudenheim, "Behavior Drugs Lead in Sales for Children," *New York Times*, May 17, 2004.

27. Dr. Zito made her comments during *Morning Edition*, September 22, 2003, during the segment entitled "Mental Illness Diagnosis in Children on the Rise." Go to http://www.npr.org/programs/morning/ index.html, click on Archives. See also Dr. Zito's paper, "Psychotropic Practice Patterns in Youth," *Archives of Pediatrics and Adolescent Medicine*, 157(1):17–23, 2003.

28. See Dr. Zito's paper in *Archives of Pediatrics and Adolescent Medicine* (the reference cited in the previous note), Table 3.

29. Shankar Vedantam, "More Kids Receiving Psychiatric Drugs," *Washington Post*, January 14, 2003, p. A1. Emphasis added.

30. H. J. Cummins, "Preschool Bullies Get Extra Help," *Minneapolis Star-Tribune*, February 5, 2003.

Chapter Nine: Lesbian, Gay, Bisexual, Transgender, Sissy, and Tomboy

1. Simon LeVay, "A Difference in Hypothalamic Structure between Heterosexual and Homosexual Men," *Science*, 253:1034–37, 1991.

2. William Byne, Stuart Tobet, and associates, "The Interstitial Nuclei of the Human Anterior Hypothalamus: An Investigation of Variation with Sex, Sexual Orientation, and HIV Status," *Hormones and Behavior*, 40:86–92, 2001. See also another recent paper from Dr. Byne's laboratory at New York University: "A Lack of Dimorphism of Sex or Sexual

Orientation in the Human Anterior Commissure," *Brain Research*, 936:95–98, 2002.

3. Dr. LeVay's paper for *Science* was the last scientific paper he ever published. He went on to write a series of popular books about homosexuality with titles like *Queer Science* and *The Sexual Brain*. You can learn more about Dr. LeVay at his personal homepage, http://members. aol.com/slevay/index.html.

4. For a brief review of evidence that male homosexuality is based at least in part on genetic factors, please go to www.gender differences.org/mz-dz.htm.

5. Dennis McFadden and Edward G. Pasanen, Spontaneous Otoacoustic Emissions in Heterosexuals, Homosexuals, and Bisexuals," *Journal of the Acoustic Society of America*, 105:2403–13, 1999. See also an earlier article by McFadden and Pasanen: "Comparison of the Auditory Systems of Heterosexuals and Homosexuals: Click-Evoked Otoacoustic Emissions," *Proceedings of the National Academy of Sciences*, 95(5): 2709–13, 1998.

6. Dennis McFadden, "Masculinization Effects in the Auditory System," *Archives of Sexual Behavior*, 31:99–111, 2002.

7. S. J. Robinson and J. T. Manning, "The Ratio of 2nd to 4th Digit Length and Male Homosexuality," *Evolution and Human Behavior*, 21:333–45, 2000.

8. A. F. Bogaert and S. Hershberger, "The Relation between Sexual Orientation and Penile Size," *Archives of Sexual Behavior*, 28:213–21, 1999.

9. William Masters and Virginia Johnson, *Homosexuality in Perspective* (Philadelphia: Lippincott, Williams & Wilkins, 1979).

10. Elisabeth Griffith, Ph.D., personal communication, November 6, 2003.

11. Nicholas Fonseca, "They're Here! They're Queer! And They Don't Like Your End Tables!" *Entertainment Weekly*, August 8, 2003, pp. 24–28. This story was the cover story for the August 8 issue of *Entertainment Weekly*. The cover proclaimed the show to be the "summer's outrageous breakout hit."

12. Louis Bayard, "Not All of Us Can Accessorize," *Washington Post*, August 10, 2003, p. B2.

13. Lisa Serbin, "Sex-Role Socialization: A Field in Transition," in B. B. Lahey and A. E. Kazdin, eds., *Advances in Clinical Child Psychology*, vol. 3 (New York: Plenum, 1980), pp. 41–96. See especially pages 84–85.

14. Alan Bell, Martin Weinberg, and Sue Hammersmith, *Sexual Preference:*

Its Development in Men and Women (Bloomington: Indiana University Press, 1981).

15. See, for example, David Seil, "Truman Capote: Homosexual or Transgendered?" *Gender & Psychoanalysis*, 5:67–80, 2000.

16. Frank Kruijver, Dick Swaab, and associates, "Male-to-Female Transsexuals Have Female Neuron Numbers in a Limbic Nucleus," *Journal of Clinical Endocrinology and Metabolism*, 85:2034–41, 2000.

17. You can learn more about Sir Ian at his personal Web site, www.mckellan.com.

18. Richard Lippa, "Gender-Related Traits in Transsexuals and Non-transsexuals," *Archives of Sexual Behavior*, 30:603–14, 2001.

19. Jennifer Finney Boylan, "Altered State: Living over 40 Years as a Man, Then Becoming a Woman, Still Didn't Answer All the Questions about the Opposite Sex," *Allure*, September 2003, pp. 150, 152. You can read Boylan's book-length description of the transition from male to female in her recent book, *She's Not There: A Life in Two Genders*, published in 2003 by Broadway Books.

20. See, for example, Masters & Johnson, *Homosexuality in Perspective* (Philadelphia: Lippincott, Williams & Wilkins, 1979), especially pages 56–58 and pages 316–21.

21. Debra Peters and Peggy Cantrell, "Factors Distinguishing Samples of Lesbian and Heterosexual Women," *Journal of Homosexuality*, 21:1–15, 1991.

22. Lisa Diamond, "Was It a Phase? Young Women's Relinquishment of Lesbian/Bisexual Identities over a 5-Year Period," *Journal of Personality and Social Psychology*, 84:352–64, 2003.

23. See, for example, Cindy Hazan and Phillip Shaver, "Romantic Love Conceptualized as an Attachment Process," *Journal of Personality and Social Psychology*, 52:511–24, 1987; and Cindy Hazan and Phillip Shaver, "Love and Work: An Attachment-Theoretical Perspective," *Journal of Personality and Social Psychology*, 59:270–80, 1990.

24. Lisa Diamond, "What Does Sexual Orientation Orient? A Biobehavioral Model Distinguishing Romantic Love and Sexual Desire," *Psychological Review*, 110:173–92, 2003. The quotation comes from page 175.

25. Wendy Waters, Michael Ziegler, and Janice Meck, "Postspaceflight Orthostatic Hypotension Occurs Mostly in Women and Is Predicted by Low Vascular Resistance," *Journal of Applied Physiology*, 92:586–94, 2002.

26. Jerome Kagan and associates, "Temperament and Allergic Symptoms," *Psychosomatic Medicine*, 53:332–40, 1991. See also Iris Bell, Mary

Jasnoski, Jerome Kagan, and David King, "Is Allergic Rhinitis More Frequent in Young Adults with Extreme Shyness?" *Psychosomatic Medicine*, 52:517–25, 1990. See also Anne-Charlotte Lilljeqvist, Dag Smørvik, and Asbjørn Faleide, "Temperamental Differences between Healthy, Asthmatic, and Allergic Children before Onset of Illness," *Journal of Genetic Psychology*, 163:219–27, 2002.

27. Jerome Kagan, *Galen's Prophecy: Temperament in Human Nature* (New York: Basic Books, 1994), chapter 5, "The Physiology of Inhibited and Uninhibited Children," and chapter 7, "Infant Reactivity and Sympathetic Physiology."

28. Doreen Arcus and Jerome Kagan, "Temperament and Craniofacial Variation in the First Two Years," *Child Development*, 66:1529–40, 1995.

29. Jerome Kagan, *Galen's Prophecy: Temperament in Human Nature* (New York: Basic Books, 1994), especially chapter 6, "Early Predictors of the Two Types."

30. Patricia Cayo Sexton, *The Feminized Male: Classrooms, White Collars, and the Decline of Manliness* (New York: Random House, 1969).

31. The song is "I Am a Rock," from the album *Sounds of Silence*, first released in January 1966.

32. Patricia Cayo Sexton, *The Feminized Male: Classrooms, White Collars, and the Decline of Manliness* (New York: Random House, 1969), p. 35.

33. Jerome Kagan, *Galen's Prophecy: Temperament in Human Nature* (New York: Basic Books, 1994), p. 205.

34. Kagan, *Galen's Prophecy*, chapter 6, "Early Predictors of the Two Types," pp. 204–7.

35. Patricia Cayo Sexton, *The Feminized Male* (New York: Random House, 1969), p. 178.

36. Sexton, *The Feminized Male*, p. 129.

37. Sexton, *The Feminized Male*, p. 93.

Chapter 10: Beyond Pink and Blue

1. You can read Gallagher's column (published September 16, 2003) at http://www.townhall.com/columnists/maggiegallagher/mg20030916.shtml.

2. Jean Twenge, "Changes in Women's Assertiveness in Response to Status and Roles: A Cross-Temporal Meta-Analysis," *Journal of Personality and Social Psychology*, 81:133–45, 2001. See especially Figure 1, page 134.

3. Medical school freshman classes have been about 50 percent female for

about five years now. See, for example, the article by Dr. Ellen More and Dr. Marilyn Greer, "American Women Physicians in 2000: A History in Progress," *Journal of the American Medical Women's Association*, 55:6–9, 2000.

4. In my own field, psychology, the change has been dramatic. Fifty years ago, more than 90 percent of psychologists were male. Today more than 70 percent of graduate students in psychology are female. See also Ilene Philipson's book, *On the Shoulders of Women: The Feminization of Psychotherapy* (Guilford Press, 1993).

5. Jean Twenge, "The Age of Anxiety? Birth Cohort Change in Anxiety and Neuroticism, 1952–1993," *Journal of Personality and Social Psychology*, 79:1007–21, 2000.

6. Jennifer Yunger, Priscilla Carver, and David Perry, "Does Gender Identity Influence Children's Psychological Well-Being?" *Developmental Psychology*, 40:572–82, 2004.

7. Joan Jacobs Brumberg, *The Body Project: An Intimate History of American Girls* (New York: Random House, 1997).

8. Start with *Cultural Anthropology* by Marvin Harris and Orna Johnson (Boston: Allyn & Bacon, 1995), especially chapter 15, "Gender Hierarchies." For more about gender-separate mechanisms by which different cultures pass on cultural standards of masculinity, see David Gilmore's book *Manhood in the Making: Cultural Concepts of Masculinity* (New Haven: Yale University Press, 1990).

9. Deborah Roffman, "Smashing the Line between Adult and Preteen," *Washington Post*, December 22, 2002, p. B4.

10. Linda Perlstein, *Not Much Just Chillin': The Hidden Lives of Middle Schoolers* (New York: Farrar, Straus & Giroux, 2003), p. 87.

11. Joan Jacobs Brumberg, *The Body Project: An Intimate History of American Girls* (New York: Random House, 1997).

12. *Balancing the Equation: Where Are Women and Girls in Science, Engineering and Technology?* National Council for Research on Women monograph, 2001. Press release online at www.ncrw.org/ research/scipress.htm.

13. The quotes from Mr. Hunter come from Elizabeth Buie's article, "Today's Sexual Evolution," published November 21, 2000, in the *Glasgow Herald*, p. 16.

14. All quotes in this paragraph come from Jennifer Wolcott's article for the *Christian Science Monitor*, "No Girls Allowed: A Help to Boys?" May 25, 2004, pp. 12, 14.

15. For more information about how single-sex classrooms increase

girls' participation in subjects such as physics, advanced math, and computer science, please go to www.genderdifferences.org/ single-sex.htm.

16. Abigail Norfleet James and Herbert Richards, "Escaping Stereotypes: Educational Attitudes of Male Alumni of Single-Sex and Coed Schools," *Psychology of Men and Masculinity*, 4:136–48, 2003.

17. Neville Bruce and Katherine Sanders, "Incidence and Duration of Romantic Attraction in Students Progressing from Secondary to Tertiary Education," *Journal of Biosocial Science*, 33:173–84, 2001.

18. Jacqueline Granleese and Stephen Joseph, "Self-perception Profile of Adolescent Girls at a Single-Sex and a Mixed-Sex School," *Journal of Genetic Psychology*, 154(4):525–30, 1993.

19. James Coleman, *The Adolescent Society: The Social Life of the Teenager and Its Impact on Education* (New York: Free Press, 1961). The quotations are from pages 51 and 55.

20. See *Music, My Love* by Jean-Pierre Rampal with Deborah Wise (New York: Random House, 1989); and also *James Galway: An Autobiography*, by James Galway (London: Coronet, 1979).

21. Johnetta Coles made this remark during an interview for the NPR radio program *The Merrow Report*, recorded December 5, 2000. You can listen to the interview online at http://www.pbs.org/merrow/tmr_radio/pgm15/index.html.

22. Educator Bruce Cook made this assertion at the 2003 meeting of the International Coalition of Boys' Schools. His findings were reported by Andrew West in the *Sydney Morning Herald*, July 6, 2003. You can read the story online at http://www.smh.com.au/articles/2003/07/05/1057179204769.html.

23. The book was *Hardwired to Connect*, jointly sponsored by the YMCA of the USA, Dartmouth Medical School, and the Institute for American Values. The authors included child psychiatrist Elizabeth Berger, Harvard University professor Robert Coles, and Stephen Suomi of the National Institutes of Health, among others. The lead authors were Kathleen Kovner Kline and Arthur Maerlender, both of Dartmouth Medical School. The quote comes from page 24.

24. *Hardwired to Connect* (see previous note), p. 24.

25. *Hardwired to Connect*, pp. 24, 57.

26. Steve Inskeep, "Cyndi Lauper's Standard Issue," NPR, *All Things Considered*, January 24, 2004. Available online at www.npr.org. Emphasis added.

Afterword

1. You can read the full text of Larry Summers's remarks at this link: http://www.president.harvard.edu/speeches/2005/nber.html

2. See Linda Chavez, "The Shibboleths of Academe," January 19, 2005, available online at http://www.townhall.com/columnists/lindachavez/lc20050119.shtml; also Cathy Young's essay "Summers Spoke the Truth," *Boston Globe,* February 28, 2005.

3. Harvard physics professor Howard Georgi reportedly said: "It's crazy to think that it's an innate difference. It's socialization. We've trained young women to be average. We've trained young men to be adventurous." Quoted in Sara Rimer and Patrick Healy, "Furor Lingers as Harvard Chief Gives Details of Talk on Women," *New York Times,* February 18, 2005.

4. Technically, the faculty vote of March 15, 2005, was a vote of no confidence in Dr. Summers's leadership, not a direct call for his resignation. However, it did mark the first time in Harvard's 370-year history that the faculty had taken any such action against the president of the college or university. The faculty has no authority to appoint or depose the president.

5. In one study, girls attending single-sex high schools were six times more likely subsequently to major in subjects like computer science and physics compared with girls who attended coed high schools (12 percent compared with 2 percent). A summary of this study is available online at http://www.ncgs.org/type0.php?pid=52. More studies demonstrating the benefits of single-sex education in encouraging girls to study math and science are posted online at http://www.single-sexschools.org/computers.html#2.

6. M. Elizabeth Tidball, "Baccalaureate Origins of Recent Natural Science Doctorates," *Journal of Higher Education,* 57:606–20, 1986.

7. Kim Tolley, *The Science Education of American Girls: A Historical Perspective* (New York: RoutledgeFalmer, 2003), chapter 2.

8. Anat Zohar and David Sela, "Her Physics, His Physics: Gender Issues in Israeli Advanced Placement Physics Classes," *International Journal of Science Education,* 25:245–68, 2003.

9. Risheng Xu, "Women in Science Discuss Changes," *Harvard Crimson,* February 23, 2005.

10. "Mixed messages," *Harvard Crimson,* February 25, 2005.

11. Marcella Bombardieri and Jenna Russell, "Summers' Critics Are Wary, but More Hopeful," *Boston Globe,* May 22, 2005.

12. Jo Sanders and Sarah Cotton Nelson, "Closing Gender Gaps in Science," *Educational Leadership,* November 2004.

13. Mark Bauerlein and Sandra Stotsky, "Why Johnny Won't Read," *Washington Post,* January 25, 2005, p. A15.

14. Margarita Bauza, "Boys Fall Behind Girls in Grades," *Detroit News,* January 9, 2005.

15. National Center for Education Statistics, U.S. Department of Education, *Gender Differences in Participation and Completion of Undergraduate Education and How They Have Changed Over Time,* Washington, D.C., 2005; online at http://nces.ed.gov/pubsearch/pubsinfo.asp?pubid=2005169.

16. John Merrow, "Women in Science," *The NewsHour with Jim Lehrer,* PBS, first broadcast on June 1, 2005.

17. James Gallagher, "National Security and Educational Excellence," *Education Week,* May 25, 2005, pp. 32, 40.

Extra Material

1. *Exploring the Biological Contributions to Human Health: Does Sex Matter?* Published in April 2001 by the National Academy Press in Washington, DC. See especially the discussion on pages 17–19, headlined "Defining the Terms *Sex* and *Gender.*" You can access the report at www.nap.edu.

2. Anne Fausto-Sterling was one of the experts chosen by the National Academies to write this monograph—including the definitions of "sex" and "gender." You may recall that Fausto-Sterling was the author of *Sexing the Body: Gender Politics and the Construction of Gender* (see note 5 in chapter 1).

3. My principal source for these questionnaires was Janet Boldizar's paper, "Assessing Sex Typing and Androgyny in Children: The Children's Sex Role Inventory," *Developmental Psychology,* 27:505–15, 1991.

4. See note 3.

5. Donald McCreary, Doris Sasse, Deborah Saucier, and Kim Dorsch, "Measuring the Drive for Muscularity: Factorial Validity of the Drive for Muscularity Scale in Men and Women," *Psychology of Men and Masculinity,* 5:49–58, 2004.

PERMISSIONS ACKNOWLEDGMENTS

The following figures have been reproduced with permission of the copyright holder:

Pg. 13: Figure 1, "Zebra finch gynandromorph with male plumage on its right side and female plumage on its left side," from the article "Neural, not gonadal, origin of brain sex differences in a gynandromorphic finch" by Robert J. Agate, William Grisham, Juli Wade, Suzanne Mann, John Wingfield, Carolyn Schanen, Aarno Palotie, and Arthur P. Arnold, *Proceedings of the National Academies of Sciences*, vol. 100, pp. 4873–4878, 2003. Copyright 2003, National Academy of Sciences, U.S.A.

Pg. 14: Figure 6, "Photomicrographs of *in situ* hybridization in brain sections using Z and W chromosome-specific probes," from the article "Neural, not gonadal, origin of brain sex differences in a gynandromorphic finch," by Robert J. Agate, William Grisham, Juli Wade, Suzanne Mann, John Wingfield, Carolyn Schanen, Aarno Palotie, and Arthur P. Arnold, *Proceedings of the National Academies of Sciences*, vol. 100, pp. 4873–4878, 2003. Copyright 2003, National Academy of Sciences, U.S.A.

Pg. 20: Figure 1, "Schematic illustration of neuronal connections between the eyes and the LGN . . ." from the article "Early divergence of magnocellular and parvocellular functional subsystems in the embryonic primate visual system," by Claude Messirel, Kenneth Wikler, Leo Chalupa, and Pasko Rakic, *Proceedings of the National Academies of Sciences*, vol. 94, pp. 5900–5905, 1997. Copyright 1997, National Academy of Sciences, U.S.A.

Pg. 21: Figure 1 from the article "Sexual dimorphism and aromatase in the rat retina," by David L. Salyer, Trent D. Lund, Donovan E. Fleming, Edwin D. Lephart, and Tamas L. Horvath, *Developmental Brain Research*, vol. 126, pp. 131–36, 2001. Copyright 2001, Elsevier Science Publishing (New York & Amsterdam).

Pg. 30: Figure 15.2 from *Neuroanatomy: Text and Atlas*, by John Martin, Ph.D. (illustrations by Michael Leonard), New York: Elsevier Science Publishing, 1989.

Pg. 57: Photograph of "Jeffrey" is reproduced with his permission.

Pg. 94: Figure I.1 from *Neuroanatomy: Text and Atlas*, by John Martin, Ph.D. (illustrations by Michael Leonard), New York: Elsevier Science Publishing, 1989.

Pg. 100: Figure 2(b) from the article "Are sex differences in navigation caused by sexually dimorphic strategies or by differences in the ability to use the strategies?" by Deborah M. Saucier, Sheryl M. Green, Jennifer Leason, Alastair MacFadden, Scott Bell, and Lorin J. Elias, *Behavioral Neuroscience*, vol. 116, pp. 403–10, 2002. Copyright 2002, American Psychological Association (Washington, DC).